Les
Bons
Mots

Formerly a member of the Department of English and Comparative Literature at Columbia University, Eugene Ehrlich is the co-editor of *The Oxford American Dictionary* and the author of numerous books, including *A Dictionary of Latin Tags and Phrases/Say it in Latin!* (also published by Hale).

Also by Eugene Ehrlich

A Dictionary of Latin Tags and Phrases

Say it in Latin!

*This book is dedicated
to nine fine grandchildren who never cease to make
Norma and me happy and proud:
Sam, Mickey, Hazel, Rebecca, Margie,
Alice, Harry, Ruth, and Danny.*

ISBN 0 7090 6226 5

Robert Hale Limited
Clerkenwell House
Clerkenwell Green
London EC1R 0HT

2 4 6 8 10 9 7 5 3 1

Printed in Great Britain by
St Edmundsbury Press Limited, Bury St Edmunds
and bound by
WBC Book Manufacturers Limited, Bridgend

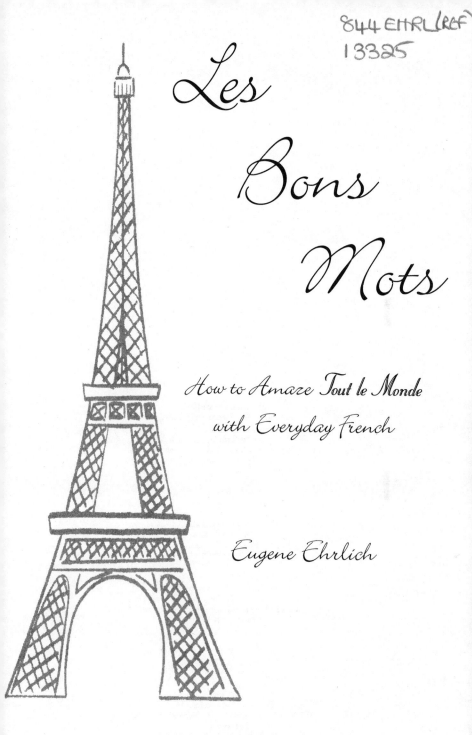

Les Bons Mots

How to Amaze Tout le Monde with Everyday French

Eugene Ehrlich

ROBERT HALE · LONDON

$\mathcal{C}$ontents

$\mathcal{P}$reface

Over the years, American tourists have relied on French phrase books to assist them in communicating with people during a journey through France. These helpful books—usually pocket-size—are typically organized as miniature, easily accessed reference books comprising phrases essential for the situations travelers customarily face, for example, in buying airline tickets, checking in at a hotel, ordering a meal, asking directions, renting a car, finding and communicating with a physician, and the like. I think of such books as verbal Band-Aids, meeting urgent needs at specific moments, but having little long-term benefit for the reader. Once one immediate need is met, another soon presents itself and requires another Band-Aid. Gone from memory is the first phrase, to be searched for again the next time the need arises.

In addition to these phrase books, tourists may also use a pocket-size dictionary to help them read—albeit haltingly—such things as newspaper headlines and news items, public notices, and road signs. And these two resources are all the help travelers find in making their way in real time into the French language. Fortunate are those who have had even a year or two of French studies at school, no matter how many years have passed between their student years and the exciting opportunity to travel abroad.

My own years as a student of French began in earnest at Townsend Harris High School, continued at the City College of New York, and—during

World War II—concluded at Boston College, where I was trained as a French interpreter for the U.S. Army. But I always found that dictionaries available at that time, no matter how comprehensive, did not do much for me when I was faced with the task of translating most idiomatic French constructions. Typically, after I had found definitions of all the individual words in a phrase, I still had the task of putting the meanings together so I could make good sense of the entire phrase. And many times, despite my best efforts, I would come up with the wrong interpretation. If you don't understand the problems I faced, wait until you read the literal translations in the present work and compare them with the markedly different idiomatic translations of the same phrases.

So decades before I undertook to write the present book, I vowed that one day I would write a dictionary of French phrases to help others who yearn to say or read more than just a few words of French.

I learned how to write this book by first writing two books of Latin phrases: *Amo, Amas, Amat and More* and *Veni, Vidi, Vici*. In a sense these books provided the paradigm for the present book. As in both of my Latin books, readers will find that each entry in the present book is followed by an attempt to provide proper pronunciation of the entry. I say "attempt to provide" because of the difficulty of representing certain sounds in French. (More of this later, in the section called Pronunciation Notes.) Also included is a free translation of each entry—how free the translation varies from entry to entry, the reader will see. The remainder of each entry gives alternative translations and, where judged to be helpful to the reader, a literal translation plus interesting ancillary information.

The most important consideration in shaping this book was to choose among the thousands of entries that were candidates for inclusion. Because of publishing restrictions, there was space only for a limited number of entries. Therefore, I kept two principles in mind in making the final selection. First, I sought to include many French phrases that are found in books written in English. Secondly, I gave particular attention to proverbs and maxims, as well as phrases and sentences that convey uniquely French or universal attitudes and insights. Finally, I paid particular attention to words and phrases that have found their way into English, either intact or slightly altered.

It is my hope that this book will stir readers to learn more of the French language. I hope also that some of them will undertake to read French works of literature. For such readers, a brief introduction to widely appreciated French novelists, poets, and playwrights is supplied in the section called Major French Literary Figures.

$\mathcal{A}$cknowledgments

As always, I am grateful to my wife for her continuing and inspiring support through all our many years together and, especially, for her cooperation in improving many entries of this book.

Thanks as well to Nicole Grandjean for her help in creating the respelling pronunciation scheme used in this book and for her assiduous work in establishing the pronunciation of each of the entries. When Nicole and I disagreed on a pronunciation, I used the second edition of the *Collins Robert French Dictionary* (1987) as final arbiter. Even so, because representation of French sounds, regardless of the system used, is far from an exact science, readers may take issue with our best efforts in the present work. If any problems remain, the fault is only mine.

I wish also to thank Jon Winokur, who unwittingly proved helpful in moving my book to completion. Early in 1995, while I was preparing this book, Jon sent me a copy of his attractive, entertaining and, above all, already published work *Je Ne Sais* **What?** He described his book as "A Guide to *de rigueur* Frenglish for Readers, Writers, and Speakers." And an excellent guide it is.

But never before had I been at work on a book and received what I saw as a competitive book—especially a book by such an accomplished author. Talk about a dagger in the heart! Nevertheless—or perhaps because his book had appeared before mine—I worked ever harder. And now that my own book has been finished, I can only congratulate him on his fine effort and publicly acknowledge the role he played in impelling me to go on.

Finally, I wish to acknowledge the help of Mary Kay Linge, my former editor at Henry Holt, and of Kevin Ohe, my present editor, who together saw my book through all the rigors of publication. Whatever quality can be claimed for this work reflects in large part their fine efforts.

Pronunciation Notes

As much as possible, this volume avoids the use of phonetic symbols that bedevil most dictionary readers. Instead, to the fullest extent possible, it uses a simple respelling scheme to represent the sounds of French. The exceptions are given below.

Stress Stresses are shown by typographic means. Stressed syllables are written in capital letters, and unstressed syllables as well as words of a single syllable are written in lowercase. Thus **madame** is pronounced mah-DAHM, and **fils** is pronounced feess.

Vowels Certain French vowels have qualities that are influenced by the words in which they appear. The samples given here are intended to help the reader sound out the French words in the pages that follow.

Pronunciation		English	French word	French pronunciation
a	as in	pat	fin	fan*
ah	as in	father	pas	pah
ai	as in	bare	chère	shair
aw	as in	awful	bon	bawn*

Pronunciation		English	French word	French pronunciation
ay	as in	betray	mais	may
Ī	as in	title	bataille	bah-TĪYə*
ī	as in	title	paille	pīyə†
oh	as in	ghost	beau	boh
oo	as in	boot	bout	boo
uu	as in	foot	deux	duu
uh	as in	purl	peur	puhr

* See **Difficult vowel and consonant combinations** for an explanation of n and N.

† See **Other vowel sounds** for an explanation of ə.

Other vowel sounds

ə

An indistinct, or unvoiced, vowel sound is represented by this symbol, properly called a "schwa." The schwa is the term in the International Phonetic Alphabet to indicate the vowel sound of the first syllable of the English word "ago" (ə-GOH). Thus, the French word **casserole** is pronounced as two syllables, kah-SəRAWL, and the English word "casserole" is pronounced as three syllables, KA-sə-rohl.

œ

These linked letters are used to represent a sound close to the sound made by "uh" (see the chart above)—but nasalized—as in **un**, pronounced œn. This sound is discussed further under **Difficult vowel and consonant combinations**.

ü

No English vowel or combination of vowels approximates the sound made by "ü." This sound is made by a procedure that has been described as holding the lips close together and in a circle, and then trying to make the sound "ee." Thus, the French noun **plume** is pronounced in this text as plüm. And the feminine article **une** is pronounced ün.

Consonants Most of the consonants given in pronunciations supplied for French words in the text are easy to sound, since they are identical with the sounds of consonants in English.

But it is important to know that the consonant "n" loses much of its strength when it is written in italics, as *n* or *N*. In the word **bonbon**, for example, the pronunciation is given as baw*n*-BAW*N*. If you say this word correctly, you will barely sound the letter "n" in either syllable. Thus **mon** is represented as maw*n*, to indicate that the "n" is barely heard. Again, **son** is represented as saw*n*, **vent** as vah*n*, **enfant** as ah*n*-FAH*N*, and **chanson** as shah*n*-SAW*N*. Practice!

And when the "n" is not written in italics, it is pronounced as in English. Thus, **nous** is pronounced noo, **naturel** is pronounced nah-tü-RAYL, and **une** is pronounced ün.

See also, at the end of this discussion, the section entitled **Difficult vowel and consonant combinations**, which explains further the problem of making the sound of *n* or *N*.

Another anticipated difficulty in dealing with consonants lies in the frequent use of two or more consecutive consonants to represent certain sounds of French. For example, the word **froid** is pronounced frwah, and the reader must take pains to sound "frw" as a single linked sound. In the same manner, you will find the pronunciation of **les yeux** given as lay zyuu, **diable** as dyahblə, **fouet** as fway, **fièvre** as fyayvrə, **humiliant** as ü-mee-LYAH*N*, **mieux** as myuu, **premier** as pruu-MYAY, **bruit** as brwee, and **buissonière** as bwee-saw-NYAIR.

Sounds represented by s, z, and ss Consider the sound made by "s" in the words "start" and "syllable," and by "c" in the word "cent." Because English speakers are accustomed to making the sound of the letter "s" and the soft letter "c," it was practical to use "s" to represent this sound, as in the French words **son**, pronounced saw*n*, and **sortir**, pronounced sor-TEER.

Now consider the sound that "s" makes in the words "busy" and "words," which English speakers easily pronounce as BIZ-ee and wuhrdz. Obviously, the letter "z" is best for representing this sound in the pronunciation of French words. Thus, the word **mauvaise** is pronounced as maw-VAYZ, **blasé** as blah-ZAY, and **croiser** as krwah-ZAY.

When an "s" sound occurs at the end of a French syllable or word, however, "ss" is used to prevent confusion. Thus, **politesse** is pronounced paw-lee-TAYSS (rather than paw-lee-TAYS) to make certain the reader

understands that the final letters in the pronunciation represent the "s"—
not the "z"—sound.

Sound represented by sh We are accustomed in English to pronouncing the sound made by the consonant blend "sh," as in the word "shun." We
are just as accustomed to making this sound when pronouncing such words
as "sugar," "recognition," and "position." Thus, "sh" is used in pronouncing
such French words as **chaud** (shoh) and **chanteur** (shahn-TUHR).

Sound represented by zh The sound made by the final four letters of
the English words "television" and "division" may be represented as zhən,
and the full pronunciations of these words as TEL-ə-vi-zhən and di-VIZH-
ən.

Thus, in French, the sound made by the "g" in the word **genou** is represented by "zh," and **genou** is pronounced zhə-NOO. As another example,
take the common locution **je ne sais pas**, which may be pronounced as
zhuu nuu say pah. In this case, the sound of the initial letter "j" is given
as zh.

Pronouncing the sound represented by r The French do not pronounce the letter "r" in the American or English manner. And, unfortu-
nately, in this text as well as in anything written in French, there are lots of
words that include the pesky "r." How much simpler life would be for those
of us trying to improve our French pronunciation if no French word included an "r." The French pronounce it beautifully, almost from birth. The
rest of us have to learn how.

A surefire way to do so is to enlist the aid of a Frenchman or French-
woman, even a French child. Ask your helper to say the word **France**
(frahnss) once, and you will hear that the "r" embedded in the word is not
the same "r" that you hear when an English speaker says "France."

Once you have heard the sound of the French "r," ask your helper to say
France (frahnss) over and over again, while you try to say it that way over
and over again. In time you will have the knack.

If you cannot find a cooperative native speaker of French, think of "r" as
being uttered while you are clearing your throat. As you practice clearing
your throat, try to pronounce **France** (frahnss) over and over. And then
practice pronouncing **royal** (rwah-YAHL). And then practice **rien** (ryan).
And so forth. Good luck.

Difficult vowel and consonant combinations The sound made by n or N is said to be nasalized. To understand how to nasalize a sound, try passing the sound of the English syllable "ing" through your nose and shutting off the letter "g" just as you begin to make its sound. Thus, in the English words "ring," "sing," "long," and "strong," the "g" is nasalized. Keeping this effect in mind will give you something close to the pronunciation of the French article **un**, in the text of this book pronounced œn.

Another way to approximate the sound of œ in œn is to put your lips in the position used in pronouncing the short English vowel "u"—as in "but"—and make the sound "ee" instead. With the help of the oral gymnastics just described, you will be able to get admirably close to being able to pronounce **un** œn. Then check out your new skill with your cooperative speaker of French.

Major French Literary Figures

Many of the maxims given in this book are quoted from the works of well-known French authors who are recognized universally as masters of drama, poetry, or fiction. In the text, only the names of these literary figures are provided. For this reason, brief biographies are provided here to help readers who may not be familiar with French literature. When French works are mentioned that have been translated into English with changed titles, the titles are given in both languages.

Balzac, Honoré de (1799–1850). Novelist, born in Tours, educated at the Collège des Oratiens at Vendôme and, in law, at the Sorbonne. He left Tours for Paris in 1819 to become an author. Balzac's literary output was remarkable—eighty-five novels in twenty years. His first success, in 1829, came with the publication of *Les Chouans*, a historical novel about the Chouans, peasants who supported the royalist cause during the French Revolution. His masterpiece, *La Comédie humaine* (*The Human Comedy*), written over a period of twenty years, is a multivolume effort to present a complete social history of France. Among the finest—and still widely read—novels in the series are *Eugénie Grandet* (1833), *Le Père Goriot* (1835), *Illusions perdues* (1837–43), and *La Cousine Bette* (1847). Aside from *La Comédie humaine*, Balzac is known for his *Contes drolatiques*, a series of humorous stories published between 1832 and 1837.

Corneille, Pierre (1606–1684). Playwright, born in Rouen and considered, along with Racine, a prime shaper of classic French theater. Corneille moved to Paris in 1629, when *Mélite*, his first successful play, a comedy of manners, was produced. He saw his subsequent efforts—among them the comedies *Clitandre*, *La Veuve*, *La Suivante*, and *La Place*—produced, meeting with moderate success, in the next few years. His first tragedy, *Médée* (*Medea*), was produced in 1635 and was followed in 1637 by his powerful tragedy *Le Cid* (*The Cid*), which became a great popular success but incurred the disapproval of Cardinal Richelieu, who ordered the French Academy to censure it. As a result, for three years Corneille did not write for the theater. He returned to the theater with *Horace* and *Cinna* (both 1640), and *Polyeucte* (1641), as well as many additional works over the years, but never again met the acclaim he earned with *Le Cid*.

Hugo, Victor-Marie (1802–1885). Poet, novelist, and playwright, born in Besançon and educated in Paris, as well as in Madrid, Spain, and at the Ecole Polytechnique. By the time he published his first set of odes in 1822, he had already produced a tragedy, at age fourteen. He continued to write poetry, including, among many other works, his *Les Feuilles d'automne* (1831) and *Les Contemplations* (1856), leading critics to consider him France's greatest lyric poet. His plays, on themes from history, are not read today except by scholars, but his novels seem never to go out of style. Modern readers are captivated, for example, by his novels *Notre-Dame de Paris* (*The Hunchback of Notre Dame*) (1831), which many of us know well from film as well as in print; *Les Misérables* (1862), of film and stage fame; *Les Travailleurs de la mer* (*Toilers of the Sea*) (1866); and *Quatrevingt-treize* (*Ninety-Three*) (1874).

La Fontaine, Jean de (1621–1695). Poet, born in Château-Thierry. Before going off to Paris, he published in 1654 a verse translation of *Eunuchus* (*The Eunuchs*), written by the classical Roman playwright Terence. His many other works include *Contes et nouvelles en vers* (*Tales and Novels in Verse*) (1664) and *Amours de Psiché et de Cupidon* (*The Loves of Cupid and Psyche*) (1669), but what the world associates most readily with La Fontaine is his *Fables choisies*, *mises en vers* (1668), translated into many languages, and in English under a variety of titles. In these fables—many of them drawn from Aesop—the ant and the grasshopper, the fox and the crow, and his many other familiar creatures, all gifted with human speech, still go through their delightful paces all over the world, but especially in the lively, original lines of verse crafted by La Fontaine. Students who memorize any of the fables never forget the succinct and useful morals La Fontaine teaches them.

La Rochefoucauld, Duc François de (1613–1680). Writer, born in Paris. After living for many years a life of love affairs and political intrigue, La Rochefoucauld turned to writing and provided the world with an account of his experiences and observations, eventually publishing his *Mémoires* (1661) and *Réflexions, ou sentences et maximes morales* (1665). Translated into many languages, and in English under a variety of titles, this latter work provided a collection of hundreds of La Rochefoucauld's pieces of wisdom and was highly praised for its conciseness, clarity, and style. La Rochefoucauld's observations on human nature and society, searching out and revealing self-love no matter how carefully disguised, proved him a master analyst of the characters of men and women.

Molière, pen name of **Jean-Baptiste Poquelin** (1622–1673). Playwright, born in Paris and educated at the Collège de Clermont. Molière, considered the inventor of French high comedy, ranks first to this day among all French writers. After working for some years as an actor, theater manager, and producer, he embarked on his dazzling career as a playwright and saw his first success with *Les Précieuses ridicules* (*The Ridiculous Snobs*) (1659), satirizing the absurd pretensions and affectations of refined society. A listing of some of his best-known and enduring plays provides an adequate indication of his great literary output: *L'Etourdi* (*The Blunderer*) (1655) and *Le Dépit amoureux* (*The Amorous Quarrel*) (1656); *Sganarelle* (1660); *Dom Garcie de Navarre* (1661); *L'Ecole des maris* (*The School for Husbands*) and *L'Ecole des femmes* (*The School for Wives*) (both 1662); *L'Impromptu de Versailles* (1663); *Le Mariage forcé* (*The Forced Marriage*) and *La Princesse d'Elide* (both 1664); *Le Misanthrope, Le Médecin malgré lui* (*The Doctor in Spite of Himself*), and *Le Sicilien* (all 1666); *Le Tartuffe* (1667); *Amphitryon, George Dandin*, and *L'Avare* (*The Miser*) (all 1668); *Les Amants magnifiques* and *Le Bourgeois gentilhomme* (*The Would-be Gentleman*) (both 1671); *Les Femmes savantes* (*The Learned Women*) (1672); and *Le Malade imaginaire* (*The Hypochondriac*) (1673).

Proust, Marcel (1871–1922). Novelist, born in Auteuil, a district of Paris, and a semi-invalid throughout his adult life. He studied at the Lycée Condorcet and at the Sorbonne. During his student years and for a while thereafter, when he spent his time making his way in the fashionable society of Paris, he wrote sketches, poems, and short stories. His *Les Plaisirs et les jours* (*Pleasures and Regrets*) (1896), a collection of these writings, was considered by critics to be the work of a literary dilettante. But it was upon the death of Proust's mother in 1905 that the novelist's life began to change radically. He withdrew from society in 1907. Except for occasional forays outdoors, he spent days and nights in his soundproof apartment on Boulevard Haussmann, giving himself over to introspection, and soon to his life work, the writing of *A la recherche du temps perdu*, later known in English as *Remembrance of Things Past*. He completed a first draft by 1912, and in 1913 saw the publication of the first part of this work, titled *Du côté de chez Swann* (*Swann's Way*). When further publication was interrupted by World War I, Proust embarked on revisions, in the process expanding the work to almost twice its original length. The novel in final form was published originally in sixteen volumes, six appearing after Proust's death. The English translation of the novel was published in seven volumes, including, in addition to the first volume, *A l'ombre des jeunes filles en fleurs* (*Within a Budding Grove*), *Le Côté de Guermantes* (*The Guermantes Way*), and *Sodome et Gomorrhe* (*Cities of the Plain*). The posthumous volumes were *La Prisonnière* (*The Captive*), *Albertine disparue* (*The Sweet Cheat Gone*), and *Le Temps retrouvé* (*Time Regained*).

Rabelais, François (1494?–1553). Satirist, believed born near Chinon, about 140 miles southwest of Paris, and educated by Benedictine and Franciscan friars. Rabelais soon entered a Franciscan monastery and, later, a Benedictine monastery, where he learned Greek, Hebrew, and Arabic and immersed himself in Latin and old French writings, as well as the sciences, medicine, and mathematics. He delighted in satirizing the social institutions and practices of his time, and his masterwork, *Gargantua and Pantagruel*, is considered to have inspired generations of writers in English as well as in French. This five-volume novel, which appeared under various French titles and at first did not carry the name of Rabelais as author, appeared between 1532 and 1564 and immediately became a great success. The novel recounts the wild adventures of a heroic giant named Gargantua and his prodigiously strong son Pantagruel, and at the same time provides a satirical picture of monasticism, scholastic education, and the pedantry of theologians at the Sorbonne. In the last volumes of *Gargantua and Pantagruel*, Pantagruel becomes progressively less the fabulous giant, more the personification of the Renaissance man, always in search of learning and the good life.

Racine, Jean (1639–1699). Playwright and poet, born at La Ferté-Milon, about forty miles northeast of Paris, and educated at the Collège d'Harcourt in Paris. It was there that Racine became interested in the world of the theater. In 1664 Molière's theater company produced Racine's first tragedy, *La Thébaïde ou les frères ennemis*, and in the next year produced his second tragedy, *Alexandre le Grand*. Racine's reputation was established. There followed the plays considered to be Racine's greatest: *Andromaque* (1667), *Les Plaideurs* (*The Litigants*) (1668), *Bajazet* (1672), *Mithridrate* (1673), *Iphigénie en Aulide* (1675), and *Phèdre* (1677). Racine, whose works have been translated into many languages, had the gift of being able to portray figures in his tragedies as flesh-and-blood people, thus humanizing classical French drama. Racine and Corneille are considered to be the great figures in the development of classical French drama.

Voltaire, pseudonym of **François-Marie Arouet** (1694–1778). Satirist, philosopher, dramatist, and poet. Born in Paris and educated at the Jesuit seminary of Collège Louis-le-Grand, Voltaire was known especially for his biting wit and his abhorrence of fanaticism, superstition, and organized religion. His life was one of perpetual dispute with people high in French court circles and was marked by periodic emigrations from his homeland to avoid punishment. Voltaire served a sentence of almost a year in the Bastille—he was charged with insulting the regent—and soon was threatened with a second imprisonment. Nevertheless, he was forever on the attack against intolerance. There is room here to list only a few of Voltaire's best-known works: his highly successful tragedy *Oedipe* (1718), written while Voltaire was in the Bastille; *La Ligue ou Henri le Grand* (1723), a long poem on Henri IV perceived as too vigorously supporting Protestantism; *Brutus* (1730); the Oriental drama of jealousy and love *Zaïre* (1732), considered one of his best plays; the dramas *Mahomet ou le fanatisme Tancrède* (1741), *Mérope* (1743), and *L'Orpheline de la Chine* (1755), and *Tancrède* (1760). Voltaire also wrote the short novel *Zadig ou la Destinée* (1748) and his most popular philosophical novel, *Candide ou l'optimisme* (1759), still widely read today. In addition, he wrote many works of history.

Zola, Emile (1840–1902). Novelist and journalist, born in Paris. In addition to his work as a journalist, he wrote many effective short stories and turned eventually to the novel form. His *Thérèse Raquin* (1867) is a powerful study of passion and remorse. But Zola wrote many more memorable novels. His interest in the effects of heredity and environment impelled him to write a series of twenty brutally realistic novels between 1871 and 1893 tracing the decay of the Rougon-Macquart family as a result of alcoholism, disease, and degeneracy. It is these novels that are considered to be Zola at his best. Four of his still widely read novels in this series are *L'Assommoir* (formerly known in English as *The Dram Shop*) (1877), on the demoralizing effects of alcoholism on the lives of the working class; *Nana* (1880), on the life and eventual dissipation of a woman who becomes a courtesan; *Germinal* (1885), on the sufferings of coal miners; and *La Terre* (*The Earth*) (1888), on the lives of poor farm workers. Zola also wrote many other novels, but with the publication of his celebrated article *J'accuse* (*I Accuse*) in 1898 he became involved in the twelve-year-long fight against the unfair treatment of Alfred Dreyfus, a Jewish artillery captain in the French Army. Because of Zola's involvement in this case, he was considered to have impeached the government and was sentenced to a prison term. He escaped imprisonment by fleeing to England, where he remained for a year. On Zola's return to France after receiving amnesty, he was given a hero's welcome. Thus, while Zola's literary reputation remains strong, it is his role in the Dreyfus affair that has ensured his public celebrity and made the condemnatory "J'accuse" an enduring symbol of determination to fight the good fight against oppression by a government. (See the entry J'ACCUSE in the text for a fuller treatment of the Dreyfus affair.)

à bas! (ah bah)
down with!

Useful in such locutions as **à bas le communisme!** (luu kaw-mü-NEESMə, "communism"), or **à bas** anything or anyone else you're not fond of.

à bâtons rompus (ah bah-TAWN rawn-PÜ)
by fits and starts

Also translated as "fitfully" and, literally, as "with broken sticks." This is hardly the best way to work when you are serious about accomplishing anything. Steady does it.

à bientôt (ah byan-TOH)
see you soon

A phrase useful in making your good-byes; literally, "until soon."

à bis ou à blanc (ah beess oo ah blahn)
by hook or by crook

Also freely translated as "in one way or another." Useful when you intend to accomplish something by any means available, whether completely ethical or not. The literal translation is "in grayish brown or in white." The word **bis** in this locution is not to be confused with the opera fan's **bis!** (beess), originally Italian, meaning "repeat!" or "encore!" and pronounced identically. The French word **encore** (ahn-KOR) in this sense means "more" or "again."

à bon appétit il ne faut point de sauce   (ah bawn nah-pay-TEE eel nuu foh pwahn duu sohss)
hungry people don't have to be coaxed to eat
   Literally, "a good appetite needs no sauce." Good for anxious parents to keep in mind when watching children pick at their food. Also helpful for cooks who think they have to go to elaborate lengths in preparing food they serve. If one's children or guests are hungry, don't worry—they will eat.

à bon chat, bon rat   (ah bawn shah bawn rah)
set a thief to catch a thief
   Literally, "to a good cat, a good rat," conveying the meaning "it takes cunning to outwit cunning." (See also À CORSAIRE, CORSAIRE ET DEMI and À FRIPON, FRIPON ET DEMI.)

à bon chien, il ne vient jamais un bon os   (ah bawn shyan eel nuu vyan zhah-MAY œn bawn nawss)
nice guys finish last
   Literally, "a good bone never comes to a good dog." The sad intent here is to tell us "the squeaky wheel receives the oil" or "merit is rarely re-warded." So be prepared.

à bon commencement bonne fin   (ah bawn kawm-mahn-SMAHN bawn fan)
start off on the right foot
   More literally, "a good beginning makes a good ending," a proverb first recorded in English in the fourteenth century.

abondance de biens ne nuit pas   (ah-bawn-DAHNSS duu byan nuu nwee pah)
you can't be too rich or too thin
   Also rendered freely as "opulence does no harm," and literally as "abun-dance of good things does no harm." And this is why we're told that if you've got it, flaunt it!

à bon entendeur, salut (ah bawn nahn-tahn-DUHR sah-LÜ)
speech is silver, silence is golden

The Persian proverb given above in English counsels against speaking out of turn, now more commonly expressed as "shooting off one's mouth." The French proverb, literally, "to a good listener, safety," incorporates the same wisdom.

à bon vin point d'enseigne (ah bawn van pwahn dahn-SAYNYə)
who needs Madison Avenue?

We all know that if we build a better mousetrap the world will beat a path to our door. More formally, any product that has real merit does not have to be advertised. This thought is expressed by the French proverb given here, literally, "good wine needs no sign," and by a sixteenth-century English proverb that expressed the thought as "good wine needs no bush." In the English proverb, "bush" goes back to the ivy bush, which for a long time was seen on the sign hung outside taverns. Why an ivy bush? In ancient Rome it was sacred to Bacchus, god of wine.

à brebis tondue Dieu mesure le vent (ah bruu-BEE tawn-DÜ dyuu muu-ZÜR luu vahn)
God tempers the wind to the shorn lamb

This French proverb makes good sense to true believers, who know that God in his goodness moderates conditions so as not to harm any defenseless person, here represented as a poor little lamb that has lost its coat.

à cause de la grève (ah kohz duu lah grayvə)
owing to the strike

Whether we blame our troubles on baseball team owners or on the players, a phrase of particular interest to all who follow big-league baseball.

à chacun sa chacune (ah shah-KœN sah shah-KÜN)
don't despair, there's someone out there for everybody

An English proverb dating back to the seventeenth century tells us "every Jack has his Jill," meaning that every man will eventually be able to find a wife of his own. In the French version given above, the masculine **chacun** and the feminine **chacune** both mean "each one," so, literally, "to each him, his own her." Not an elegant phrase in this translation.

Not surprisingly, Gilbert and Sullivan said it more felicitously and more realistically in *The Yeomen of the Guard*:

> It is purely a matter of skill,
> Which all may attain if they will:
> But every Jack,
> He must study the knack
> If he wants to make sure of his Jill!

à chacun selon son mérite (ah shah-KœN suu-LAWN sawn may-REET)
to each according to his worth

A slogan evocative of Karl Marx's dictum "from each according to his abilities, to each according to his needs," but quite different in intent. The emphasis in the French phrase is on the social contribution made by the individual, not on the needs of the individual.

à chacun son heure de gloire (ah shah-KœN sawn nuhr duu glwahr)
every dog has its day

Literally, "to each of us an hour of glory"—recent evidence has it that fame is measured in minutes—suggesting that while a person at some time may appear to be on the top of the heap, we can be certain that eminence is transitory. Soon enough, there will be someone else in his place. (See also À CHACUN VIENT SA CHANCE.)

à chacun son métier (ah shah-KœN sawn may-TYAY)
shoemaker, stick to your last

A thought originally given in Latin, with the popular English translation given above. The French advice translates literally as "every man to his own trade." But the Latin, the French, and the English convey the same meaning—no one should presume to interfere in matters in which he or she is not qualified. In short, mind your own business!

à chacun vient sa chance (ah shah-KœN vyan sah shahnss)
my turn will come tomorrow

Also translated as "every dog has its day," literally, "everyone gets a chance." This is the way life is, and it has nothing to do with democratic government or with America, the land of opportunity. Thus, you are enjoined not to crow today, because tomorrow you may see me enjoying my chance. (See also À CHACUN SON HEURE DE GLOIRE.)

à chaque jour suffit sa peine (ah shahk zhoor sü-FEE sah payn)
every day there's trouble enough to go round

A French translation of Matthew in the New Testament: "sufficient unto the day is the evil thereof."

à chaque oiseau son nid est beau (ah shahk wah-ZOH sawn nee ay boh)
every bird thinks its own nest is fine
 Not just birds, of course, but the rest of us too, young as well as old. Maybe this is part of the mind-set of well-adjusted people, who manage to get through their lives without being consumed by envy. Or maybe it's because there are more than enough rose-colored glasses to go round.

à chaque saint sa chandelle (ah shahk san sah shahn-DAYL)
honor to whom honor is due
 Literally translated as "to each saint his candle," an allusion to the practice of lighting candles to honor the memory of saints.

acheter chat en poche (ahsh-TAY shah ahn pawsh)
buy a pig in a poke
 Unless you and I are exceptionally wary, we may be inclined at least once in our lives to buy a pig in a poke. The French so inclined may, literally, "buy a cat in a pocket." And why not? The English word "pocket" is a diminutive of "poke." Of course, neither language speaks approvingly in these idioms. English speakers are led to think they are buying a pig in a sack and fail to look inside before plunking down hard cash. In the old confidence game, a swindler would actually have a cat—instead of a pig—in the poke. Thus, the French saying is more accurate in that the dupe is actually buying a cat when he thinks he's buying a pig. Take note: **acheter chat en poche** extends to any purchase we contemplate. Especially ten-dollar Rolex watches offered by sidewalk vendors. Maybe we should all subscribe to *Consumer Reports*.

acheter quelque chose pour une bouchée de pain (ahsh-TAY kaylkə shohz poor ün boo-SHAY duu pan)
buy something for a song
 The dream of every flea market devotee, literally translated as "buy something for a mouthful of bread."

à cheval donné on ne regarde pas la bride (ah shuu-VAHL dawn-NAY awn nuu ruu-GAHRD pah lah breed)
never look a gift horse in the mouth

The allusion in the translation given is to the practice of assessing the age of a horse by examining its front teeth. The French expression, however, does not speak of teeth. Rather, it says, literally, "don't look at the bridle of a gift horse." Notwithstanding, in both cases the advice carries the same meaning. When someone gives you a gift, you know it ain't nice to ask the donor how much the gift is worth.

à coeur ouvert (ah kuhr oo-VAIR)
unreservedly
Also translated as "without holding anything back" and, literally, "with open heart."

à corsaire, corsaire et demi (ah kor-SAIR kor-SAIR ay də-MEE)
set a thief to catch a thief
We are told that when you wish to catch a rascal, hire a bigger rascal, literally, "against a pirate, a pirate and a half." (See also À BON CHAT, BON RAT and À FRIPON, FRIPON ET DEMI.)

à coups de dictionnaire (ah koo duu deek-shawn-NAIR)
with continual reference to the dictionary
Literally translated as "with strokes of the dictionary," and hardly intended as a compliment. The allusion is to the writer who searches for obscure words he considers elegant, rather than choosing readily understood words that come easily to mind. The result is a text that sends most readers on frequent dictionary searches of their own to try to figure out what the writer is trying to say.

à des prix très étudiés (ah day pree tray zay-tü-DYAY)
prices cut to the bone
The French idiom for suggesting that merchandise is being offered at rock-bottom prices, more literally, "at the lowest possible prices." The verb **étudier** means "study," giving us in this idiom the image of a merchant staying up late at night looking for ways to help clients get the most for their money. Get real!

à deux (ah duu)
two at a time
Also translated as "of two," "for two," and "by twos." Two phrases employing **à deux** are of interest: **à deux fins** (fan), meaning "for two uses *or*

purposes," as a horse suitable for riding and jumping; and **à deux mains** (man), meaning "with both hands" and, literally, "with *or* for two hands."

adieu la voiture, adieu la boutique (ah-DYUU lah vwah-TÜR ah-DYUU lah boo-TEEK)
go belly up
    Bankruptcy has been around for a long time, so it's no surprise that the French have this idiom, literally, "good-bye automobile, good-bye shop" to indicate that it's all over—bankruptcy, here I come! But wouldn't you agree that "good-bye automobile, good-bye shop" has a special poignancy? We can almost see the tearful shopkeeper standing at his door while creditors haul away his every last possession.

adieu paniers, vendanges sont faites (ah-DYUU pah-NYAY vawn-DAHNZH sawn fayt)
turn off the respirator, it's all over
    Literally, "farewell, baskets, the vintage is over." The image is of the final day of the annual grape harvest, but the words speak to all of us. There comes a time when we all must make our final farewells—the game is over, there's no hope left, there's nothing more to be done.

affaire (ah-FAIR)
affair
    This useful word gives us the following phrases: **affaire d'amour** (dah-MOOR) is a love affair, as is **affaire de coeur** (duu kuhr), which has the literal meaning of "affair of the heart." **Affaire de moeurs** (duu muhr, "of morals") is a sex scandal or sex case. **Affaire d'honneur** (daw-NUHR) is a duel, literally an "affair of honor."

à fils de cordonnier point de chaussures (ah feess duu kor-daw-NYAY pwahn duu shoh-SÜR)
the shoemaker's son has no shoes
    Folk wisdom. In the course of our daily efforts to keep body and soul together by working hard at our daily tasks, many of us tend to put our families' needs last. (See also CE SONT LES CORDONNIERS QUI SONT LES PLUS MAL CHAUSSÉS.)

à fripon, fripon et demi (ah free-PAWN free-PAWN ay duu-MEE)
to catch a crook, hire a bigger crook

Almost literally, "against a rogue, set a rogue and a half." (See also À BON CHAT, BON RAT and À CORSAIRE, CORSAIRE ET DEMI.)

agent provocateur (ah-ZHAHN pro-voh-kah-TUHR)
entrapment expert
Literally, "inciting agent," which term is far from adequate as a replacement for **agent provocateur**. Indeed, there is no English term that can replace the French. So what does English do? Acting characteristically, English has taken **agent provocateur** directly into the language, and we are stuck with "agent provocateur," pronounced AY-jənt prə-VAHK-ə-TUHR. And when we define agent provocateur in either language we call attention to a secret agent employed to provoke criminal suspects to commit illegal actions that will make them liable for prosecution.

aide (ayd)
help
This verb—infinitive form **aider**, ay-DAY—appears in a variety of requests or injunctions: **aide-moi** (ayd-MWAH), "help me"; **aide-nous** (ayd-NOO), "help us"; **aide-toi, et le ciel t'aidera** (ayd-TWAH ay luu syayl tay-duu-RAH), literally, "help yourself, and heaven will help you." (This last is attributed to La Fontaine.) More commonly, we render this advice as "God helps those who help themselves."

aide de camp (ayd duu kahn)
aide-de-camp
Aide here is a noun meaning "helper," giving us, literally, "camp helper," a pallid translation; more freely and accurately, "assistant to a military officer." The term **aide de camp** is one among many specialized French military terms that have been taken into English unaltered or virtually unaltered. Consider **colonel**, colonel; **capitaine**, captain; **sergent**, sergeant; **caporal**, corporal—the list is a very long one. The only alteration in **aide de camp** is the addition of hyphens in the English word, "aide-de-camp" (ayd də kamp). And, of course, the word **aide** has retained its spelling in the English word "aide"—pronounced ayd—which is used widely to mean "assistant" in such designations as "teacher's aide" and "nurse's aide."

aimer éperdument (ay-MAY ay-pair-dü-MAHN)
love passionately
And if you think that's true love, read the next entry.

aimer quelqu'un avec frénésie (ay-MAY kayl-KœN ah-VAYK fray-nay-ZEE)
love someone wildly
  The noun **frénésie** translates literally as "frenzy," besides which desperate love is a close second, and passionate love comes in a distant third.

à l'abandon (ah lah-bahn-DAWN)
in disorder
  Literally, "in abandonment." Sometimes translated as "at sixes and sevens," more frequently, as "at random," "left uncared for," and "adrift."

à la belle étoile (ah lah bayl ay-TWAHL)
under the stars
  Also rendered as "in the open air at night"; literally, "at the beautiful star." To appreciate this phrase, imagine yourself camping out in Vermont on a starry night. Ah!

à la bonne heure (ah lah bawn uhr)
very well
  Literally, "at the good hour." Better translated as "be it so."

à l'abri (ah lah-BREE)
under cover
  Literally, "under shelter," either literally or figuratively.

à la carte (ah lah kahrt)
according to the menu
  A restaurant term indicating that dishes are ordered—and paid for—individually. Distinguished from **table d'hôte** (tahblə doht), which offers an entire meal, with fewer choices and a fixed price. (See also À PRIX FIXE.)

à la croûte! (ah lah kroot)
come and get it!
  This idiomatic expression, literally, "to the crust!" summons guests or family to put on the feed bag. While it appears to bear little relation to the word "crust," keep in mind that French chefs prepare more than one dish **en** (ahn) **croûte**, translated as "in pastry." Enough to make one's mouth water!

à la guerre comme à la guerre (ah lah gair kawm ah lah gair)
that's life, don't fight it
Literally, "in war as in war," counseling that one must take things as they come. And when we think of the difficulties encountered in devoting oneself to bucking the system, we must admit there's something to this advice.

à la lanterne! (ah lah lahn-TAIRN)
string him up!
Literally, "to the lamppost with him!" and, more freely, "lynch him!" The phrase derives from the summary executions threatened—and often carried out—during the French Revolution by Parisian street mobs. They were intent on punishing members of the aristocracy after the fall of the Bastille, in July 1789, by hanging them on street lamps. (See also LES ARISTOCRATES À LA LANTERNE!)

à la mode (ah lah mawd)
fashionable or *fashionably*
Literally, "according to the fashion" or "according to the prevailing mode." So what uses does this phrase have? First consider the French dish **boeuf** (buhf) **à la mode**, a kind of beef stew more appetizing than the mundane word "stew" implies. (For further dining pleasure, see BOEUF EN DAUBE.) Then there is the delicacy known as **tripes** (treep) **à la mode de Caen** (duu kawn), tripe cooked in cider or white wine with carrots, onions, and cow hocks. But now consider something closer to home, the all-American pie à la mode (mohd), which calls for a generous portion of ice cream served atop a slab of pie, usually apple pie. Can anything be better?

à la prochaine! (ah lah praw-SHAYN)
until next time!
Also rendered as "I'll be seeing you." However we translate **à la prochaine!** the expression conveys the feeling that friendship will continue, unlike **adieu** (ah-DYUU), which translates as "good-bye" and carries an air of finality. (See, for example, the sad expression ADIEU LA VOITURE, ADIEU LA BOUTIQUE.)

A la recherche du temps perdu (ah lah ruu-SHAIRSH dü tahn pair-DÜ
Remembrance of Things Past
This is the well-known English rendering of the title of a great literary

work by the French novelist Marcel Proust, originally published between 1913 and 1927 in sixteen volumes. The literal meaning of the French title is "in search of lost time," and that is what Proust—and the narrator in the novel—sought in prolonged ruminations that led to involuntary memories stimulated by discrete objects or circumstances, enabling the narrator of the novel to find what he saw as the true meanings of a lifetime's experiences. Note that the first word of the title, **A**, properly carries an accent as in the lowercase letter **à**.

à l'article de la mort (ah lahr-TEEKLə duu lah mor)
at the point of death
   A sad but inevitable time. (See also À L'EXTRÉMITÉ.)

à la va-comme-je-te-pousse (ah lah vah-kawm-zhtuu-POOSS)
in any old way
   Also translated as "in a slapdash manner." The idiom is especially interesting—and amusing—in that the long hyphenated word within it translates literally as "go-as-I-push-you."

à la va-vite (ah lah vah-VEET)
in a hurry
   In this idiom **va-vite** translates literally as "go quickly."

à la volée (ah lah vaw-LAY)
on the fly
   When we do something **à la volée**, we act without stopping to think. We are intent on promptly seizing the occasion.

à la vôtre! (ah lah vohtrə)
cheers!
   A common toast, more literally translated as "to your health!" with the word "health" understood.

à l'extrémité (ah laykss-tray-mee-TAY)
at the last gasp
   Literally, "to extremity"; more commonly rendered as "at the point of death"—when one has run out of options. (See also À L'ARTICLE DE LA MORT.)

à l'impossible nul n'est tenu (ah lan-paw-SEEBLə nül nay tuu-NÜ)
relax!

Literally, "no one is required to accomplish the impossible." Something to remember when you are tempted to drive yourself too far beyond your abilities and available resources. In Exodus the Israelites in Egypt were commanded by their taskmasters to make bricks without straw, an impossibility. Thus, the English observation "you can't make bricks without straw" cautions against attempting the impossible.

aller (ah-LAY)
go

This infinitive and its various verb forms appear in a variety of idioms: **aller à toute vapeur** (ah toot vah-PUHR), "go full steam ahead," a locution that evokes the image of a steamship—**vapeur** means "steam"—putting everything it has into a rapid ocean crossing. Thus, we may translate **aller à toute vapeur** as "go all out" or "go at full speed." **Aller au paddock** (oh pah-DAWK) can be translated as "turn in"; literally, "go to the paddock," the field or saddling enclosure known to all devotees of horse racing. The colloquial translations most appropriate here are "hit the hay" and "hit the sack," both of which mean "retire for the night" or "go to sleep" and have nothing to do with the sport of kings. (See also SE METTRE AU PAGE.) **Aller au tapis** (oh tah-PEE), can be translated as "go down for the count." When a boxer cannot rise from the mat—**tapis** means "mat"—the match is over. But this locution is also applied outside the manly arts. Consider barroom brawls, business failures, and the countless personal defeats even the most successful among us may suffer in the course of our strivings. **Aller de pis en pis** (duu pee zahn pee), means "go from bad to worse"; more literally, "get worse and worse." **Aller en ville** (ahn veel) means "go into town." **Aller planter ses choux** (plahn-TAY say shoo) means "retire into private life." The metaphor, literally, "go plant one's cabbages," is often translated as "retire to the country." Come to think of it, that's a lot better than installing oneself in a so-called retirement community, to spend time only with people as old and inactive as you, with little to occupy your time but shuffleboard, bridge games, and the occasional round of golf. Far better to watch a few heads of cabbage grow. **Aller sur le pré** (sür luu pray) translates as "fight a duel"; literally, "go out on the meadow." The modern counterpart would involve meeting someone out on the sidewalk or in a back alley. **Allez-vous-en!** (ah-lay-voo-ZAHN) translates as "beat it!" or, as we used to say, "off with you!" or "go away!" or "begone!" The same meaning is also conveyed by **allez-vous promener!** (praw-muu-NAY); literally, "take a walk!" **Allez-y piane-piane** (zee pyahn-pyahn) translates as "easy does it"; literally, "go gently." Also given as **allez-y piano** (zee pyah-NOH). **Allons donc!** (ah-lawn dawnk) translates as "well, really!"; literally, "let us go then!" and often rendered as "come on!" or "come now!"

à l'oeuvre on connaît l'ouvrier (ah luhvrə awn kawn-NAY loo-vree-YAY)
a man is judged by the work he does
This gentle proverb, "it is in the work that one knows the workman," adjures us to judge people by what they accomplish, not by what they say.

Alouette! Gentille alouette!
Alouette! Je te plumerai! (ah-loo-AYTə zhahn-teeyə ah-loo-AYTə ah-loo-AYTə zhuu tuu plü-muu-RAY)
Skylark! Sweet skylark! Skylark! I'm going to pluck you!
This song, known to all beginning students of French, conveys a happy mood that is belied by its translation. Its lyrics go on to say "I'm going to pluck your head" and even more. Fortunately, children singing this song don't stop to think of what is about to happen to the poor bird.

amant (ah-MAHN)
lover
The feminine form of this noun is **amante** (ah-MAHNTə), translated as "betrothed" and "mistress." One phrase employing **amant** is **amant de coeur** (duu kuhr), literally, "heart's lover."

à méchant chien court lien (ah may-SHAHN shyan koor lyan)
for a vicious dog a short chain
Something to remember: better not allow a dangerous situation to go unchecked, lest it finally become virtually uncontrollable.

âme (ahm)
soul
This noun appears in several common phrases: **âme damnée** (dah-NAY), "devoted adherent," less felicitously but accurately translated also as "dupe" or "mere tool"; literally, "a damned soul." The phrase **âme de boue** (duu boo) translates as "mean soul" or "base soul"; literally, "soul of mud."

The phrase **âme perdue** (pair-DÜ) means "desperate character" or "one morally ruined"; literally, "lost soul."

ami (ah-MEE)
friend
   This noun gives rise to a number of interesting phrases: **ami de cour** (duu koor) translates as "false friend," "superficial friend" and, literally, "court friend," which indicates how people viewed the politics of court life back when there were royal courts. There may no longer be courts and court life, but when we wish to indicate a person who makes a polite but meaningless show of friendship, the phrase of choice is **ami de cour**. By way of contrast, **ami de table** (duu tahblə), which translates as "boon companion" or, literally, "table companion," gives us a more encouraging view of life and social intercourse. Even more attractive is **ami du peuple** (dü puhplə), which translates as "friend of the people." A marvelous appellation.

amie (ah-MEE)
female friend
   Also "mistress."

amour (ah-MOOR)
love
   This noun, essential to human experience, is the core of a variety of common phrases and insights: **amour de rencontre** (duu rahn-KAWNTRə) means "brief love affair." Only that and nothing more. The noun **rencontre** means "meeting" or "encounter." (See the last entry in this paragraph for a discussion of the plural of **amour de rencontre**.) The cynical observation **amour fait beaucoup, mais argent fait tout** (fay boh-KOO may ahr-ZHAHN fay too) translates as "love is powerful, but money is all-powerful" or as "love can do much, but money can do everything." Perhaps realistic but not exactly a sanguine view of love and the power of wealth. We move on happily to **amour fou** (foo), which means "passionate love" or "mad love." Perhaps not realistic but more in line with the common perception of true love—at least for a while. Even better is **amour fraternel** (frah-tair-NAYL), which means "brotherly love," and isn't this what life is or should be all about? With a nod in the direction of youth, we have **amour juvénile** (zhü-vay-NEEL), which means "puppy love"; literally, "young love"—once the epitome of innocence, now the briefest of inter-

ludes between childhood and major social concerns. The condition known as **amour-propre** (PRAWPRə) translates as "self-love," "vanity," or "self-esteem," none of which concerns love in the most general sense. (See also L'AMOUR-PROPRE EST LE PLUS GRAND DE TOUS LES FLATTEURS for a further indication of this.) Now we come finally to **amours de rencontre** (ah-MOOR duu rahn-KAWNTRə. This plural form of **amour de rencontre**, discussed above, is best translated as "casual love affairs." And the "meetings" or "encounters" imply an element of arrangement rather than fortuity.

ancienne noblesse (ahn-SYAYN noh-BLAYSS)
the old nobility
    That is, the nobility of France before the Revolution of 1789. (See also ANCIEN RÉGIME.)

ancien régime (ahn-SYAN ray-ZHEEM)
former regime
    Also translated as "old system of government" or "old order of things." The phrase **ancien régime** was used during the French Revolution to denote the system of government that existed under the Bourbon monarchy. It is now applied more widely to any regime—within a corporation or other institution—that is no longer in favor.

anglaiser quelqu'un (ahn-glay-ZAY kayl-KœN)
fleece somebody
    Literally, "English somebody." Talk about nationalism and stereotypes!

annoncer la couleur (ah-nawn-SAY lah koo-LUHR)
lay one's cards on the table
    In general use, translated as "say where one stands"; in bridge and other card games, "declare suit." **Couleur**, usually meaning "color," in cards means "suit."

à peindre (ah pandrə)
worth painting
    Also translated as "fit to paint," as a beautiful woman, a muscled male athlete, a marvelous natural scene, or the like.

à père avare, enfant prodigue (ah pair ah-VAHR ahn-FAHN proh-DEEG)
shirtsleeves to shirtsleeves in three generations

More literally, "a miser will father a spendthrift son." Does this explain the phenomenon that economists call "redistribution of wealth"?

aplanir le chemin devant quelqu'un (ah-plah-NEER luu shuu-MAN duu-VAHN kayl-KœN)
smooth somebody's way

Lobbyists and politicians, even parents and friends, come to mind as people who might figuratively or literally, as expressed here, "level the road in front of someone." What greater boon than to accomplish this generous function for a deserving person!

à point (ah pwan)
in time

This is just one of the English expressions used to translate this useful phrase, which translates literally as "to the point." "Just in time," "at just the right moment," "opportunely," "apropos," and "to a nicety" also come immediately to mind. And for those who have not succumbed to vegetarianism, there is always the possibility of ordering steak broiled **à point**, which translates as "just right" or "to a turn." Unless, that is, you want your steak rare, or **saignant** (sayn-YAHN) or, literally, "bloody." Consult any knowledgeable epicure or chef.

appareil critique (ah-pah-RAY kree-TEEK)
critical apparatus

In Latin, *apparatus criticus*, a scholar's term for supplementary material; for example, variant readings added to a text to provide material for study and criticism.

appeler un chat un chat (ah-PLAY œn shah œn shah)
call a spade a spade

Literally, "call a cat a cat," meaning call something by its rightful name instead of resorting to euphemisms.

appuyez sur le champignon! (ah-pwee-YAY sür luu shahn-pee-NYAWN)
step on it!

An interesting idiom, usually translated as "depress the accelerator." While anyone who is even slightly familiar with French cuisine knows that the usual meaning of **champignon** is "mushroom," early automobile accelerators were thought to bear some resemblance to the fungus. Ergo, literally, "depress the mushroom."

après la mort le médecin (ah-PRAY lah mor luu mayd-SAN)
better late than never? not always
Literally, "after death the doctor." For many of us, the moment when we begin to sink irretrievably into death is the only time we can expect a physician to make a house call.

après la pluie le beau temps (ah-PRAY lah plwee luu boh tahn)
good times will come again
The optimist's view of things; literally, "after the rain, fair weather."

après moi le déluge (ah-PRAY mwah luu day-LÜZH)
after me the deluge
The suggestion that no matter what you may think of me, wait until you see how desperate things will become after I'm gone. This statement is most often attributed to French King Louis XV. A close twin carrying the same meaning is **après nous** (ah-PRAY noo) **le déluge**, "after us the deluge," which is attributed to Madame de Pompadour, mistress of Louis XV. It is not known whether she was referring to herself in the royal "us" or to her and her lover, but things did go downhill for the monarchy and hit bottom—for them, at least—by 1789.

à prix fixe (ah pree feeks)
at a fixed price
See also À LA CARTE.

à propos de bottes (ah praw-POH duu bawt)
for no earthly purpose
A phrase used to introduce a quite irrelevant topic. Thus it may also be translated as "by the way," "for no earthly reason," and "foreign to the subject." The literal translation is "speaking of boots." Irrelevant enough for you? A less colorful way of conveying the same meaning is **à propos de rien** (ryan), translated as "apropos of nothing."

à quelque chose malheur est bon (ah kaylkə shohz mah-LUHR ay bawn)
every cloud has a silver lining

More literally, "there's some good in any misfortune." Maybe Emerson was right in his essay "Compensation."

à qui cela profite-t-il? (ah kee suu-LAH praw-feetə-TEEL)
who stands to benefit?

When attempting to find out who may have perpetrated a crime, the clever investigator—Hercule Poirot and Inspector Morse come first to mind—begins by asking **à qui cela profite-t-il?**, literally, "who will profit from this?" The answer to this question immediately reduces—in detective stories, at least—the number of possible suspects.

argent comptant (ahr-ZHAHN kawn-TAHN)
ready money

Nothing like it.

à Rome il faut vivre comme les romains (ah rawm eel foh veevrə kawm lay raw-MAN)
when in Rome, do as the Romans do

"Conform to local manners and customs." This is the classic advice—literally rendered as "in Rome, one must live like the Romans"—for those who go abroad and find themselves among people of unfamiliar customs. St. Ambrose (bishop of Milan, fourth century) is said to have advised St. Augustine: "When in Rome, live as the Romans do; when elsewhere, live as they live elsewhere."

arrêt (ah-RAY)
decree

This noun is also translated as "sentence," "judgment," and "arrest." Thus, **arrêt de mort** (duu mor) means "death sentence," and **arrêt du coeur** (dü kuhr) means "cardiac arrest." Take your choice!

arrêter (ah-ray-TAY)
stop

From this infinitive, we have **arrête de pleurnicher!** (ah-RAYT duu pluhr-nee-SHAY), "stop crying!" The infinitive **pleurnicher** also means "whine" or "snivel." We also have **arrêtez votre char!** (ah-ray-TAY vawtrə shahr), a way of saying "shut up!" or "shut your trap!" The literal translation of **arrêtez votre char!** is "stop your chariot!"

arrière-pensée (ah-ree-YAIR pahn-SAY)
ulterior motive
   Also translated as "mental reservation" or as "secret intention."

arriviste (ah-ree-VEEST)
go-getter
   While "go-getter" is a benign translation, the pejorative **arriviste** is more usually interpreted as "a person of new or uncertain social or artistic success." So apt is **arriviste** that we have taken the term "arriviste" into English, with the pronunciation ar-ee-VEEST.

art nouveau (ahr noo-VOH)
the new style of art
   Art Nouveau, literally, "New Art," is applied—in English as well as in French—to a style of fine and applied art introduced toward the end of the nineteenth century.

assez bien (ah-SAY byan)
pretty well
   Literally, "well enough."

assister quelqu'un dans ses derniers moments (ah-see-STAY kayl-KœN dahn say dair-NYAY moh-MAHN)
comfort someone at death's door
   More literally, "aid someone in his last moments." Note that the verb **assister** here is used transitively and is translated as "aid" or "assist." When **assister** is used intransitively, it means "be present at," "look on," or "witness."

à tort (ah tor)
wrongly or *wrong*
   This phrase appears in **à tort et à droit** (ay ah drwah), translated literally as "wrong and right"; idiomatically as "right and wrong" and "regardless of right and wrong." Another phrase is **à tort et à travers** (ay ah trah-VAIR), translated as "at random," "indiscriminately," and "regardless of circumstances." The phrase **à tort ou à droit** (oo ah drwah) is translated idiomatically as "right or wrong." Notice that the French give "wrong" first place in **à tort et à droit** and **à tort ou à droit**, while the idiomatic English translations give "right" first place. Two cultures, two ways of seeing things.

à toutes jambes (ah toot zhahnbə)
fast as your legs can carry you
   Literally, "with all one's legs."

à trompeur, trompeur et demi (ah traw*n*-PUHR traw*n*-PUHR
ay duu-MEE)
every deceiver meets his match
   Literally, "to a cheater, a cheater and a half." Thus we may say "to catch
a cheater, send a more skillful cheater." **Trompeur** may also be translated as
"deceiver." (See also À FRIPON, FRIPON ET DEMI.)

attendre la semaine des quatres jeudis (ah-TAHNDRə lah suu-MAYN
day kahtrə zhuu-DEE)
not until the cows come home
   Also rendered as "wait forever." And why does this idiom translate as it
does? Its literal meaning is "await a week with four Thursdays"—making it
clear we will have to wait forever. (See also JUSQU'AU JOUR OÙ LES POULES
AURONT DES DENTS.)

attendre le boiteux (ah-TAHNDRə luu bwah-TUU)
don't jump to conclusions
   Also translated as "bide one's time" and, literally, "wait for the lame person," suggesting that we wait for slow-moving confirmatory news. Red Sox
fans and anyone who has ever had a mammogram or CT scan knows the
wisdom of this advice.

attendre que les alouettes vous tombent toutes rôties dans la bouche
(ah-TAHNDRə kuu lay zah-loo-AYT voo tawnbə toot roh-TEE dahn lah
boosh)
count on manna from heaven
   Or on selecting the winning numbers in a state lottery. This idiom, literally, "wait for roasted larks to fall into your mouth," advises us not to expect miracles. In this world good things just don't fall into your lap.

attends de connaître la vie pour juger (ah-TAHN duu kawn-NAYTRə
lah vee poor zhü-ZHAY)
wait till you're dry behind the ears
   Literally, "wait until you know life before you pass judgment." But how

can we convince adolescents to wait a few years before displaying their un-
challengeable knowledge to one and all?

attentat (ah-tah*n*-TAH)
attack or *assault*
   Two timely phrases employ this noun: the first, **attentat à la pudeur** (ah
lah pü-DUHR), translates both as "indecent exposure" and "indecent assault." The second, **attentat aux moeurs** (oh muhr) translates as "offense
against public decency."

attirail de cambrioleur (ah-tee-RĪ duu kah*n*-bree-yoh-LUHR)
burglar's tools
   French is beautiful even when it speaks of illicit second-story activities.
Incidentally, the noun **attirail** translates as "paraphernalia," a term far more
elegant than "jimmy," "crowbar," or "picklock."

attraper la crève (ah-trah-PAY lah krayv)
catch one's death of cold
   Less vividly and more accurately translated as "come down with a bad
cold."

au bout de son latin (oh boo duu saw*n* lah-TA*N*)
at wits' end
   Literally, "at the end of his Latin." Could it be that in France, as elsewhere, mastery of Latin appears to overtax a schoolchild's pertinacity or intellectual grasp?

au couchant (oh koo-SHAHN)
to the west
   Where the sun sets each evening; **couchant** meaning "setting." (See also
AU LEVANT.)

au courant (oh koo-RAHN)
well informed
   Also translated as "fully acquainted with," "conversant with what is
going on," and "up on the circumstances, facts, etc., of a case." The literal
meaning of the phrase is "in the current"—of events, that is.

aucun chemin de fleurs ne conduit à la gloire (oh-KœN shuu-MAN duu fluhr nuu kawn-DWEE tah lah glwahr)
life just ain't easy
    For the ambitious, an insightful observation of La Fontaine; literally, "it is no path of flowers that leads to glory." And, as if that were not discouraging enough, consider the words of eighteenth-century English poet Thomas Gray, in "Elegy Written in a Country Churchyard": "The paths of glory lead but to the grave."

aujourd'hui marié, demain marri (oh-zhoor-DWEE mah-RYAY duu-MAN mah-REE)
married today, sorry tomorrow
    Too often true. And, as we approach the end of a millennium, we may well say in English, "married today, divorced tomorrow."

aujourd'hui roi, demain rien (oh-zhoor-DWEE rwah duu-MAN ryan)
on top today, scraping bottom tomorrow
    Literally, "king today, nothing tomorrow." And that's life. Even so, isn't it better to have a moment in the sun than never to enjoy celebrity, fame, power—you name it?

au levant (oh luu-VAHN)
to the east
    Where the sun rises each morning. **Levant** means "rising." (See also AU COUCHANT.)

au milieu de la nuit (oh mee-LYUU duu lah nwee)
in the middle of the night
    For an indication of how dark things can get at that time, see also AU PLUS PROFOND DE LA NUIT.

au naturel (oh nah-tü-RAYL)
in real life
    Literally, "in the natural state" or "as in nature." Also translated as "in the nude." Note that when we cook a dish **au naturel**, the food is prepared simply or plainly. But the primary meaning intended by English speakers who use this phrase is "naked," as in "posing au naturel."

au pied de la lettre (oh pyay duu lah laytrə)
literally
   Also translated as "exactly" or "to the very letter"; literally, "to the foot of the letter."

au plus profond de la nuit (oh plü praw-FAWN duu lah nwee)
at dead of night
   Literally, "in blackest night," when, of course, the outlook may be gloomiest.

au printemps de la vie (oh pran-TAHN duu lah vee)
in the springtime of life
   When everything seems possible—or so we are told.

au secours! (oh suu-KOOR)
help!

au seuil de la mort (oh sœyə duu lah mor)
at death's door
   Literally, "on the threshold of death."

au soir de sa vie (oh swahr duu sah vee)
"September Song"
   Literally, "in the evening of life," when "the days dwindle down to a precious few."

aussitôt dit, aussitôt fait (oh-see-TOH dee oh-see-TOH fay)
no sooner said than done
   Literally, "immediately said, immediately done." Wouldn't it be wonderful if everyone were so responsive!

autant d'hommes, autant d'avis (oh-TAHN dawm oh-TAHN dah-VEE)
everybody wants to get into the act
   Literally, "so many men, so many opinions." Maybe it's not always helpful to ask everybody.

au temps de sa verte jeunesse (oh tahn duu sah vairtə zhuu-NAYSS)
when our hearts were young and gay

Usually translated as "in the first bloom of his youth"; literally, "in the period of his green youth."

autres temps, autres moeurs (ohtrə tahn ohtrə muhr)
customs change with the times
A proverb, literally, "other times, other habits *or* customs," offering us a way of responding when young people do or say something that seems rude or eccentric. As you put on years, you will begin to notice that people around you are beginning to behave differently from the way you think they should. Don't criticize them, go with the flow. If you can.

au voleur! (oh vaw-LUHR)
stop, thief!
The phrase of choice when someone picks your pocket or steals your purse on a crowded Paris street.

aux absents les os (oh zahp-SAHN lay zoh)
latecomers get the bones
Literally, "for the absent, the bones." Think of someone arriving late for a Thanksgiving Day feast or showing up at a box office just before curtain time seeking tickets for the hottest show in town. In the first example, the unfortunate wretch misses a chance for the choice parts of the turkey. In the second, he's lucky if he can find standing room. The lesson is clear: Don't be late—ever. (For affirmation of this thought, see the next entry.)

aux audacieux les mains pleines (oh zoh-dah-SYUU lay man playn)
he who hesitates is lost
Translated as "the bold are amply rewarded"; more literally, "to the bold, full hands." So if you go after something believing you'll succeed, you probably will. Or at least you'll have a good shot at it. (See also UNE MINUTE D'HÉSITATION PEUT COÛTER CHER.)

aux grands maux les grands remèdes (oh grahn moh lay grahn ruu-MAYD)
sometimes you just can't avoid a root canal job
More conventionally translated as "desperate diseases demand desperate remedies" and, literally, "for great ills, great remedies." As long as Medicare is solvent.

aux idiots l'argent file entre les doigts (oh zee-DYOH lahr-ZHAHN feel ahntrə lay dwah)
a fool and his money are soon parted
The English proverb given above dates from the sixteenth century and still serves us well. As the literal translation of the French proverb so well puts it, "money slips through fools' fingers."

à vaincre sans péril, on triomphe sans gloire (ah vankrə sahn pay-REEL awn tree-YAWNF sahn glwahr)
back when men were men
This observation of Corneille has it that "triumph without peril brings no glory." Maybe it was true in the seventeenth century, but don't you think most moderns will probably reject the thought?

avaler des couleuvres (ah-vah-LAY day koo-LUHVRə)
swallow insults
Literally, "swallow adders," meaning snakes; that is, "accept indignities without protest."

avancer (ah-vahn-SAY)
advance or *move* or *progress*
Three phrases using **avancer** are of particular interest: the first is **avancer à vitesse réduite** (ah vee-TAYSS ray-DWEET), translated as "advance slowly" or "move forward at a crawl"; literally, "move forward at a reduced speed." The second phrase is **avancer comme une écrevisse** (kawm ün ay-kruu-VEESS), translated as "move very slowly"; literally, "go forward like a crayfish." The third is **avancer comme un escargot** (kawm œn nayss-kahr-GOH), translated most appropriately as "go at a snail's pace" and literally as "go forward like a snail." Both *écrevisse* and *escargot*, of course, are slow-moving creatures that delight the epicure in need of a culinary fix. Indeed, so taken are many American and English diners with *escargots* and *écrevisses* that both words appear, in the singular, in comprehensive English dictionaries, and on menus in the plural. While dictionaries still label this pair as French words, you can be sure that in due time they will no longer be so characterized. And those who take delight in eating these creatures—as well as those among us who will never even taste these creatures—don't particularly care whether they are French or English.

avant-garde (ah-vahn-GAHRD)
vanguard
One of hundreds of terms that have been taken from French unchanged in spelling or pronunciation. In English "avant-garde," thought of as meaning "unorthodox" or "daring," is applied particularly to experimentation in the arts.

avec des si et des mais, on mettrait Paris en bouteille (ah-VAYK day see ay day may awn may-TRAY pah-REE ahn boo-TAYə)
wishful thinking
Literally, "with ifs and buts, one could put Paris in a bottle." Also given in English as "if wishes were horses, beggars could ride." Best of all captured in a nineteenth-century proverb:

> *If Ifs and Ans were pots and pans*
> *There'd be no trade for tinkers.*

"Ans" here is the plural form of "an," an old form that meant "if."

avec la régularité d'un métronome (ah-VAYK lah ray-gü-lah-ree-TAY dœn may-traw-NAWM)
like clockwork
Literally, "with the regularity of a metronome."

avec plaisir (ah-VAYK play-ZEER)
with pleasure
One of those welcome locutions that have become almost automatic in facilitating human intercourse.

à verse (ah vairssə)
in torrents
Thus, we may say **il pleut à verse,** "It's raining cats and dogs." Note that **verse** is a form of the verb **verser** (vair-SAY, "pour") and quite different from **vers** (vair, "verse"). Confusing enough?

avez-vous du feu? (ah-vay-VOO dü fuu)
do you have a light?
When cigarettes were king, the English expression given above was heard everywhere in the United States. Its French counterpart, still heard

in the land of Gauloises—long the most popular French brand of cigarettes and readily identifiable by its unmistakably pungent aroma—literally means "do you have fire?"

à vieux comptes nouvelles disputes (ah vyuu kawnt noo-VAYL deess-PÜT)
old reckonings create new disputes
Literally, "on old accounts new disputes."

avise la fin (ah-VEEZ lah fan)
consider the end
Excellent counsel whenever you contemplate an unusual or extreme action.

avocat marron (ah-vaw-KAH mah-RAWN)
crooked lawyer
Also translated as "ambulance chaser." The noun **marron** means "chestnut," but the adjective means "brown," as well as "crooked" and "shady." What the connection is between the noun and the last two adjectival meanings is unclear, but English has many comparable mysteries, so we must not be too surprised. Let us instead be grateful for **marron glacé** (glah-SAY), the marvelous dish properly translated as "glazed chestnut," but always called "marron glacé" even in American and English restaurant menus.

avoir bec et ongles (ah-VWAHR bayk ay awnglə)
ready for a fight
Translated freely as "be ready or well equipped to fight back"; literally, "have beak and claws." At the ready, that is.

avoir bu un verre de trop (ah-VWAHR bü œn vair duu troh)
be tipsy
Also translated freely as "have half a load on"; literally, "to have drunk one drink too many." (See also AVOIR UN VERRE DANS LE NEZ.)

avoir d'autres chats à fouetter (ah-VWAHR dohtrə shah ah fway-TAY)
have other fish to fry
Literally, "have other cats to flog." Oh well, all languages have their metaphors.

avoir de l'argent en caisse (ah-VWAHR duu lahr-ZHAHN ahn kayss)
have cash on hand
Literally, "have money in the cashbox," where it is available for immediate disbursement. (See the next entry.)

avoir de l'argent plein les poches (ah-VWAHR duu lahr-ZHAHN plan lay pawsh)
rolling in money
This phrase translates freely as "have plenty of ready money"; literally, "have pockets stuffed with cash."

avoir de l'estomac (ah-VWAHR duu layss-taw-MAH)
have guts
The literal meaning of this idiom is "have the stomach," meaning have the inclination to do something. The English idiom "have the stomach for something" dates from the sixteenth century and is still frequently heard.

avoir de quoi faire bouillir la marmite (ah-VWAHR duu kwah fair boo-YEER lah mahr-MEET)
able to keep body and soul together
Literally, "have enough to keep the pot boiling," but extending as well to all necessities of life.

avoir des fourmis dans les jambes (ah-VWAHR day foor-MEE dahn lay zhahnb)
be on pins and needles
More literally, "have ants in one's legs," but **fourmis** is also translated as "pins and needles." You know the sensation. (See also J'AI LES PIEDS QUI FOURMILLENT.)

avoir dix dixièmes à chaque oeil (ah-VWAHR dee dee-ZYAYM ah shahk œyə)
20/20 vision
Literally, "have ten tenths in each eye." The French measure visual acuity from a distance of ten, rather than twenty, feet.

avoir du pain sur la planche (ah-VWAHR dü pan sür lah plahnsh)
have a lot on one's plate
Also translated as "have a lot to do"; literally, "have bread on one's

plank." The metaphor becomes clear when we consider that French bread is normally cut on a board, or plank. While most of us relish the prospect of having a lot to do, we must also keep in mind that there are too many families overloaded with responsibilities and the need to work long hours. A little moderation, please!

avoir du sang dans les veines (ah-VWAHR dü sahn dahn lay vayn)
have courage
    More expressively translated as "have guts"; literally as "have blood in one's veins." So we have red-blooded Frenchmen as well as red-blooded Americans.

avoir du toupet (ah-VWAHR dü too-PAY)
have a nerve
    Literally, "have a tuft of hair," *toupet* being the ancestor of the English word "toupee," with the meaning of "wig" or "hairpiece." Incidentally, the French word for "toupee" is **postiche** (pawss-TEESH), and the English word "postiche" (paw-STEESH) means "sham," "pretense," and—you guessed it—"hairpiece."

avoir la dent dure (ah-VWAHR lah dahn dür)
have a sharp tongue
    Literally, "have a hard tooth." Tongue, tooth—you pays your money and takes your choice. What's in an idiom?

avoir la gueule de bois (ah-VWAHR lah guhl duu bwah)
have a hangover
    Literally, "have a wooden mouth." Not a surprising metaphor for those of us thus afflicted. (See also GDB.)

avoir la guigne (ah-VWAHR lah geenyə)
be jinxed
    Less colorfully, "have rotten luck."

avoir la langue (ah-VWAHR lah lahng)
have the tongue
    A number of noteworthy idioms begin thus: **avoir la langue bien affilée** (byan ah-fee-LAY), "have a sharp tongue"; **avoir la langue bien pendue** (byan pawn-DÜ), "have the gift of gab," literally, "have the well-hung

tongue"; **avoir la langue déliée** (day-lee-AY), meaning "talk glibly," literally, "have the tongue untied"; and **avoir la langue fourchue** (foor-SHÜ), "speak deceitfully," literally, "have the forked tongue."

avoir la main (ah-VWAHR lah man)
have the hand

A number of common idioms begin thus, among them **avoir la main légère** (lay-ZHAIR), "rule mercifully"; literally, "rule with the light hand." Contrast this with **avoir la main lourde** (loordə), "be heavy-handed," as a judge who dispenses justice with a heavy hand. At the same time, **avoir la main lourde** may be translated as "be overly generous," as in rewarding someone. In either case, the almost literal translation is "have a heavy hand." Departing markedly from consideration of human behavior, consider **avoir la main verte** (vairt), translated as "have a green thumb"; literally, "have the green hand." Can it be that the French need five fingers to garden successfully, while the English and Americans need only a thumb?

avoir la mite à l'oeil (ah-VWAHR lah meet ah lœyə)
sandman's doing his work

An idiom meaning "fall asleep" or, with a bow toward folklore, "welcoming the sandman." The literal translation is "have the clothes moth in one's eyes." Which makes you more comfortable, sand or a moth?

avoir la tête (ah-VWAHR lah tayt)
have the head

A number of common idioms begin thus: **avoir la tête comme une passoire** (kawm ün pah-SWAHR), meaning "be forgetful" or "have a faulty memory," literally, "have a head like a sieve"; **avoir la tête près du bonnet** (pray dü bawn-AY), meaning "be quick-tempered," literally, "have the head near the hat." A mystery: where else can it be? Much easier to comprehend is **avoir la tête qui tourne** (kee toornə), meaning "feel giddy," literally, "have the head that turns," easily understood by anyone who has experienced full-fledged giddiness.

avoir le cafard (ah-VWAHR luu kah-FAHR)
have the blues

There are many ways to express this idiom in English, among them "be down in the dumps," "be in a funk," and "be depressed," today's most stylish expression. When asked to supply the literal meaning of **avoir le cafard**, one must say "have the cockroach" and quickly change the subject.

avoir le coeur malade (ah-VWAHR luu kuhr mah-LAHD)
have a weak heart
   Or "have a heart condition." Neither translation gives joy, nor does the literal translation "have a sick heart."

avoir le coeur sur les lèvres (ah-VWAHR luu kuhr sür lay layvrə)
wear your heart on your sleeve
   Literally, "have your heart on your lips." Wear? Have? Whichever word you prefer, we mean "lack in normal reserve."

avoir le nez en marmelade (ah-VWAHR luu nay ahn mahr-muu-LAHD)
be beaten to a pulp
   More literally, "have one's nose reduced to a pulp."

avoir les foies (ah-VWAHR lay fwah)
shake in one's boots
   Also translated as "be scared to death"; literally, "have the livers." The French seem to enjoy fattening animal livers and, as a consequence, contributing to damage in human livers.

avoir les jambes comme des fils de fer (ah-VWAHR lay zhahnbə kawm day feel duu fair)
have legs like matchsticks
   The literal translation is "have legs like wires." Just as nasty as the English translation given above. Note that **fils** here is the plural of **fil**, "wire." **Fils**, thus, must not be confused with **fils** (feess), meaning "son." (By way of contrast, see ELLE A DE BONS GIGOTS.)

avoir l'haleine forte (ah-VWAHR lah-LAYN fort)
have bad breath
   Literally, "have strong breath."

avoir l'oeil américain (ah-VWAHR lœyə ah-may-ree-KAN)
really sharp
   This idiom, translated also as "have a quick eye" and literally as "have an American eye," is not meant as an insult.

avoir l'orgueil de quelque chose (ah-VWAHR lor-GœYə duu kayl-KUU shohz)
take justifiable pride
   More closely translated as "pride oneself in something." But take note that **orgueil**, meaning "pride," may also be translated as "arrogance."

avoir mal à la tête (ah-VWAHR mahl ah lah tayt)
have a headache
   The idiom, literally "have a pain in the head," learned first by most American students of French.

avoir mal au coeur (ah-VWAHR mahl oh kuhr)
feel sick
   Literally, "have a pain in the heart."

avoir quelqu'un dans le nez (ah-VWAHR kayl-KœN dahn luu nay)
bear a grudge
   Literally, "have someone in the nose." Wow!

avoir réponse à tout (ah-VWAHR ray-PAWNSS ah too)
never at a loss
   Literally, "have an answer for everything," describing the kind of person born to be disliked.

avoir un besoin (ah-VWAHR œn buu-ZWAHN)
where's the restroom?
   Literally, "have a need"—to find a toilet, that is.

avoir un chagrin d'amour (ah-VWAHR œn shah-GRAN dah-MOOR)
be disappointed in love
   Also, "have an unhappy love affair."

avoir une aventure avec quelqu'un (ah-VWAHR ün ah-vahn-TÜR ah-VAYK kayl-KœN)
have an affair with someone

avoir une cervelle d'oiseau (ah-VWAHR ün sair-VAYL dwah-ZOH)
be birdbrained
   Hardly a compliment.

avoir une mine de déterré (ah-VWAHR ün meen duu day-tay-RAY)
look like death warmed over
 Literally, "look like someone who's been exhumed."

avoir un verre dans le nez (ah-VWAHR œn vair dahn luu nay)
have one too many
 Literally, "have a glass in the nose." (See also AVOIR BU UN VERRE DE TROP.)

à voleur voleur et demi (ah vaw-LUHR vaw-LUHR ay duu-MEE)
it takes one to know one
 As the seventeenth-century English proverb has it, "set a thief to catch a thief."

à votre santé! (ah vawtrə sahn-TAY)
l'chaim!
 Also "cheers!" and, literally, "to your health!"

baba au rhum (bah-BAH oh ruum)
baba au rhum
 A French delight—a spongelike cake steeped in rum syrup—which in English is never called anything but "baba au rhum" and pronounced as in French.

bâcler sa toilette (bah-KLAY sah twah-LAYT)
a lick and a promise
 Translated as "have a quick wash," **bâcler** meaning "hurry over."

badaud (bah-DOH)
gaping idler
 Also translated as a "foolishly curious and credulous person."

bâiller à s'en décrocher la mâchoire (bah-YAY ah sahn day-kraw-SHAY lah mah-SHWAHR)
yawn one's head off
Literally, "yawn to the point of unhinging one's jaw." Now that's a yawn!

bal costumé (bahl kawss-tü-MAY)
fancy-dress ball
Literally, "a costume ball," an event still seen among the rich and celebrated. **Bal masqué**, or "masked ball," is an equivalent phrase.

ballon d'essai (bah-LAWN day-SAY)
trial balloon
Also a "feeler," that is, a remark, announcement, or the like designed to test the opinions of others. (See also REGARDER DE QUEL CÔTÉ LE VENT SOUFFLE.)

bàtir des châteaux en Espagne (bah-TEER day shah-TOH ahn nayss-PAHNYə)
kid oneself
Literally, "build castles in Spain," a metaphor in English as well, dating from the fourteenth century.

battre l'eau avec un bâton (bahtrə loh ah-VAYK œn bah-TAWN)
try in vain
Literally, "beat water with a stick." If you don't immediately understand this metaphor, find a stick and try to beat water.

battre le fer pendant qu'il est chaud (bahtrə luu fair pahn-DAHN keel ay shoh)
make hay while the sun shines
This French proverb translates literally as "strike while the iron is hot," which also is a fourteenth-century English proverb understandable to anyone who has watched a blacksmith at his job. "Make hay while the sun shines" is itself a sixteenth-century English proverb counseling farmers not to harvest hay in wet weather, lest the hay rot in storage. Whatever the frame of reference, we all are instructed—both in French and English—to take advantage of opportunity that is presented.

battre quelqu'un comme plâtre (bahtrə kayl-KœN kawm plahtrə)
beat the living daylights out of someone
Literally, "beat someone like plaster."

beau geste (boh zhayst)
conciliatory gesture

Also translated as "magnanimous gesture" and "graceful gesture"; literally, "beautiful gesture." Early in the twentieth century, English novelist P. C. Wren wrote *Beau Geste*, a work still in print that continues to enthrall impressionable boys with its rousing portrayal of brave soldiers of the French Foreign Legion. If you wish to understand **beau geste** completely, read the novel—or find a video of the 1939 Hollywood movie made from it. (See also *Beau Sabreur* by the same author, and BEAU SABREUR below.)

beau monde (boh mawndə)
high society

"Beau monde" has been taken into English, with the meaning of "fashionable society" or "the world of fashion." The literal French translation is "fine world," denoting the people who make up the coterie of fashion.

beau sabreur (boh sah-BRUHR)
dashing cavalryman or *soldier*

Literally, "fine swordsman." *Beau Sabreur* is the title of a novel by P. C. Wren glamorizing the exploits of members of the French Foreign Legion. (See also BEAU GESTE.)

belle amie (bayl lah-MEE)
mistress

Literally, "fair friend."

belle époque (bayl lay-PAWK)
beautiful era

La Belle Epoque was the name given to the Edwardian Era, roughly the period between 1890 and the beginning of World War I, remembered in Europe as a time of affluence and gentility. The English monarch during most of this period was Edward VII (1841–1910).

belle passion (bayl pah-SYAWN)
the tender passion

Also translated as "ardent affection" and plain old "love."

belles-lettres (bayl-LAYTRə)
belles lettres
   Taken as "writings of a purely literary nature" or "literature regarded as a fine art"; literally, "fine letters." You can see why the succinct "belles lettres" has been welcomed into the English language, where it is pronounced bel LEH-trə.

bête noire (bayt nwahr)
bugaboo
   Also translated as "pet aversion"; literally, "black beast."

beurre (buhr)
butter
   And there are various types of **beurre**, for example, **beurre d'anchois** (dahn-SHWAH), "anchovy paste"; **beurre de cacahuètes** (duu kah-kah-WAYT), "peanut butter"; **beurre fondu** (fawn-DÜ), "melted butter"; and **beurre roux** (roo), "browned butter." **Roux** here translates literally as "auburn."

bien (byan)
well
   This adverb introduces many locutions, for example: **bien conservé pour son âge** (kawn-sair-VAY poor sawn nahzh), "well-preserved for his age," a demeaning characterization, translating more loosely as "in good shape for an old man." In better taste are **bien élevé** (nayl-VAY), "well-mannered," and **bien entendu** (ahn-tahn-DÜ), "of course," "agreed," and "assuredly"; literally, "well understood." By way of a compliment we have **bien joué!** (zhoo-AY), translated as "attaboy!" and "well played!" or, as the English say, "well done!" Moving on to the inevitable proverbs, we have **bien mal acquis ne profite jamais** (mahl ah-KEE nuu praw-FEET zhah-MAY), "ill gotten, ill spent"; literally, "ill-gotten gains never prosper." Then there is **bien perdu, bien connu** (pair-DÜ byan kaw-NÜ), literally "well lost, well known," better translated as "some things are not missed till you've lost them" or "once lost, then prized."

bienvenue à vous! (byan-vuu-NÜ ah voo)
welcome!
   More literally, "you are welcome!" A happy greeting for arriving guests.

bifteck haché (beef-TAYK ah-SHAY)
ground beef
   The hamburger appears to be universal. (See also HACHIS.)

billet doux (bee-YAY doo)
love letter
   Literally, "sweet letter."

blagueur (blah-GUHR)
joker
   Also, "comedian."

blanc comme un cachet d'aspirine (blah*n* kawm œn kah-SHAY dahss-
pee-REEN)
white as a sheet
   Literally, "white as an aspirin tablet."

boeuf en daube (buhf ah*n* dohb)
beef stew
   Comprising beef prepared with vegetables, herbs, and seasonings. Delicious and nutritious. (See also DAUBE.)

boire (bwahr)
drink
   This verb gives us many locutions and idioms, beginning with **boire à la
santé de quelqu'un** (ah lah sah*n*-TAY duu kayl-KœN), translated as "drink
to someone's health," and going on to several expressions that all mean
"drink to excess": **boire avec excès** (ah-VAYK ayks-SAY), literally, "drink
to excess"; **boire comme un trou** (kawm œn troo), literally, "drink like a
hole"; **boire comme un troupier** (kawm œn troo-PYAY), literally, "drink
like a trooper"; and **boire comme une éponge** (kawm ün ay-PAWNZHə),
literally, "drink like a sponge." For a change of pace, there is **boire les
paroles de quelqu'un** (lay pah-RUHL duu kayl-KœN), meaning "swallow
whole"; more literally, "drink in someone's words," which idiomatic Amer-
ican-English expresses as "lap up someone's words." Going back to real
drinking, there is **boire le whisky nature** (luu wee-SKEE nah-TÜR),
"drink whiskey straight." (See also IL PREND SON WHISKY SEC.) Going even
further back, there are **boire outre mesure** (ootrə mə-ZÜR), "get smashed,"
"drink overmuch," and, of course, "drink to excess"; and **boire sec** (sayk),

"drink hard"; literally, "drink dry," which describes a heavy drinker. On a
more convivial note there is **boire un coup devant le zinc** (œn koo duh-
VAHN luu zank), translated as "have a drink at the bar." But, going back to
excess for one last time, there is **boire un verre de trop** (œn vair duu troh),
"have a drink too many."

bois tordu fait feu droit (bwah tor-DÜ fay fuu drwah)
everything has its use
    Literally translated as "crooked wood makes a straight fire."

bon ami (bawn ah-MEE)
lover
    Literally, "good friend." (See also BONNE AMIE.)

bon an, mal an (bawn nahn mahl lahn)
wait till next year
    The French phrase, literally "good year, bad year," conveys the meaning
"taking the good with the bad" and drives home the message that you can't
win 'em all.

bon à rien (bawn nah ryan)
ne'er-do-well
    More literally, "good-for-nothing."

bon avocat, mal voisin (bawn nah-vaw-KAH mahl vwah-ZAN)
good lawyer, bad neighbor
    Telling us, as though we needed the prompting, that those of us who
have a lawyer as a neighbor may well anticipate being sued or at least being
threatened with a suit.

bon gré, mal gré (bawn gray mahl gray)
willy-nilly
    Also translated as "willing or unwilling"; literally, "good grace, bad
grace."

bonhomie (bawn-naw-MEE)
geniality
    Also translated as "good nature" and "unaffected affability."

bon jour, bonne oeuvre (bawn zhoor bawn uhvrə)
better the day, better the deed
　　Literally, "good day, good work."

bon mot (bawn moh)
witticism
　　Also translated as "witty saying or repartee"; literally, "good word." "Bon mot" has been taken into English, usually with the French pronunciation. The infrequently heard English pronunciation is so strange to the ear that it has been omitted here.

bonne amie (bawn ah-MEE)
sweetheart or *mistress*
　　Literally, "good friend." (See also BON AMI.)

bonne bouche (bawn boosh)
choice morsel
　　Also, "delicious tidbit"; literally, "good mouth," suggesting an agreeable taste left in the mouth.

bonne renommée vaut mieux que ceinture dorée (bawn ruh-naw-MAY voh myuu kuu san-TÜR daw-RAY)
a good name is better than wealth
　　Literally, "a good name is worth more than a golden girdle." A golden girdle formerly meant a purse of gold, from the custom of carrying money in the belt or in a purse suspended from it.

bonnet de nuit (bawn-NAY duu nwee)
nightcap
　　An item of apparel, not the last drink of the day.

bon sang ne saurait mentir (bawn sahn nuu soh-RAY mahn-TEER)
blood will tell
　　Loosely given as "what's bred in the bone will come out in the flesh"; literally, "good blood cannot lie." Whichever translation is used, the meaning is "a natural propensity cannot be repressed." (See also CHASSEZ LE NA-TUREL, IL REVIENT AU GALOP.)

bon voyage (bawn vwah-YAHZH)
enjoy your trip
   A fine sentiment expressed to a friend leaving on vacation; literally, "good journey" or "good voyage."

bouche à bouche (boosh ah boosh)
face-to-face
   Literally translated as "mouth to mouth."

bouche cousue! (boosh koo-ZÜ)
mum's the word!
   Literally translated as "mouth sewn up."

bouillie pour les chats (boo-YEE poor lay shah)
fruitless labor
   A devastating characterization of a failed effort that was seriously pursued; literally, "pap for cats."

bouleversé (bool-vair-SAY)
thrown for a loop
   Also translated as "upset" and "shattered"; literally, "turned upside down." Anyone who ends up **bouleversé** has been thoroughly discomposed, thrown into complete disorder. For example, **bouleversé par la peur** (pahr lah puhr) means "distraught with fear."

bourgeois (boor-ZHWAH)
middle-class or *common*
   As a noun, "member of the middle class." **Bourgeois gentilhomme** (zhahn-tee-YAWM) is usually translated as "tradesman turned gentleman." (See also LE BOURGEOIS GENTILHOMME.)

brassière (brah-SYAIR)
bra
   Also given in English as "brassiere" (brə-ZEER), a word now only rarely heard. (See also SOUTIEN-GORGE.)

briller par son absence (bree-YAY pahr sawn nahb-SAHNSS)
be conspicuous by one's absence
   Literally, "shine by one's absence."

broder n'est pas mentir mais farder la vérité (braw-DAY nay pah mahn-TEER may fahr-DAY lah vay-ree-TAY)
color the truth
   Literally translated as "to embellish *or* embroider is not to lie but to gloss over the truth."

broder sur un sujet (braw-DAY sür œn sü-ZHAY)
expatiate
   Also translated as "elaborate on a subject"; literally, "embroider on a subject."

brûler la chandelle par les deux bouts (brü-LAY lah shahn-DAYL pahr lay duu boo)
burn the candle at both ends
   This metaphor, dating from the seventeenth century in English and more prosaically given as "live it up without a thought for tomorrow," owes much of its present renown to the poem "First Fig," written by the American poet Edna St. Vincent Millay in the twentieth century:

> My *candle burns at both ends;*
> *It will not last the night;*
> *But, ah, my foes, and, oh, my friends—*
> *It gives a lovely light.*

C

cabinet (kah-bee-NAY)
toilet
   Note that **cabinet** means "office" or "closet," which reminds one of the English euphemism "water closet."

cabrer quelqu'un (kah-BRAY kayl-KœN)
get someone's back up
   Literally, "make someone rear up"—as a fractious horse rears up, that is.

ça coûte les yeux de la tête (sah koot lay zyuu duu lah tayt)
it costs an arm and a leg
> More politely, "that's exorbitant"; literally, "that costs the eyes of the head."

ça coûte trois fois rien (sah koot trwah fwah ryan)
it's dirt cheap
> Also translated as "it costs next to nothing"; literally, "it costs three times nothing." And every upstanding student knows that even a million times zero still means nothing.

cadeau (kah-DOH)
present or *gift*
> Thus, something given **en** (awn) **cadeau** is given as a present.

ça fait très habillé (sah fay tray zah-bee-YAY)
it looks very smart
> More literally, "it looks very dressy."

ça ira (sah ee-RAH)
it will go on
> The refrain from a song popular during the French Revolution:

> *Ah, ça ira, ça ira, ça ira!*
> *Les aristocrates à la lanterne!*

Suffice it to say that the second line is designed to incite street mobs to string up the aristocrats. (See also À LA LANTERNE.)

caisse de prévoyance (kayss duu pray-vwah-YAHNSS)
contingency fund
> The noun **caisse** means "box" or "cashbox," and **prévoyance** means "foresight."

ça me donne le frisson (sah muu dawn luu free-SAWN)
it gives me the willies
> Or "creeps" or "shivers" or "shudders." The entire locution is also translated as "it makes me shudder." The English word "frisson," usually pro-

nounced as in French, is taken to mean "sudden, passing sensation of excitement" or "shudder of emotion."

canaille (kahn-NAHYə)
rabble or *riffraff*
> Be careful! **Canaille** also translates as "bastard" or "crook."

ça ne fait rien (sah nuu fay ryan)
it doesn't matter
> Also translated as "never mind!"

ça n'empêche rien (sah nahn-PAYSH ryan)
it makes no nevermind
> Usually translated as "it makes no difference," literally as "it doesn't prevent anything."

ça ne va pas tarder (sah nuu vah pah tahr-DAY)
it's in the mail
> Usually translated as "it won't be long in coming."

ça ne vaut pas un radis (sah nuu voh pah œn rah-DEE)
it's worthless
> Usually translated as "it's not worth a penny"; literally, "it's not worth a radish."

carte (kahrt)
card or *map* or *chart*
> In a restaurant, "bill of fare." This noun also gives us several useful phrases: **carte blanche** (blahnsh), translated as "full discretionary power," literally, "blank card"; **cartes des vins** (day van), "wine list"; **carte du jour** (dü zhoor), in a restaurant, "the bill of fare for the day"; **carte du pays** (dü pay-EE), translated as "lay of the land," literally, "map of the country"; and **cartes sur table** (sür tahblə), "aboveboard"; literally, "cards on the table."

casaque tourner (kah-ZAHK toor-NAY)
change sides
> Literally, "turn one's coat *or* blouse."

ça sent le fagot (sah sahn luu fah-GOH)
it smacks of heresy
Literally translated as "it smells of firewood," an allusion to burning at the stake, historically the fate of heretics.

ça sent le poisson ici (sah sahn luu pwah-SAWN ee-SEE)
something is rotten in the state of Denmark
Leaving Shakespeare out of it, often translated as "I smell something fishy"; literally, "it smells fishy in here." (See also IL Y A ANGUILLE SOUS ROCHE.)

ça se vaut (sah suu voh)
it's all the same
Also translated as "it's all one" and as "six of one and half a dozen of the other"—all by way of saying there's nothing to choose between proposed alternatives.

cassage de gueule (kah-SAHZH duu guhl)
fistfight
Also translated as "brawl," literally as "breaking of a mouth." Ugh!

casser les pieds à quelqu'un (kah-SAY lay pyay ah kayl-KœN)
bore someone to death
Less dramatically translated as "wear someone out," "bore someone stiff," or "get on somebody's nerves." The literal translation is "break someone's legs." The French take boredom seriously.

casserole (kah-SəRAWL)
saucepan
Also food prepared in it.

casser sa pipe (kah-SAY sah peep)
kick the bucket
Literally translated as "break his pipe." Clearly, the person in question has smoked—and done everything else—for the last time.

casse-tête (kahss-TAYT)
headache
Also translated as "brainteaser"; literally, "head breaker."

catalogue raisonné (kah-tah-LAWG ray-zaw-NAY)
catalogue raisonné
Literally, "reasoned catalog," suggesting a catalog that has been well thought out. This French term has come into English to denote a descriptive catalog arranged according to subjects. Thus, in a catalogue raisonné of paintings or books—the usual subjects covered in such a catalog—notes and commentaries are generally supplied for the items listed. The pronunciation of the English term is reasonably close to the French pronunciation. (See also RAISONNÉ.)

cause célèbre (kohz say-LAYBRə)
cause célèbre
Yet another apt French phrase that has come into English unchanged, with the literal meaning of "famous case" and denoting "a trial that has attracted great public interest" or "a widely debated controversial issue."

causeur (koh-ZUHR)
conversationalist
Literally translated as "talker." **Causeuse** (koh-ZUHZ) is the feminine form of **causeur**, and also means "love seat"—and what could be better for carrying on an intimate conversation?

ça va (sah vah)
OK
A commonly heard locution, also translated as "all right," "not bad," and the like. With a question mark—**ça va?**—the meaning becomes "how are things?" or "how are you?" The literal translation of **ça va** is "it goes," which leads the discussion to a large number of useful idiomatic expressions. In alphabetic order, the first is **ça va de compagnie avec** (duu kawn-pah-NYEE ah-VAYK), translated as "it goes hand in hand with" or, as Americans formerly were inclined to say and sing of love and marriage, "you can't have one without the other." The second is **ça va être la corrida!** (aytrə lah kaw-ree-DAH), meaning "all hell is going to break loose!" more literally translated as "there's going to be a bullfight!" In the same vein we have **ça va gueuler** (guh-LAY), freely translated as "all hell is going to break loose" and "there's going to be a hell of a row." **Gueuler** means "bawl" or "bellow," so we know there will be much yelling if the prediction holds true. Two additional locutions are **ça va mal tourner** (mahl toor-NAY), translated as "no good will come of it," "it's sure to turn nasty," as well as

"that'll lead to trouble," and **ça va tourner au vilain** (toor-NAY oh vee-LAN), which can be translated similarly. Finally, on a somewhat more sanguine note, there is **ça va tout doux** (too doo), translated freely as "it's neither a smash hit nor a disaster" or "things are going so-so."

ça vaut bien un fromage sans doute (sah voh byan œn fraw-MAHZH sahn doot)
it's well worth a piece of cheese
 Every schoolchild who has had to memorize the fables of La Fontaine knows that this locution concludes a lesson delivered to a silly crow by a wily fox. In the fable the crow holds a piece of cheese in its bill but drops it when the naive crow is inveigled into favoring the fox with a song. The lesson is "flatterers live at the expense of those who listen to them."

ce jeune homme ira loin (suu zhuhn nawm ee-RAH lwan)
this kid will make it
 Freely translated as "keep your eye on him," literally as "this young man will go far." That is, he will surely achieve success.

cela ne fait rien (suu-LAH nuu fay ryan)
that doesn't matter

cela va sans dire (suu-LAH vah sahn deer)
it goes without saying
 Also translated as "it's understood" or "it's a matter of course."

ce ne sont que des seconds couteaux (suu nuu sawn kuu day suu-GAWN koo-TOH)
they're only small fry
 Also translated as "they don't count for much," more literally "they're nothing but second-rate knives."

ce n'est pas . . . (suu nay pah)
it isn't . . .
 A common locution used in making many types of statements, a few of which are given here: **ce n'est pas à son âge qu'on apprend de nouveaux trucs** (zah sawn nahzh kawn nah-PRAHN duu noo-VOH trük), translated as "it's hard to teach old dogs new tricks"; literally, "it's not at his advanced age that one learns new tricks." (The idiom **à son âge** translates as "at his

advanced age.") All this by way of saying that elderly people are not adaptable. When we wish to express incredulity, there is **ce n'est pas croyable** (krwah-YAHBLǝ), "it's unbelievable." For an insight more profound, there is **ce n'est pas être bien aise que de rire** (aytrǝ byan nayz kuu duu reer), translated as "don't be misled by a laugh"; more literally, "laughter is not always a sign of a mind at ease." The source of this insight is Saint-Evremond, a seventeenth-century French writer and wit. And when we want someone to do a favor, we may reassure that person with **ce n'est pas la mer à boire!** (lah mair rah bwahr), freely translated as "I'm sure it's no great hardship," also as "I'm not asking the impossible of you," and literally as "it's not drinking the sea." By way of criticism we have **ce n'est pas marrant** (mah-RAHN), "it's no joke" or "it ain't funny," **marrant** meaning "funny," or, with greater intensity, **ce n'est pas pensable** (pahn-SAHBLǝ), "it's unthinkable." When we wish to reject a suggestion or offer, we may say **ce n'est pas très intéressant pour moi** (tray zan-tay-ray-SAHN poor mwah), "it's not worth my while" or "it's not really worth it for me." Yet another way to do so is to say **ce n'est pas une sinécure** (zün see-nay-KÜR), "it's no pushover," or "it's not a bed of roses," **sinécure** meaning the same thing as the English word "sinecure." Finally, we have the ironic comment **ce n'est pas un génie** (zœn zhay-NEE), "he's no Einstein" or, more literally, "he's not a genius."

ce n'est que de l'argent, c'est fait pour être dépensé (suu nay kuu duu lahr-ZHAHN say fay poor aytrǝ day-pahn-SAY)
easy come, easy go
   Literally, "it's only money; it's made to be spent."

ce n'est que la première ébauche (suu nay kuu lah pruh-MYAIR ay-BOHSH)
this is just a rough draft
   The French phrase of choice, literally, "it's only the first outline," for students showing trepidation as they hand a term paper to a teacher, for young employees submitting what they fear is an unacceptable business plan, for writers trembling as they deliver a worked and reworked iteration of a manuscript.

ce n'est que le premier pas qui coûte (suu nay kuu luu pruh-MYAY pah kee koot)
the first step on the slippery slope

Literally, "it's only the first step that costs," making it clear that further steps will soon be taken and that certain disaster lurks in the wings.

ce qui est bon pour l'un l'est pour l'autre (suu kee ay bawn poor lœn lay poor lohtrə)
what's sauce for the goose is sauce for the gander
Literally, "what is good for one is good for the other," giving us a principle that usually ends in mutual recriminations and a failed partnership, whether of husband and wife or of any other duo.

ce qui est différé n'est pas perdu (suu kee ay dee-fay-RAY nay pah pair-DÜ)
some things are best put off
Literally translated as "what is put off is not lost," which makes a lot more sense than "never put off until tomorrow what you can do today." Surely you can do something today, but wouldn't a little more thought—perhaps another day's effort—enable you to do it differently and better?

ce qui guérit l'un tue l'autre (suu kee gay-REE lœn tü lohtrə)
one man's meat is another man's poison
One of life's ironies; literally, "what cures one kills the other."

ce qu'il est suant! (suu keel ay swee-AHN)
what a pain in the neck!
The adjective **suant** is translated freely as "dull" and literally as "sweaty." So while this idiomatic construction can be translated freely as "what a bore he is!" and "he's a real drag," a literal translation should be avoided, since it would make no sense at all and would leave readers uncomfortable.

ce sont les cordonniers qui sont les plus mal chaussés (suu sawn lay kor-daw-NYAY kee sawn lay plü mahl shoh-SAY)
papa's too busy making a living
Usually given in English as "the cobbler's children are always the worst shod," heightening the literal meaning of the French proverb, "it's the cobblers who are worst shod." (See also À FILS DE CORDONNIER POINT DE CHAUSSURES.)

c'est-à-dire (say-tah-DEER)
that is
Also given as "i.e."; literally, "that is to say."

c'est à l'oeil qu'on connaît l'ouvrier (say tah lœyə kawn kaw-NAY loo-vree-YAY)
a man is judged by his works
Also translated as "we know the workman by what we see," that is, by his product, not by the claims made for his product.

c'est à l'usage que l'on peut juger de la qualité d'une chose (say tah lü-ZAHZH kuu lawn puu zhü-ZHAY duu lah kah-lee-TAY dün shohz)
don't judge by appearances
Literally translated as "performance is the true test of the quality of anything." Or, as the seventeenth-century English proverb has it, "the proof of the pudding is in the eating." It is worthwhile to point out that in Great Britain, "pudding" is a word often used for "dessert." In French, **dessert** (day-SAIR) means "dessert." Clear?

c'est à se cogner la tête contre les murs (say tah suu kaw-NYAY lah tayt kawntrə lay mür)
it's enough to drive you up the wall
Literally translated as "it's enough to make you knock your head against the walls."

c'est bonnet blanc et blanc bonnet (say bawn-NAY blahn ay blahn bawn-NAY)
six of one, half dozen of the other
Also translated as "it amounts to the same thing"; literally, "it's a white hat and a white hat." Thus, as we are wont to say pejoratively, "it's the same no matter which way you cut it." The most interesting aspect of the French locution is its demonstration that French adjectives may modify an immediately preceding noun as well as an immediately following noun. So **bonnet blanc** is identical in meaning with **blanc bonnet**. English adjectives may also be moved back and forth, but this is done far less frequently than with French adjectives.

c'est bon pour les chiens (say bawn poor lay shyan)
it's for the birds
Literally translated as "it's good for the dogs." Birds or dogs, either way you express the thought, "it's no good at all." Get rid of it. Try something else.

c'est ça (say sah)
it's so
> Literally translated as "it is that."

c'est dans la poche (say dahn lah pawsh)
it's in the bag
> Literally translated as "it's in the pocket." Of course, when we say "he has the governor in his pocket," we are suggesting criminal behavior. The French expression merely tells us that a bet, for example, is a sure thing— "you can bet the farm on it."

c'est dans le besoin que l'on connaît ses vrais amis (say dahn luu buu-ZWAN kuu lawn kawn-NAY say vray zah-MEE)
a friend in need is a friend indeed
> The Romans used this proverb—in Latin, of course—to tell us that "you'll know who your true friends are when you are in need of them." Another way to say this in French is **c'est dans le malheur qu'on connaît ses amis** (say dahn luu mah-LUHR kawn kawn-NAY say zah-MEE), **malheur** being translated as "adversity."

c'est de l'hébreu pour moi (say duu lay-BRUU poor mwah)
it's Greek to me
> Literally "it's Hebrew to me."

c'est dommage! (say daw-MAHZH)
what a shame!
> Literally "it's a shame!"

c'est du déjà-vu (say dü day-zhah-VÜ)
it's nothing new
> Literally translated as "we've already seen it." (See also DÉJÀ VU.)

c'est du flan (say dü flahn)
it's the bunk
> Also translated as "it's hooey"; literally, "it's custard." (See also FLAN.)

c'est du gâteau (say dü gah-TOH)
it's a snap
> Or "it's a cinch" or "it's a piece of cake," "cake" being an accurate translation of **gâteau**. The same meaning is conveyed by **c'est du nougat** (noo-

GAH), translated literally as "it's nougat," the chewy or brittle candy adored by many who are afflicted with a sweet tooth.

c'est du trompe-l'oeil (say dü trawnpə-LœYə)
it's hogwash
Or "eyewash," or "humbug." In short, "it's nonsense."

c'est du vol organisé (say dü vawl or-gah-nee-ZAY)
it's a racket
Literally, "it's organized theft." An excellent way to describe an illicit enterprise.

c'est en forgeant qu'on devient forgeron (say tahn for-ZHAHN kawn duu-VYAN for-zhuu-RAWN)
practice makes perfect
The path to competence in any occupation or profession. Also freely translated as "one learns by doing," literally as "one becomes a blacksmith by working as a blacksmith." Right on!

c'est entendu (say tahn-tahn-DÜ)
it's agreed
Also translated as "all right," "granted," and "it's understood."

c'est entré comme dans du beurre (say tahn-TRAY kawm dahn dü buhr)
it's easy as pie
Also, "it's a pushover" and, almost literally, "it went through it like a knife through butter."

c'est fait! (say fay)
that's it!
Literally, "it's done!"

c'est juste bon à mettre aux ordures (say zhüst bawn ah maytrə oh zor-DÜR)
get rid of it!
More literally, "it's fit only for the garbage can," **ordures** meaning "dirt" or "filth." It is worth pointing out that the English word "ordure" means "dung," "manure," or "excrement."

c'est la carte forcée! (say lah kahrt for-SAY)
we've no choice!

An allusion to the situation in a game of cards in which a player is forced to play a certain card, so he has no choice at all. Also translated as "it's Hobson's choice!" Thomas Hobson, who rented horses in Cambridge, England, centuries ago, insisted that his customers accept the horse that stood nearest the stable door or do without one, thus giving us an English phrase meaning "no choice at all."

c'est la fin de tout (say lah fan duu too)
that's the last straw

The last straw being the one that breaks the camel's back. The literal translation of **c'est la fin de tout** is "that's the end of all," a prosaic phrase. Conveying the same sense, but more vividly, we have **c'est la goutte d'eau qui fait déborder le vase** (say lah goot doh kee fay day-bor-DAY luu vahz), almost literally, "it's the last drop of water that causes the vase to overflow."

c'est la guerre (say lah gair)
forget it!

Literally, "that's war." Or, as Americans are wont to say, "that's baseball."

c'est là le diable (say lah luu dyahblə)
there's the rub

By way of identifying a difficulty or impediment; literally, "there's the devil." Another way of saying this is **c'est là la difficulté** (say lah lah dee-fee-kül-TAY), which needs no translation.

c'est la mer à boire (say lah mair rah bwahr)
it's an impossibility

Also translated as "it's an endless task"; literally, "it's the sea to drink." Endless enough for you?

c'est la Pitié qui se moque de la Charité (say lah pee-TYAY kee suu mawk duu lah shah-ree-TAY)
how can you accuse anyone?

Usually translated as "it's the pot calling the kettle black"; literally, "it's Pity ridiculing Charity." The pot and kettle metaphor is seen somewhat more directly in French in **c'est la poêle qui se moque de chaudron** (say lah pwahl kee suu mawk duu shoh-DRAWN); literally, "it's the stove ridiculing the cauldron." (See also C'EST L'HÔPITAL QUI SE MOQUE DE LA CHARITÉ.)

c'est la série noire (say lah say-REE nwahr)
it's one calamity after another
 Also given as "it's a string of disasters" or "it's a run of bad luck" and, literally, as "it's a dark series."

c'est le cas ou jamais (say luu kah oo zhah-MAY)
this is it!
 An idiom also translated as "it's now or never"; literally, "it's the situation or never."

c'est le chéri de ses parents (say luu shay-REE duu say pah-RAHN)
he's the apple of his parents' eye
 Literally, "he's his parents' beloved," making us all the fonder of the apple metaphor.

c'est le commencement de la fin (say luu kaw-mahn-SəMAHN duu lah fan)
it's the beginning of the end

c'est le jour et la nuit (say luu zhoor ray lah nwee)
different as day and night
 Literally, "it's day and night." Or, as the fourteenth-century English proverb has it, "it's chalk and cheese"—try to think of two materials more different than these.

c'est le monde renversé (say luu mawndə rahn-vair-SAY)
what are we coming to?
 An expression of disillusionment heard most often from those of middle age and from the Social Security crowd: "the world's going to hell" or "whatever happened to our country?" or, literally, "the world is upside down."

c'est le premier pas qui coûte (say luu pruu-MYAY pah kee koot)
get off your duff!
 Usually translated as "it's the first step that is difficult *or* that costs," to

which some us respond with "don't kid yourself, it never gets easier." But that is not what the French aphorism says.

c'est le reflet de son père (say luu ruu-FLAY duu sawn pair)
the spitting image of his dad
   Literally, "he's the reflection of his father." At any rate, the idea is that he and his father look alike. (See also C'EST SON PÈRE TOUT CRACHÉ.)

c'est le tonneau des Danaïdes (say luu taw-NOH day dah-nah-EEDə)
it's a Sisyphean task
   Literally translated as "it's the cask of the Danaides," a reference to the fifty daughters of Danaus in classical mythology, of whom forty-nine were condemned in Hades to pour water forever into leaky casks. Why were they thus condemned? They had murdered their husbands on their wedding nights. And why had they committed these murders? Their daddy told them to.

c'est l'hôpital qui se moque de la charité (say law-pee-TAHL kee suu mawk duu lah shah-ree-TAY)
pot calling the kettle black
   Or, more literally, "it's the hospital looking down its nose at kindness." (See also C'EST LA PITIÉ QUI SE MOQUE DE LA CHARITÉ.)

c'est l'usage (say lü-ZAHZH)
it's what done
   Or "it's the custom" or "it's the way things are done." The noun **usage** means "custom."

c'est ma bête noire (say mah bayt nwahr)
it's my pet peeve
   Literally translated as "it's my black beast." And maybe that's why we have taken "bête noire" untranslated into English to mean "pet aversion." What is a black beast anyway?

c'est magnifique, mais ce n'est pas la guerre (say mah-nyee-FEEK may suu nay pah lah gair)
it's magnificent, but it's not warfare
   Attributed to French General Bossuet on viewing the charge of the British cavalry against the Russians at Balaklava. And anyone who remem-

bers Tennyson's "Charge of the Light Brigade" knows that things didn't turn out too well for the brigade. "Theirs not to reason why, theirs but to do and die. . . ." And they didn't, and they died!

c'est pas de la tarte (say pah dəlah tahrt)
it's no pushover
Nor is it a cream puff. The French locution is usually translated as "it's no easy matter" or "it's no joke" and, somewhat more literally, "it's not a piece of cake," and even more literally as "it's not a tart"—not a type of pastry, that is.

c'est pas fait pour les chiens! (say pah fay poor lay shyan)
it's there to be used
By people, that is. A principle of family life—literally "it's not made for dogs"—uttered by frustrated parents who see children rejecting good food. We throw scraps—not food—to dogs.

c'est plus qu'un crime, c'est une faute (say plü kœn kreem say tün foht)
it's more than a crime, it's a blunder
Attributed to Talleyrand and others, on the execution of the duc d'Enghien by Napoleon's soldiers.

c'est quelque chose de très recherché (say kaylkə shohz duu tray ruu-shair-SHAY)
it's in great demand
Literally, "it's something much sought after." **Recherché** has been taken over unchanged in English with several meanings, including "precious," "affected," and "pretentious." (See also RECHERCHÉ.)

c'est reculer pour mieux sauter (say ruu-kü-LAY poor myuu soh-TAY)
await a better opportunity
An intelligent tactic based on careful study of an ongoing situation. Almost literally, "it's stepping back to go forward better"; more literally, "it's stepping back in order to leap better." This French phrase is also taken as "it's just putting off the evil day" or as "it's just delaying the day of reckoning." It all depends on the context in which the statement is made.

c'est son père tout craché (say sawn pair too krah-SHAY)
spitting image of his dad

A dandy way to say "he's the living image of his father," that is, an exact likeness or close resemblance. The French, like the English "spitting image" (also given as spit 'n' image), suggests of the son that "he was spat out of his father's mouth" and so was an exact likeness. (See also C'EST LE REFLET DE SON PÈRE.)

c'est toujours . . . (say too-ZHOOR)
it's always . . .
The opening words of five interesting and useful phrases: **c'est toujours la même chanson** (lah maym shahn-SAWN), translated as "it's always the same old story;" more literally, "it's always the same old song." In the same vein, there is **c'est toujours la même histoire** (lah maym ees-TWAHR), "it's always the same old story." Again, **c'est toujours la même musique** (lah maym mü-ZEEK), "here we go again!" or "it's always the same refrain." Notice that **musique** here translates as "refrain," so what is to be said of **c'est toujours le même refrain** (luu maym ruu-FRAN)? **Refrain**, rather than translating as "refrain," here means "story," so "it's always the same story." Could anything be simpler? Finally, by way of further obfuscation, consider **c'est toujours le même topo** (luu maym taw-POH), which is also translated as "it's always the same old story" or "it's always the same old spiel."

c'est toujours le même tabac (say too-ZHOOR luu maym tah-BAH)
it's always the same old thing
Sometimes given as "any way you slice it, it's still baloney"; more literally and only a little less broadly, "whatever you call it, it's always the same tobacco."

c'est tout à fait exclu (say too tah fay aykss-KLÜ)
forget it!
Usually translated as "it's just not done," more literally as "it's entirely out of the question."

c'est un bled perdu (say tœn blayd pair-DÜ)
it's a godforsaken place
Or "it's a hole in the middle of nowhere." Next time you are inclined to speak of a place as being in the boondocks, try **c'est un bled perdu**.

c'est un cadavre ambulant (say tœn kah-DAHVRə ahn-bü-LAHN)
he's skin and bones
Or "he's a living corpse"; literally, "he's a walking corpse."

c'est un dictionnaire ambulant (say tœn deek-syaw-NAIR ahn-bü-lahn)
he's a walking dictionary

Just the kind of person we love to hate—someone who knows all the words, especially the rare ones.

c'est une affaire (say tün nah-FAIR)
it's a business or *matter*

The first words of several interesting locutions. **C'est une affaire en or** (ahn nor): in shopping, "it's a real bargain"; in business, "it's a gold mine." Closely related in meaning is **c'est une affaire qui marche** (kee mahrsh), "it's a flourishing business." Less happy is **c'est une affaire louche** (loosh), "it's a shady business," so watch out! (See also IL Y A DU LOUCHE DANS CETTE AFFAIRE.) Finally, there is **c'est une autre affaire** (nohtrə ah-FAIR), "that is another matter."

c'est une autre paire de manches (say tün nohtrə pair duu mahnsh)
that's another story

A great idiom: "that's a different kettle of fish"; literally, "that's another pair of sleeves."

c'est une peau de vache (say tün poh də vahsh)
he's a bastard

This idiom can also be translated as "she's a bitch." So what is the literal meaning of **peau de vache**? "Cowhide." Figure this one out!

c'est une sainte nitouche (say tün sant nee-TOOSH)
don't trust her

Also construed as "she looks as if butter won't melt in her mouth"; more literally, "she's hypocritically pious."

c'est un éternel fauché (say tœn nay-tair-NAYL foh-SHAY)
a real Chapter 11

As we are wont to say, "he doesn't have a penny" or "he doesn't have two pennies to rub together"; literally, "he's permanently broke."

c'est une vraie girouette (say tün vray zheer-WAYT)
anything but consistent

Well translated as "he changes his mind with the weather"; literally, "he's a real weather vane." Thus, as we say, he changes his opinion depending on which way the wind is blowing.

c'est un homme qui a une grande information (say tœn nawm kee ah ün grahndə an-for-mah-SYAWN)
talk about smart
   The French equivalent of a walking encyclopedia; literally, "he's a man with a great fund of knowledge."

c'est un homme qui s'éparpille beaucoup trop (say tœn nawm kee say-pahr-PEEYə boh-KOO troh)
specialize, specialize!
   A useful idiom describing someone who has too many strings in his bow, often translated as "he's a man who dissipates his efforts"; more literally, "he's a man who scatters his shots." The message is "concentrate on what you know or do best!"

c'est un mort en sursis (say tœn mor an sür-SEE)
living under a death sentence
   Usually translated as "he's a condemned man," literally as "he's a dead man on reprieve."

c'est un peloteur (say tœn plaw-TUHR)
watch out for this guy!
   Why? Because he's a dirty old man: he can't keep his hands to himself. Literally, "he's a caresser." The verb **peloter** (plaw-TAY)—associated with the noun **peloteur**—means "caress" or "paw."

c'est un sacré dragueur (say tœn sah-KRAY drah-GUHR)
women, beware!
   Translated as "he's a real sweet-talker"; literally, "he's a holy minesweeper." Match that metaphor!

c'est un touche-à-tout (say tœn too-shah-TOO)
he's into everything
   Also translated, when applied to a child, as "he's a meddler"; when applied to an adult, as "he dabbles in everything."

c'est un vrai concierge (say tœn vray kaw*n*-SYAIRZH)
he's a real busybody
   (See also CONCIERGE.)

c'est un vrai marchand de tapis (say tœn vray mahr-SHAHN duu tah-PEE)
he's a haggler
   Where we say "he drives a hard bargain," the French in this metaphor say "he's a real rug dealer."

cet écrivain est un second Hemingway (sayt ay-kree-VAN ay tœn suu-GAWN ay-meen-GWAY)
a real comer
   Literally, "this writer is a second Hemingway." One of countless thousands so characterized?

chacun à son goût (shah-KœN ah sawn goo)
everyone to his own taste
   The best way to terminate a disagreement that hinges on a matter of personal taste and therefore cannot be resolved. Also given as **chacun son goût**.

chacun de nous a payé son écot (shah-KœN duu noo ah pay-YAY sawn nay-KOH)
we went Dutch
   More formally, "each of us paid his own way"; literally, "each person paid his own share of the bill."

chacun est l'artisan de sa fortune (shah-KœN ay lahr-tee-ZAHN duu sah for-TÜN)
you cannot blame others
   Usually translated as "everyone is the architect of his own fortune."

chambre (shahnbrə)
room
   But of course there are various types of rooms, for example, **chambre à coucher** (ah koo-SHAY), translated as "bedroom." Then there is **chambre avec salle de bain** (ah-VAYK sahl duu ban), "room and bath," that is,

a room with its own bathroom. Finally, there is **chambre séparée** (say-pah-RAY), "private room." It pays to know these terms when traveling abroad.

change de disque! (shahnzh duu deesk)
give it a rest!
   Also translated as "change the subject!" or "let's drop it!" The literal meaning is "change the record!"

changer de peau (shahn-ZHAY duu poh)
become a different person
   Literally, "shed one's skin."

chansons de geste (shahn-SAWN duu zhayst)
chansons de geste
   English has no phrase to specifically characterize these old French epic poems celebrating the exploits of knights, even though we may lamely translate the term as "songs of deeds." The most famous *chanson de geste* is the eleventh-century *Chanson de Roland* (raw-LAHN), *Song of Roland*, relating heroic battles and the eventual death of this, the most famous of Charlemagne's paladins.

chant du cygne (shahn dü seenyə)
swan song
   The phrase used to denote "the last work of a poet or musician immediately before his death"; more loosely, "any performer's final public appearance." Superstition has it that a dying swan—never having sung at all before—sings beautifully once before it dies. A marvelous conceit holding out hope for all of us who've been publicly labeled listeners.

chaque (shahk)
each
   The first word of several worthwhile observations, for example, **chaque chose en son temps** (shohz ahn sawn tahn), translated as "everything in its own time," and thus counseling "don't burn your bridges before you come to them." Then there is **chaque homme naît libre** (kawm nay leebrə), "every man is born free." Finally, there is **chaque pays a son guide** (pay-EE ah sawn geed), "each country has its own customs"; literally, "each country has its own ways."

charbonnier est maître chez soi (shahr-baw-NYAY ay maytrə shay swah)
don't enter without a warrant!

Freely translated as "the humblest man is master in his own home" and "an Englishman's home is his castle." Literally, "the charcoal burner is master in his own home." A humble man if ever there was one.

charité bien ordonnée commence par soi-même (shah-ree-TAY byan nor-daw-NAY kaw-MAHNSS pahr swah-MAYM)
charity begins at home

Literally, "proper charity begins at one's home." **Charité** in this sense means something close to Christian love or **l'amour fraternel** (lah-MOOR frah-tair-NAYL), "brotherly love," and **bien ordonné** means "proper" or "well-ordered."

chassez le naturel, il revient au galop (shah-SAY luu nah-tü-RAYL eel ruu-VYAN toh gah-LOH)
what's bred in the bone comes out in the flesh

Translated almost literally, "drive out the natural, it comes back in a hurry." At any rate, try as we may, we cannot easily change our essential natures. (See also BON SANG NE SAURAIT MENTIR.)

chat échaudé craint l'eau froide (shah ay-shoh-DAY kran loh frwahd)
once bitten twice shy

This proverb is translated literally as "a scalded cat fears cold water."

chat en poche (shah ahn pawsh)
pig in a poke

Literally, "cat in a bag," something we should not buy, lest we find that we have paid good money for something worthless.

chaud comme une caille (shoh kawm ün kīyə)
snug as a bug in a rug

Literally, "warm like a quail."

chauffeur du dimanche (shoh-FUHR dü dee-MAHNSH)
Sunday driver

This expression, suggesting a driver who has too little practice in the arcane art of safe driving, may not be known to some younger readers.

chef-d'oeuvre (shay-DUHVRə)
masterpiece

This term has been taken into English as "chef d'oeuvre" and pronounced as in French. That means it will usually be mispronounced. So practice!

chemin de fer (shuu-man duu fair)
a railroad

Literally, "iron road."

cher ami (shair rah-MEE)
dear friend

Also, "lover," the feminine form being **chère amie**, with the same pronunciation.

chercher (shair-SHAY)
seek or *look for*

Four interesting locutions begin with this infinitive or with one of its verb forms: **chercher la bagarre** (lah bah-GAHR), translated as "be spoiling for a fight"; literally, "be looking for a fight." Then there is the famous **cherchez la femme** (shair-SHAY lah fahm), literally, "look for the woman." Every devotee of detective stories knows that there must be a woman in the case who, once identified, will lead the gumshoe unerringly to the heart of the matter. Less glamorous is **chercher la petite bête** (lah puu-TEET bayt), translated as "nitpick" or "be excessively finicky." The literal translation is "search for the little bug," which takes us back to nitpick and to certain creepy-crawlies and the minute eggs they lay in human hair. To end on an uplifting theme, we have **chercher le merle blanc** (luu mairlə blahn), "dream the impossible dream" or "chase rainbows" or "seek the impossible"; literally, "search for the white blackbird."

cheval de bataille (shuu-VAHL duu bah-TĪYə)
war horse

Or "charger." Figuratively, "strong point," "favorite subject," or "hobby." In some contexts, **cheval de bataille** means "mainstay," "favorite theme," or "chief reliance." A useful term.

chichi (shee-SHEE)
fuss

A noun adopted by English and pronounced SHEE-shee.

chose promise, chose due (shohz praw-MEEZ shohz dü)
don't make promises lightly
   Also translated as "promises are made to be kept," literally as "thing promised, thing owed."

chose qui plaît est à demi vendue (shohz kee play ay tah duu-MEE vahn-DÜ)
a thing that pleases is half sold
   Ask any alert merchandiser.

chou (shoo)
cabbage
   This splendid plant finds its way into several words and phrases. For ex-ample, **choucroute** (shoo-KROOT) is "sauerkraut," and **choucroute garnie** (gahr-NEE) is "sauerkraut with sausage," which sounds less attractive than the literal translation "garnished sauerkraut." And then there is **chou-fleur** (shoo-FLUHR), good old "cauliflower." And when we get to **chou pour chou** (shoo poor shoo), we are in the grips of a cabbage idiom meaning "taken all in all"; literally, "cabbage for cabbage." (For some more cabbage pleasure, see MON PETIT CHOU.)

çi gît . . . (see zhee)
here lies . . .
   The beginning of many a tombstone inscription.

cirrhose du foie (see-ROHZ dü fwah)
cirrhosis of the liver
   For a nation of wine drinkers, a very important term. But also for a na-tion of beer and whiskey drinkers.

cocu (kaw-KÜ)
cuckold
   Both a noun and an adjective. The verb is **cocufier** (kaw-kü-FYAY).

coeur de lion (kuhr duu lyawn)
a lionheart
   One who has the courage of a lion, especially Richard I of England.

coeur de marbre (kuhr duu mahrbrə)
heart of stone

With all the phrase implies. Literally, "heart of marble." Also given as **coeur de pierre** (pyair), **pierre** meaning "stone."

coiffer Sainte Catherine (kwah-FAY sant kah-TREEN)
live a virgin

Literally, "braid St. Catherine's tresses." Needless to say, the martyr St. Catherine, who died ca. A.D. 310, was a virgin who was tied to a wheel to be tortured, but was quickly beheaded instead when her bonds were miraculously broken. For centuries her martyrdom was painted over and over again in all its bloodiness. The best that can be said of the grisly occurrence is that the pleasure of her tormentors was cut short.

combat au finish (kawn-BAH oh fee-NEESH)
fight to the finish

A phrase showing vividly that the exchange of nouns between French and English is a two-way street.

comme il faut (kawm eel foh)
as it should be

Also, "proper," "correct," "in good form," and "well-bred."

comme le berger mène ses moutons, ainsi le pasteur guide ses ouailles
(kawm luu bair-ZHAY mayn say moo-TAWN an-SEE luu pahss-TUHR geed say zwahyə)
recipe for pastoral behavior

Literally translated as "just as the shepherd leads his sheep, so does the minister guide his flock."

comment (kawm-MAHN)
how

A word appearing in many phrases, for example, **comment allez-vous?** (kawm-MAHN tah-lay-VOO), "how are you?" Not much different are **comment ça va?** (sah vah), "how's everything?" and **comment ça va, mon vieux?** (sah vah mawn vyuu), "how are you, old buddy?" as well as **comment vous portez-vous?** (voo por-tay-VOO), "how do you do?" Finally, there is **comment dit-on ça en français?** (dee-TAWN sah ahn frahn-SAY), "what's the French word for that?" or, literally, "how do you say that in French?"

comme on fait son lit, on se couche (kawm awn fay sawn lee awn suu koosh)
as you sow, so shall you reap
    More literally, "as you make your bed, so you must lie in it." In short, we can't blame our fate on anyone but ourselves.

commettre un impair (kawm-MAYTRə œn an-PAIR)
make a booboo
    More elegantly, "make a faux pas." (See also FAIRE UN FAUX PAS.)

comme un cheveu sur la soupe (kawm œn shuu-VUU sür lah soop)
at the most awkward moment
    Literally, "like a hair in the soup." A metaphor used, for example, to characterize the arrival of an uninvited guest.

comme un éléphant dans un magasin de porcelaine (kawm œn nay-lay-FAHN dahn zœn mah-gah-zan duu por-suu-LAYN)
like a bull in a china shop
    Literally, "like an elephant in a china shop."

communiqué de presse (kaw-mü-nee-KAY duu PRAYSS)
press release or *bulletin*
    Communiqué, meaning "official communication" or "statement," is another of the French words we have taken unchanged into English, with pronunciation almost unchanged.

comparaison n'est pas raison (kawn-pah-ray-ZAWN nay pah ray-ZAWN)
comparisons are odious
    More literally, "comparison isn't reasonable," so take care to make valid comparisons.

concessions mutuelles (kawn-say-SYAWN mü-tü-AYL)
give-and-take
    Literally, "mutual concessions." Isn't compromise, based on forbearance and consideration, the best way to settle a dispute?

concierge (kawn-SYAIRZH)
doorkeeper

Also translated as "hall porter" and "janitor." This apartment building employee functions as manager of the building, screening visitors, accepting mail for tenants, and the like. (See also C'EST UN VRAI CONCIERGE.)

concours (kawn-KOOR)
competition
   Two popular competitions are **concours de beauté** (duu boh-TAY), "beauty contest," and **concours hippique** (ee-PEEK), "horse show."

confidences sur l'oreiller (kawn-fee-DAHNSS sür law-ray-YAY)
pillow talk
   More traditionally translated as "intimate confidences," but be aware that **oreiller** means "pillow" and **oreille** (aw-RAYə) means "ear." A logical linguistic connection.

connaître bien des vicissitudes (kawn-NAYTRə byan day vee-see-see-TÜDə)
have one's share of troubles
   Also translated as "know good times and bad."

connaître le dessous des cartes (kawn-NAYTRə luu duu-SOO day kahrt)
be on the inside
   Or "know the secret"; literally, "know the underside of the cards." In a card game, that is.

connaître les ficelles du métier (kawn-NAYTRə lay fee-SAYL dü may-TYAY)
know how to work the system
   Also translated as "know the ropes"—**ficelles** are "strings"—and "know the tricks of the trade"; **métier** is "trade" or "occupation."

conseil (kawn-SAYə)
council
   Giving us at least three common terms: **conseil d'administration** (dahd-mee-nee-strah-SYAWN), translated as "board of directors"; **conseil de famille** (duu fah-MEEYə), "family council"; and **conseil d'état** (day-TAH), "council of state."

considérer le pour et le contre (kawn-see-day-RAY luu poor ay luu kawntrə)
how about a trade-off study?
Literally translated as "consider the pros and cons." Useful before making a decision.

conte à dormir debout (kawnt tah dor-MEER duu-BOO)
old wives' tale
Or "rigmarole"; literally, "story that would put one to sleep on one's feet."

conte de fée (kawnt duu fay)
tall story
Literally, "fairy tale."

contentement passe richesse (kawn-tahn-tə-MAHN pahss ree-SHAYSS)
contentment surpasses riches
Best translated as "enough is as good as a feast" or "happiness is worth more than wealth." So whether poor or well off, be happy!

conter (kawn-TAY)
tell or *relate*
Giving us two locutions of interest: **conter des fariboles** (day fah-ree-BAWL), translated as "talk nonsense," or "stuff and nonsense," or "twaddle"; and **conter fleurettes** (fluh-RAYT), "whisper sweet nothings," better translated as "make love to." And what are **fleurettes**? Literally, "little flowers." (But see FLEURETTE for more information.)

contretemps (kawn-truu-TAHN)
glitch
Also, "hitch," "mischance," "untoward accident," but best of all, "contretemps." Yes, this is another English word taken directly from French, and pronounced slightly differently.

coq-à-l'âne (kawk-kah-LAHN)
cock-and-bull story
Or "nonsense"; literally, "rooster to the donkey." One small change in the cast of characters, but useful in both languages for characterizing a breakdown in communication.

coq au vin (kawk koh van)
coq au vin
   Commonly described as "chicken braised in wine," but always given in French even in American or English restaurants. Take note that **coq** really means "rooster."

coquilles Saint-Jacques (kaw-KEEYə san-ZHAHK)
scallops baked and served in a scallop shell
   Lovers of fine food are aware that in English this dish, usually served as an appetizer, is commonly called "coquilles St. Jacques" and pronounced as in French. Take note that **coquilles** is defined both as "scallops" and as "scallop shells." These shells were once worn as badges by pilgrims to the shrines of **Saint-Jacques**, in English "Saint James."

corbeille à pain (kor-BAYə ah pan)
breadbasket
   Not to be taken figuratively.

cordon-bleu (kor-dawn-BLUU)
Julia Child
   Short for a "cordon bleu cook," that is, a "first-rate cook." **Cordon bleu**—notice that the hyphen is absent—literally means "blue ribbon," now a conventional mark of distinction awarded in animal shows, chili contests, and a host of other competitions, but once worn by knights of the Holy Ghost.

corps de ballet (kor duu bah-LAY)
corps de ballet
   The term is used unchanged in English and pronounced as in French to denote ballet dancers who perform as a group and have no solo parts. Originally, the term meant "company of ballet dancers."

coterie littéraire (kawt-REE lee-tay-RAIR)
literary set
   Note that English has adopted "coterie," with the same meaning but pronounced KOH-tə-ree.

coucher sous les ponts (koo-SHAY soo lay pawn)
live as a tramp

Literally, "sleep under the bridges," an allusion to the wonderful Parisian bridges across the Seine, under which many homeless people sleep each night.

coucheuse (koo-SHUHZ)
fast woman
To replace one euphemism with another, "woman who sleeps around."

couleur de rose (koo-LUHR duu rohz)
bright side of things
Also translated as "in a favorable light"; literally, "rose color" or "rose-colored."

coup (koo)
blow or *stroke*
This noun launches many useful phrases, for example: **coup de bec** (duu BAYK), meaning "peck," "taunt," or "gibe"; literally, "blow of a beak." An apt metaphor for the many critics who can almost be heard cackling as they peck away at the reputation of a creator of a literary or artistic work. Happier phrases are **coup de bonheur** (duu bawn-NUHR), translated as "stroke of good fortune," useful next time you win the lottery; and **coup de bourse** (duu boorss), translated as "successful stock speculation." Then we have **coup de courage** (duu koo-RAHZH), "bold stroke"; literally, "stroke of courage." Another way of saying "bold stroke" is **coup d'éclat** (day-KLAH), better translated as "brilliant exploit." A phrase with a double meaning is **coup de foudre** (duu foodrə), literally, "thunderclap" or "thunderbolt," figuratively, "love at first sight." And isn't a thunderclap what this too common phenomenon engenders? More ominous is **coup de grâce** (duu grahss), "death blow"; literally, "blow of mercy," especially one intended to end the suffering of a mortally wounded person. This phrase has been taken into English and incorrectly pronounced by almost every American who has ever undertaken to use it. Somewhat less lethal are **coup de langue** (duu lahng), translated as "backbiting," "slander," and "invective," literally, "stroke of the tongue"; and **coup de main** (duu man), literally, "stroke of the hand," but meaning "surprise attack," "bold stroke," or "sudden, vigorous onslaught." A much more positive phrase is **coup de maître** (duu maytrə), "masterstroke." Three phrases to reckon with are **coup de pied** (duu pyay), "kick"; **coup de poing** (duu pwahn), "punch"; and **coup de soleil** (duu saw-LAYə), "sunstroke." The best-known phrase in this series of **coup** phrases is **coup d'état** (day-TAH), a usually violent change in

government, which is best translated as "coup" or "coup d'état," both of which have made their way into English without change in pronunciation. Finally, there is **coup d'oeil** (dœyə), "general view" or "rapid and comprehensive glance," literally, "stroke of the eye." (See also UN COUP DE PIED AU DERRIÈRE.)

coupe de cheveux (koop duu shə-VUU)
haircut
    Coupe is readily understood as "cutting," giving us the literal translation of "cutting of hair."

couper l'herbe sous les pieds (koo-PAY lairb soo lay pyay)
pull the rug out from under you
    Literally, "cut the grass under your feet."

couper un cheveu en quatre (koo-PAY œn shuu-VUU ahn kahtrə)
split hairs
    Also translated as "quibble." Almost literally, "cut a hair in four parts." (See also FENDRE UN CHEVEU EN QUATRE.)

courage sans peur (koo-RAHZH sahn puhr)
fearless courage
    Literally, "courage without fear." By courageous people considered an impossibility. Ask any person who has distinguished himself or herself by an act of courage.

coureur de nuit (koo-RUHR duu nwee)
philanderer
    Sometimes translated as "man who keeps late hours"; literally, "night runner." In any case, you can be sure that the person so characterized is up to no good.

courir (koo-REER)
run or roam
    This verb introduces five common phrases: **courir après le vent** (ah-PRAY luu vahn), "go on a wild goose chase," literally, "run after the wind"; and **courir comme un zèbre** (kawm œn zaybrə), meaning "run like the wind," literally, "run like a zebra." Less sanguine is **courir au désastre** (oh day-ZAHSTRə), "head straight for disaster." There is nothing straight about **courir les rues** (lay rü), "roam the streets." And when you wish to

talk about speed, consider **courir ventre à terre** (vahn trah tair), "run flat out" and "run at top speed"; literally, "run belly to earth."

court plaisir, long repentir (koor play-ZEER lawn ruu-pahn-TEER)
for a few moments of pleasure!
Literally, "brief pleasure, long repentance." A great slogan for an ad campaign—you name the sponsor.

coûte que coûte (koot kuu koot)
cost be damned!
Or "cost what it may," "at any cost," or "come what may."

couvrir quelqu'un de honte (koo-VREER kayl-KœN duu awnt)
disgrace someone
Literally, "cover someone with shame."

cracher son venin (krah-SHAY sawn vuu-NAN)
spit out one's venom
Figuratively, of course.

crèche (kraysh)
crib or *manger*
Also "day care center." The best-known **crèche** of them all, usually written **Crèche**, is the manger in which the newborn Christ was laid.

crécher (kray-SHAY)
hang out
Often used to mean "crash," in the sense of "bed down."

crème (kraym)
cream
This delicious word introduces several sublime phrases: **crème à la glace** (ah lah glahss) is, of course, heavenly "ice cream," also known as **crème glacée** (glah-SAY). The noun **glace** means "ice," and **glacée** means "icy." To move from the sublime to the superlative, there is **crème de la crème** (duu lah kraym), translated as "the choicest" and literally "cream of the cream," but never expressed in English as anything but "crème de la crème" (pronounced krem duu la krem). To top off this fattening discussion we have **crème fouettée** (fway-TAY), "whipped cream."

crêpage de chignon (kray-PAHZH duu shee-NYAWN)
free-for-all

Also translated as "set-to." The literal meaning of **crêpage** is "crimping" or "backcombing," and **chignon** is "hair bun." The entire phrase sounds like a hairdresser's term, quite different from its idiomatic meaning, but that's the joy of language. Don't think we speakers of English are immune. Consider "get a bun on," meaning "drink to excess," which has nothing to do with hair or with the roll we order with our coffee of a morning. "Chignon" (SHEEN-yahn), of course, has been taken into English to denote a woman's hairstyle in which a knot of hair is worn at the back of the head. But be sure to avoid a **crêpage de chignon** when you suggest that your hairdresser has not quite achieved the effect you desire.

crépuscule (kray-püss-KÜL)
twilight or *dusk*

Included here because of the wonderful sound the word makes and because it evokes the beauty of Paris just as the city lights turn on. Note that the word is used figuratively as well to convey the sense of "twilight of life."

crève-coeur (krayvə-KUHR)
heartbreak

Also translated as "crushing sorrow" and "heartbreaking thing." If you enjoyed your studies of American literature, you may recall Michel Guillaume Jean de Crèvecoeur, the French writer who emigrated to America and wrote *Letters from an American Farmer* (1782). He is included here only because he might have called himself "Mike Heartbreak," but instead used the pseudonym "J. Hector St. John." Go figure!

crever (kruh-VAY)
burst or *puncture*

Four idioms are launched by this verb: **crever de graisse** (duu grayss), idiomatically translated as "become a tub of lard," that is, "be extraordinarily fat" and literally "burst with fat." (See also PRENDRE DE LA GRAISSE.) Then there is **crever de jalousie** (duu zhah-loo-ZEE), "be green with envy"; literally, "burst with jealousy." On a lighter note, we have **crever de rire** (duu reer), "split one's sides"; literally, "burst with laughter." Finally, there is **crever le coeur à quelqu'un** (luu kuhr ah kayl-KœN), "break someone's heart." Alas!

cri du coeur (kree dü kuhr)
heartfelt cry
   Literally, "cry from the heart"; in English usually written "cri de (pronounced duu) coeur."

crier comme un veau (kree-YAY kawm œn voh)
bawl one's head off
   Literally, "cry like a calf."

crier famine sur un tas de blé (kree-YAY fah-MEEN sür œn tah duu blay)
plead poverty without justification
   Literally, "cry famine on a heap of wheat."

crise (kreez)
crisis or *attack* or *fit* or *rage* or *tantrum*
   The French use **crise** in quite a few locutions, among them **crise de confiance** (duu kawn-FYAHNSS), "crisis of confidence," and **crise de foie** (duu fwah), "king-size bellyache." The second of these is more precisely "liver attack," which bellyache American tourists are wont to blame on misbehavior of their gall bladders. Whatever the precise source of the pain, both conditions seem to appear after sustained and intemperate eating and drinking. More interesting is **crise de la quarantaine** (duu lah kahrahn-TAYN), translated as "midlife crisis"; literally, "crisis of the forties." Implicit in the phrase is the knowledge that the condition will pass, as will **crise de larmes** (duu lahrmə), "fit of tears," and **crise de nerfs** (duu nair), "attack of nerves," also translated as "fit of hysterics." More serious is **crise du pouvoir** (dü poo-VWAHR), "leadership crisis"; literally, "crisis of power." And even more serious is **crise religieuse** (ruu-lee-ZHYUUZ), "crisis of belief"—religious belief, of course. (See also PIQUER UNE CRISE.)

critiquer les autres, c'est s'exposer à la critique (kree-tee-KAY lay zohtrə say saykss-paw-ZAY ah lah kree-TEEK)
people who live in glass houses
   Should, of course, never throw stones. Less idiomatically translated as "those who are in a morally vulnerable position shouldn't criticize others."

croissant (krwah-SAH*N*)
crescent
Adopted by English speakers in need of morning coffee and a "croissant" (abominably mispronounced), who delight in a marvelously buttery pastry roll baked in a crescent shape.

croissez et multipliez! (krwah-SAY ay mül-tee-plee-YAY)
be fruitful and multiply
From Genesis: "be fruitful, and multiply, and replenish the earth." An injunction that often comes to mind when one thinks about this overpopulated planet.

croque-madame (krawk-mah-DAHM)
toasted cheese sandwich with chicken
Not half as popular as its companion. (See the next entry.)

croque-monsieur (krawk-muu-SYUU)
toasted cheese sandwich with ham
Yum!

croqueuse de diamants (kraw-KUHZ duu dyah-MAHN)
fortune hunter
Also translated as "gold digger," but literally, "diamond cruncher." Maybe diamonds really are a girl's best friend.

croûte au fromage (kroot oh fraw-MAHZH)
Welsh rabbit
For those who've never experienced this admirable dish, be it understood that it is little more than cheese on toast, but remember that **croûte** translates literally as "crust" and the **fromage** is melted.

cul-de-sac (kü-duu-SAHK)
dead end
Also translated as "blind alley"; literally, "bottom of the bag." The English word "cul-de-sac," with the same free meanings, is pronounced KUL-duu-sak.

d'accord (dah-KOR)
agreed
   Also translated as "granted," suggesting that a person uttering this phrase agrees to comply with someone's request. The literal translation is "in accord" or "in agreement."

daignez agréer mes respectueux hommages (day-NYAY ah-gray-AY may rayss-payk-tü-UU zaw-MAHZH)
yours truly
   Hard to believe that this tongue twister is a formal way to close a letter, saying almost literally "be so good as to accept my respectful compliments." Oh, those French! (See also VEUILLEZ AGRÉER L'EXPRESSION DE MES SENTIMENTS LES MEILLEURS.)

dalle funéraire (dahl fü-nay-RAIR)
tombstone
   It is important to note that **dalle** means "flagstone," and this is of special interest in the American West. The Dalles (pronounced dalz), in Oregon, took its name from the perception of early French settlers that the Columbia River rapids there reminded them of gutters lined with flagstones.

dans (dahn)
in or *into* or *from* or *out of*
   The introductory preposition for many popular locutions and proverbs, for example, **dans le doute, abstiens-toi** (luu doot ahb-styan-TWAH), "when in doubt, don't." An excellent bit of advice. Then there is **dans l'épaisseur de la nuit** (lay-pay-SUHR duu lah nwee), "in darkest night" or, literally, "in the depths of the night." A cheerful saying is **dans les petites boîtes les bons onguents** (lay puh-TEET bwaht lay bawn zawn-GAHN), translated as "good things come in little packages"; literally, "in the little boxes the good ointments." For the introspective, there is **dans le tréfonds de son âme** (luu tray-FAWN duu sawn nahm), translated as "deep down in

his soul" or "in the deepest recesses of his soul." Turning to family life, consider **dans l'intimité conjugale** (lan-tee-mee-TAY kaw*n*-zhü-GAHL), translated as "in the bosom of one's family"; literally, "in the intimacy of married life." Finally, we have the morbid characterizations **dans un coma dépassé** (zœn kaw-MAH day-pah-SAY), translated as "brain-dead," literally, "in a state beyond a coma"; and **dans un état voisin de la folie** (zœn nay-TAH vwah-ZAN duu lah faw-LEE), "in a state akin to madness" or, more literally, "in a state bordering on madness."

danse (dah*n*ss)
dance

Two well-known dances come to mind: **danse du ventre** (dü vah*n*tr∍), literally, "belly dance"; and **danse macabre** (mah-KAHBR∍), literally, "dance of death," which every schoolchild subjected to a course in music appreciation learns from hearing skeletons' bones rattle in the short work by Camille Saint-Saëns of that title. But few schoolchildren know that **danse macabre** represents the allegorical dance of Death with all conditions of men, as represented in medieval art.

daube (dohb)
a stew

A manner of stewing and seasoning certain braised dishes. (See, for example, BOEUF EN DAUBE.)

de bon (duu baw*n*)
of good

When a French phrase begins with these two words, we know we're going to hear something favorable, for example, **de bon augure** (noh-GÜR), "of good omen," and **de bon goût** (GOO), "in good taste." Then there is **de bon gré** (gray), "willingly"; literally, "of good taste." The next two phrases employ the feminine form, **bonne** (bawn), because in both "good" modifies a feminine noun: **de bonne grâce** (bawn grahss) "willingly"; literally, "with good grace"; and **de bonne heure** (bawn nuhr), "early," **heure** meaning "hour." A happy phrase is **de bons copains** (duu bawn kaw-PAN), "great buddies" or "great pals."

débordé de travail (day-bor-DAY duu trah-VĪ)
swamped with work

A phrase not completely happy, but promising eventual reward for those of us who work for a living. Also translated as "overburdened" or, as we might say, "up to one's eyeballs in work."

décampez d'ici (day-kahn-PAY dee-SEE)
scram!
   Also translated as "clear out!" and "beat it!" And we see within this phrase the English verb "decamp," which means "depart," especially "depart quickly."

décolleté plongeant (day-kawl-TAY plawn-ZHAHN)
plunging neckline
   The borrowed English adjective "décolleté," meaning "low-necked," and applied to a woman's dress or blouse, is pronounced DAY-kohl-TAY. An associated noun, **décolletage** (day-kawl-TAZH), also taken into English, means "low-cut neckline."

défaillance (day-fah-YAHNSS)
weakness
   This less than sanguine term leads to two specific uses, neither of which is especially attractive: **défaillance cardiaque** (kahr-DYAHK), "heart failure"; and the less threatening **défaillance de mémoire** (duu may-MWAHR), "memory lapse."

de fond en comble (duu fawn tahn kawnblə)
from top to bottom
   Also translated as "entirely," "thoroughly," "utterly," and, literally, "from foundation to roof timbers."

de gaieté de coeur (duu gay-TAY də kuhr)
gladly or willingly
   Also translated as "wantonly" or "sportively"; literally, "from lightness of heart."

dégustation de vins (day-güss-tah-SYAWN duu van)
wine tasting
   Better translated as "wine sampling" or "session of wine tasting."

de haute lutte (duu oht lüt)
with authority
   Also, "by force"; literally, "by main strength."

de haut en bas (duu oh tahn bah)
superciliously or *scornfully*

Also, "from head to foot"; literally, "from top to bottom," giving us a thumbnail description of someone who looks us over in this objectionable manner. This phrase is also given as **du** (dü) **haut en bas**, with the same meanings.

déjà vu (day-ZHAH vü)
seen before

An illusion of something previously experienced, made commonplace for Americans, particularly baseball fans, by Yogi Berra, master of the gloriously quotable redundancy, in "it's déjà vu all over again."

déjeuner sur l'herbe (day-zhuu-NAY sür lairb)
picnic lunch

Included here primarily to remind us of *Déjeuner sur l'herbe*, the marvelous, and in its time scandalous, painting by Edouard Manet (1832–1883). For those who cannot readily bring the painting to mind, a hint: not all its attractive, picnicking subjects were dressed conventionally, yet no one seemed to be bothered by bees or ants.

de jour en jour (duu zhoor rahn zhoor)
day by day

Literally, "from day to day," the way most of us live.

de l'audace, encore de l'audace, et toujours de l'audace (duu loh-DAHSS ahn-KOR duu loh-DAHSS ay too-ZHOOR duu loh-DAHSS)
don't give up!

Literally, "boldness, boldness again, boldness always." The closing words of Danton expressing defiance at the foes of France in his 1792 address before the French Legislative Assembly. Easily translated into a motto for business speculators and other audacious moderns.

de luxe (duu lüks)
sumptuous

Also translated as "elegant"; literally, "of luxury," characterizing something of special elegance or quality. Taken into English unchanged in pronunciation.

de mauvais genre (duu maw-VAY zhahnrə)
ill-bred

Also translated as "ungentlemanly" or "unladylike." Literally, "of bad type."

de mes propres yeux (duu may prawprə zyuu)
eyewitness

Literally, "with my own two eyes." **Propre**, plural **propres**, means "own."

demeurer dans la pénombre (də-muh-RAY dahn lah pay-NAWNBRə)
stay in the background

Pénombre and its English cognate "penumbra" mean "partial shadow." In this case implying that the shadow is caused by someone else.

demi (duu-MEE)
half

In Hollywood parlance the name of an outrageously popular young star, which makes red-blooded youth wonder whether there is another half waiting to be seen. As a prefix, **demi** makes perfectly good sense in such terms as **demi-douzaine** (doo-ZAYN), "half dozen"; **demi-jour** (zhoor), "twilight," literally, "half-light"; and **demi-mondaine** (mawn-DAYN), "woman of dubious character" or "woman of doubtful reputation"—**demi-monde** (mawnd) meaning "class of women who have lost their standing in respectable society," because they are financially dependent on their lovers. Finally, there is an especially interesting term, **demi-vierge** (vyairzh), translated as "someone who hasn't gone all the way," that is, "someone who is a virgin in name only," taken to mean someone who lacks full sexual experience.

dénouement (day-noo-MAHN)
outcome

Also "conclusion" or "catastrophe"; literally, "an untying." The allusion is to the unraveling of a story or plot. The French term has been taken into English as "denouement" with pronunciation unchanged.

dénué de bon sens (day-nü-AY duu bawn sahnss)
senseless

More literally, "devoid of good sense."

dépêche-toi! (day-paysh-TWAH)
step on it!
  Also, "hurry up!" and "hustle!"

dépenser son argent en bêtises (day-pahn-SAY sawn nahr-ZHAHN ahn bay-TEEZ)
spend money foolishly
  More literally, "squander one's money on trash."

dépourvu de (day-poor-VÜ duu)
lacking in
  Or "wanting in." A phrase ingrained in the memory of students of French who once knew by heart La Fontaine's fable of the grasshopper and the ant. The grasshopper found herself entirely lacking in food for the oncoming winter because she had frittered away her summer instead of providing for the winter months, as had the wise ant.

de provenance étrangère (duu praw-və-NAHNSS ay-trahn-ZHAIR)
made abroad
  Literally, "of foreign origin." **Provenance** is best translated as "provenance," meaning "place of origin," not as "provenience," a failed attempt to Anglicize the French term.

dépucelage d'une fille (day-pü-SLAHZH dün feeyə)
deflowering of a girl
  More often translated as "robbing a girl of her virginity."

depuis que le monde est monde (duu-PWEE kuu luu mawndə ay mawndə)
since the big bang
  More commonly translated as "from time immemorial"; literally, "since the world has been the world." And that's straight talk.

de rigueur (duu ree-GUHR)
obligatory
  Also translated as "indispensable," "imperative," and "required by etiquette."

dernier cri (dair-NYAY kree)
the latest thing
Also translated as "the last word"; literally, "the last cry."

dernier ressort (dair-NYAY ruu-SOR)
the last resort
Also translated as "desperate expedient."

descendre quelqu'un en flammes (day-SAHNDRə kayl-KœN ahn flahm)
wipe someone out
Also translated as "demolish someone"; more literally, "bring *or* shoot someone down in flames."

déshabillé (day-zah-bee-YAY)
undressed
Also translated as "careless," "being dressed carelessly," and "in dishabille," the last term being taken directly from French, made to look like English, and almost never used. Note that **déshabillé** as a noun means "negligee," another borrowing from French—**négligée** (nay-glee-ZHAY)—and never satisfactorily translated except as "negligee." (See also EN DÉSHABILLÉ.)

des habitudes de vieux garçon (day zah-bee-TÜD duu vyuu gahr-SAWN)
bachelor ways
Literally, "of the habits of an old boy." But note that **vieux garçon** is well translated as "bachelor."

dessiller les yeux de quelqu'un (day-see-YAY lay zyuu duu kayl-KœN)
open somebody's eyes
To the truth, that is, or to something else that may not please.

de trop (duu troh)
superfluous
Also translated as "unwanted," "in the way," "unwelcome," and, literally, "too much" and "too many."

dette de jeu, dette d'honneur (dayt duu zhuu dayt daw-NUHR)
never welsh

Best and literally translated as "a gambling debt (is) a debt of honor."
But remember to feed and clothe your children!

deux avis valent mieux qu'un (duu zah-VEE vahl myuu kœn)
two heads are better than one
　　Literally, "two opinions are worth more than one." That's one plus
your own. But don't even think of seeking a third! The third leads to a
fourth, and the fourth to a fifth, and so on ad infinitum. (See also next
entry.)

deux précautions valent mieux qu'une (duu pray-koh-SYAWN vahl
myuu kün)
you can't be too careful
　　Also translated as "better safe than sorry"; literally, "two precautions are
worth more than one." (See also DEUX AVIS VALENT MIEUX QU'UN.)

devenir complètement givré (də-vuu-NEER kawn-playt-MAHN zhee-
VRAY)
go nuts
　　Also translated as "go crazy" or "go completely off one's rocker"; literally,
"become completely cracked."

Dieu (dyuu)
God
　　As one might expect, **Dieu** introduces aphorisms and proverbs galore,
among them **Dieu aide trois sortes de personnes: aux fous, aux enfants,
et aux ivrognes** (ayd trwah sort duu pair-SAWN oh foo oh zahn-FAHN ay
oh zee-VRAWNYə), translated as "God helps three kinds of people: fools,
children, and drunkards"—we hope! Genesis gives us **Dieu créa l'homme à
son image** (kray-AH lawm ah sawn nee-MAHZH), translated as "God created man in his own image." Or should one say "created people in his own
image"? A self-centered wish: **Dieu défend le droit** (day-FAHN luu
drwah), translated as "may God defend the right," meaning our side. Then
there is a saying quoted by Voltaire: **Dieu est toujours pour les gros bataillons** (ay too-ZHOOR poor lay groh bah-tah-YAWN), translated as "God is
always on the side of the strong"; literally, "God is always for the big battal-
ions." Not exactly orthodox in outlook, was he? And then there is the
motto of English monarchs since the time of Henry VI: **Dieu et mon droit**
(ay mawn drwah), translated as "God and my right." Always useful are

Dieu m'en garde (mahn gahrd), "God forbid!" and "Heaven preserve me from it!" and **Dieu seul le sait** (suhl luu say), "only God knows." By way of gratitude we have **Dieu soit loué!** (swah loo-AY), "thank God!" or "God be praised!" And finally, by way of benediction, **Dieu vous bénisse!** (voo bay-NEESS), "may God bless you!" and **Dieu vous garde** (voo gahrd), "may God preserve you."

dîner aux chandelles (dee-NAY oh shahn-DAYL)
live it up
Literally translated as "dine by candlelight."

dîner par coeur (dee-NAY pahr kuhr)
skip dinner
A most apt metaphor for "go hungry"; literally, "dine from memory." Also translated as "make do without dinner."

dire (deer)
say or *talk*
This useful infinitive is variously employed in many phrases, including **dire des crudités** (day krü-dee-TAY), translated as "talk dirty" and "make coarse remarks." Then there is **dire des extravagances** (day zaykss-trah-vah-GAHNSS), translated as "talk wildly" and "speak extravagantly." A more enticing expression is **dire des fadeurs à une dame** (day fah-DUHR ah ün dahm), "murmur sweet nothings," more precisely, "pay insipid compliments to a woman," **fadeurs** being translated usually as "platitudes." Getting back to more everyday experiences, we have **dire des inepties** (day zee-nayp-SEE), translated as "talk rubbish" or "talk nonsense," and **dire des malpropretés** (day mahl-praw-pruu-TAY), "talk dirty" or "tell dirty stories," **malpropretés** being translated as "dirtiness." But there are more in the same vein: **dire des méchancetés à quelqu'un** (day may-shahn-STAY ah kayl-KœN), "say nasty things to someone"; **dire des ordures** (day zor-DÜR), "talk dirty" and "utter obscenities"; **dire des saletés** (day sahl-TAY), "talk dirty," literally, "say filthy things"; and **dire des saloperies** (day sah-law-PREE), with the same meanings. Finally, there is **dire du mal de quelqu'un** (dü mahl duu kayl-KœN), "criticize someone behind his back"; literally, "speak ill of somebody behind his back."

discours plein de mordant (deess-KOOR plan duu mor-DAHN)
punchy words

Literally, "speech full of bite," the noun **mordant** being translated as "punch" and "bite." As an adjective **mordant** means "caustic," as does the English "mordant," pronounced MOR-dənt.

dis donc! (dee dawnk)
by the way!
   An interjection, also translated as "I say!" or "Hey!"

diseur (dee-ZUHR)
talker
   Three phrases employing this noun are of interest. One is **diseur de bonne aventure** (duu bawn nah-vahn-TÜR), "fortune-teller," **bonne aventure** being translated as "good affair" or "good venture." And who would want to consult someone who sees anything but good signs in the cards or in a crystal ball? In an entirely different sense, we have **diseur de bons mots** (duu bawn moh), "wit"; literally, "sayer of clever things." (See also BON MOT.) Finally, there is **diseur de riens** (duu ryan), "idle talker"; literally, "talker about nothings," and surely the world has a plethora of such **diseurs**.

dis-moi ce que tu manges, et je dirai ce que tu es (dee mwah suu kuu tü mahnzh ay zhuu dee-RAY suu kuu tü ay)
you are what you eat
   A dictum, literally, "tell me what you eat, and I will tell you what you are," set forth by the illustrious Brillat-Savarin (bree-YAH sah-vah-RAN, 1755–1826), the French politician, gastronome, and writer whose pronouncements on the art of dining are taken as Holy Writ. His *Handbook of Gastronomy* is still in print and still read.

dominer de la tête et des épaules (daw-mee-NAY duu lah tayt ay day zay-POHL)
be a superstar
   Literally, "be head and shoulders above others."

donner (daw-NAY)
give
   Introducing a number of interesting locutions, for example, **donner à quelqu'un un gage d'amour** (ah kayl-KœN œn gahzh dah-MOOR), on the Broadway stage interpreted as "don't talk of love; show me!"—more

conventionally translated as "give someone a token of one's love," with **gage** having the literal meaning of "evidence." Then there is the French translation of a famous line from the New Testament: **donner de la confiture aux cochons** (duu lah kawn-fee-TÜR oh kaw-SHAW*N*), translated as "cast pearls before swine." In Matthew we read "Give not that which is holy unto the dogs, neither cast ye your pearls before swine." In the French we have, literally, "give jam to pigs." And knowing what delicious experience lurks in most **confitures**, we can easily make the leap from the literal "jams" to the figurative "pearls." More prosaically, we have **donner le fouet à quelqu'un** (luu fway ah kayl-Kœ*N*), translated as "give someone a whipping or flogging," with **fouet** denoting "whip"; and the happier **donner le sein à un bébé** (luu sa*n* ah œ*n* bay-BAY), translated as "suckle a child," literally, "give the breast to a baby." Departing the domestic scene, there is the metaphoric **donner quelqu'un en pâture aux fauves** (kayl-Kœ*N* ahn pah-TÜR oh fohv), usually translated as "throw someone to the wolves," more literally as "feed someone to wild animals" or "give food to wildcats." (See also FAUVES.) For those of independent mind, there is **donner son congé** (sawn kawn-ZHAY), heroically translated as "I quit!" but more conventionally as "give one's notice." By way of contrast, we have **donner son plein** (sawn pla*n*), translated as "go all out," "give one's all," or "do one's best." More satisfying to the recalcitrant is **donner un coup de pied dans les tibias à quelqu'un** (œ*n* koo də pyay dah*n* lay tee-BYAH ah kayl-Kœ*N*), literally, "kick someone in the shins." Finally, there is the aphorism **donner un oeuf pour avoir un boeuf** (œ*n* nuhf poor ah-VWAHR œ*n* buhf), meaning "make a concession in the hope of a bigger return" and literally translated as "give an egg to have an ox," but in the most idiomatic English version, "throw a sprat to catch a mackerel." This is what chess players call a gambit, a move that sacrifices a pawn or other minor piece to entrap an opponent into a damaging line of play.

dorer la pilule (daw-RAY lah pee-LÜL)
gild the pill

What is meant here is "make an unattractive thing at least appear desirable." The allusion is to the practice of physicians of an earlier time who attempted to improve the appearance—and taste—of their nauseating pills by gilding them with a thin coating of sugar. Which is comparable to what manufacturers of breakfast cereals do to make their product more attractive to children—as well as to many consenting adults.

dormir à la belle étoile (dor-MEER ah lah bayl lay-TWAHL)
camp out
   Usually translated as "sleep under the stars" or "sleep out in the open."

double entente (dooblə ahn-TAHNT)
ambiguity
   An indelicate play on words; literally, "double meaning," often given in English as "double entendre," a locution that can convey two meanings, one of which is usually risqué—itself a borrowing from French that is well understood as "off-color."

drapeau tricolore (drah-POH tree-kaw-LOR)
tricolor
   The flag of the French Republic.

droit du seigneur (drwah dü say-NYUHR)
right of the first night
   Literally, "lord's right," the supposed right of the feudal lord to deflower the bride of a vassal on her wedding night. While this privilege seems to have been exercised in medieval Europe, it was more often seen as an excuse for exacting taxes in lieu of exercising this privilege.

du fort au faible (dü for oh fayblə)
on an average
   Also translated as "one thing with another"; literally, "from the strong to the weak."

d'une oreille distraite (dün naw-RAYə deess-TRAYT)
abstractedly
   A way of not hearing what one is supposedly listening to; also translated as "with half an ear." The best practitioners of this art go undetected.

d'une seule voix (dün suhl vwah)
unanimously
   Literally, "with one voice."

E

eau (oh)
water

As one might suspect, French has many phrases introduced by this vital word: the terms **eau bénite** (bay-NEET), "holy water," and **eau bénite de cour** (bay-NEET duu koor), literally, "holy water of the court," are an interesting pair. The former denotes water that has been blessed by a priest, but the latter means "empty promises," "smooth, insincere words," or "blarney." So much for court life! Other common locutions are **eau courante** (koo-RAHNT), "running water," and **eau de Seltz** (duu sayltz), "seltzer water." But moving on to straightforward metaphor, we have **eau de vie** (duu vee), translated as "brandy"; literally, "water of life." An image of reviving a swooning maiden comes to mind in this phrase, especially when combined with mouth-to-mouth resuscitation. But on to the commonplace **eau dormante** (dor-MAHNT), translated as "stagnant water," literally, "sleeping water," and to **eau douce** (dooss), "fresh water," literally, "sweet water." And then we have **eau gazeuse** (gah-ZUHZ), "carbonated water" and "soda water," literally, "gaseous water"; **eau minérale** (mee-nay-RAHL), "mineral water"; **eau morte** (mort), "still water"; and **eau vive** (veevə), "spring water" and "running water."

ébats amoureux (ay-BAH ah-moo-RUU)
lovemaking

Also translated as "love frolics" or "love gambols." Makes the activity seem quite innocent as well as enjoyable, doesn't it?

échanger son cheval borgne contre un aveugle (ay-shahn-ZHAY sawn shuu-VAHL bornyə kawntrə œn nah-VUHGLə)
make a bad bargain

Literally, "swap a one-eyed horse for a blind one."

éclat (ay-KLAH)
brilliance

Also translated as "splendor," "striking effect," and "brilliant light." The original meaning was "splinter" or "fragment." This noun has also been taken into English as "éclat," with the pronunciation unchanged and meaning "brilliance of success" and "showy display."

écouter d'une oreille attentive (ay-koo-TAY dün naw-RAYə ah-tahn-TEEV)
listen attentively
Literally, "listen with an attentive ear."

écrasez l'infâme (ay-krah-ZAY lan-FAHM)
crush the abomination!
Also translated as "Crush the infamous thing," a favorite expression of Voltaire, with reference to the entrenched orthodoxy of pre-Revolutionary France.

effondré de douleur (ay-fawn-DRAY duu doo-LUHR)
grief-stricken
More literally, "crushed by grief."

élan (ay-LAHN)
dash
Also translated as "impetuous ardor."

élan vital (ay-LAHN vee-TAHL)
vital, creative force
Literally, "vital ardor." The French philosopher Henri Bergson (1859–1941) advanced the idea that a creative force of living things is responsible for growth, change, and desirable adaptations of organisms. The phrase was taken into English without change of meaning or pronunciation, indicating that there is no better way to express élan vital.

élevé dans la rue (aylə-VAY dahn lah rü)
brought up in the street
No happier a phrase than the following.

élevé dans le ruisseau (aylə-VAY dahn luu rwee-SOH)
brought up in the gutter

elle a (ayl lah)
she has

And what does she have? Read on: **elle a beaucoup de poitrine** (boh-KOO duu pwah-TREEN), translated as "she's stacked"; more literally, "she has a big bosom." Also given by **elle a un beau châssis** (œn boh shah-SEE), "she has a figure that never quits," more literally as "she has some chassis." More adulation: **elle a ce qu'il faut** (suu keel foh), translated as "she has what it takes." For example, **elle a de bons gigots** (duu bawn zhee-GOH), "she has great legs." Then there is **elle a du chien** (dü shyan), "she's a real looker"; literally, "she has something of the dog." We do admire dogs, don't we? And we do put on the dog. But **elle a** also leads us to a metaphor less complimentary: **elle a un appétit d'ogresse** (œn nah-pay-TEE daw-GRAYSS), "she really packs it in," also given as "she has an appetite like a horse"; literally, "she has the appetite of an ogress," which may give offense when you consider the cannibalistic proclivities imputed to ogres and ogresses. Then consider **elle a le coeur dur** (luu kuhr dür), meaning "nothing moves her" or "she has a heart of stone"; literally, "she has a hard heart." And, finally, its opposite, **elle a le coeur sensible** (luu kuhr sahn-SEEBLə), meaning "she has a soft heart," "she's tenderhearted," and "she's compassionate." Good to end on a pleasant note.

elle devient chameau avec l'âge (ayl duu-VYAN shah-MOH ah-VAYK lahzh)
age ill becomes her

Also translated as "age does not improve her disposition"; more literally, "as she ages she becomes more and more like a camel." Beastly, that is.

elle est . . . (ayl lay)
she is . . .

Leading us into several colorful characterizations, including **elle est bien balancée** (byan bah-lahn-SAY), translated as "she's stacked," also as "she has a figure that won't quit"; literally, "she is well balanced." Then there is **elle est cavaleuse** (kah-vah-LUHZə), translated as "she chases anything in pants," "she is a man chaser," and "she's a hot number." Among other uncomplimentary locutions, there is **elle est plate comme une limande** (plahtə kawm ün lee-MAHNDə), translated as "she's no Marilyn Monroe"; literally, and more cruelly, "she's flat-chested as a dab"—a European flatfish, that is. Much happier is **elle est plusieurs fois millionnaire** (plü-ZYUHR fwah mee-lyaw-NAIR), translated as "she's as rich as Rockefeller"; more literally, "she's a millionaire several times over." Good for her! Another compliment is paid by **elle est très soignée de sa personne** (tray swah-NYAY duu sah pair-SAWN), translated as "she is well groomed."

elle l'a incendié du regard (ayl lah ahn-sahn-DYAY dü ruu-GAHR)
she cut him dead
   Also translated as "she shot him a baleful look" and "she looked daggers at him"; somewhat more literally as "her glance burned him to a crisp."

elle ne dit ni oui ni non (ayl nuu dee nee wee nee nawn)
she's on the fence
   Also translated as "she's not committing herself either way"; more nearly literally as, in the words of an old song, "she wouldn't say yes, she wouldn't say no."

embarras de richesses (ahn-bah-RAH duu ree-SHAYSS)
too much of a good thing
   Meaning "an embarrassing amount of wealth or other good things"; literally translated as "embarrassment of riches." I should be so embarrassed!

embrasser quelqu'un à pleine bouche (ahn-brah-SAY kayl-KœN ah playn boosh)
kiss somebody on the lips
   Not peck on or near the cheek, in the manner of modern close—or, in some circles, not-so-close—friends.

émeutes (ay-MUHTə)
riots
   Or "rioting," as declaimed by Gilbert and Sullivan's policemen's chorus in *The Pirates of Penzance*: "For when threatened with émeutes (pronounced ee-MYOOTS), and your heart is in your boots."

émigré (ay-mee-GRAY)
emigrant
   Taken into English as "émigré," without change in pronunciation.

éminence grise (ay-mee-NAHNSS greez)
éminence grise

Although this phrase can be translated as "gray eminence," it usually goes untranslated when used in English or may be translated as "power behind the throne." The allusion is to a trusted counselor of Cardinal Richelieu, whose policies he influenced without attracting undue attention to himself.

emmener déjeuner quelqu'un (ahn-muu-NAY day-zhuu-NAY kayl-KœN)
let's do lunch
Literally translated as "take someone out to lunch."

empire des lettres (ahn-PEER day laytrə)
the domain of letters
More often translated as "world of letters"; literally, "empire of letters."

en amour l'éloignement rapproche (ahn nah-MOOR lay-lwah-nyə-MAHN rah-PRAWSH)
absence makes the heart grow fonder
Also given as "distance lends enchantment." But, recalling "out of sight, out of mind," let us not carry this thought too far. (See also LOIN DES YEUX LOIN DU COEUR.)

en arrière (ahn nah-RYAIR)
in or *to the rear*
Note that this phrase also carries the meaning "in arrears."

en avant! (ahn nah-VAHN)
forward!
This command may also be construed as "march on!"

en bloc (ahn blawk)
wholesale
This merchant's term—also an astute shopper's term—translates more closely as "in a lump" or "as a whole."

en bon français (ahn bawn frahn-SAY)
in plain English
Also translated as "in plain terms" or "without dancing around" or "like a true Frenchman," but literally, "in good French."

en bon train (ahn bawn tran)
going well
  Literally, "in good train," a translation that teaches us once again how far an idiom can get from its accepted meaning.

en chair et en os (ahn shair ray ahn nawss)
as large as life
  Also translated as "in the flesh"; literally, "in flesh and bone." Nothing like being accurate.

en costume d'Adam (ahn kawss-TÜM dah-DAHN)
naked as a jaybird
  Also translated as "in his birthday suit" or "naked as the day he was born," he being Adam. Then there's **en costume d'Eve** (daivə), "in her birthday suit" or "naked as the day she was born," she being Eve.

en déshabillé (ahn day-zah-bee-YAY)
in a state of undress
  Also translated as "naked." In pathetic English—the kind of English that pretends we are always fully clothed and pure of mind—this phrase is sometimes given as "in dishabille," less frequently as "in deshabille."

en Dieu est ma confiance (ahn dyuu ay mah kawn-fee-YAHNSS)
in God is my trust
  An inscription familiar to numismatists as "in God we trust."

en effet (ahn nay-FAY)
in reality
  Also translated as "really" or "substantially" or, literally, as "in effect."

en faire une jaunisse (ahn fair ün zhoh-NEESS)
with nose out of joint
  Also translated as "be pretty miffed" or with the meaning of "be green with envy," which latter translation is pretty close to the literal meaning of **jaunisse**, "jaundice," and its metaphoric meaning, "jealousy." Do English speakers turn green with envy instead of yellow because they yearn to be in Paris in the spring? Correspondence is invited on this subject.

en famille (ahn fah-MEEYə)
informally
   Also translated as "among ourselves" or "in the family."

enfant (ahn-FAHN)
child
   As one might expect, **enfant** leads to many idiomatic expressions, for example, **enfant de l'amour** (duu lah-MOOR), commonly translated as "love
child," a euphemism matched in evasiveness only by the translation "natural child" and considered preferable to the ugly translations "bastard" and
"illegitimate child." Turning to a phrase that condemns parents for rearing
rather than siring, we have **enfant gâté** (gah-TAY), "spoiled child." Then,
focusing attention on a child's accomplishments, consider **enfant prodige**
(praw-DEEZH), "child prodigy." And lest we think we have become excessively benign in our outlook, there is **enfant prodigue** (praw-DEEG),
"prodigal son," which explicitly condemns the child for wasting his inheri-
tance. Then there are **enfants à charge** (ah shahrzh), "dependent children," and **enfants perdus** (pair-DÜ), literally, "lost children," but carrying
the meaning of "forlorn hopes" and "lost souls," referring especially to soldiers sent out on especially dangerous duty. In modern times **enfants perdus** may also be applied very expansively to any men or women given
especially hazardous, even career-threatening, assignments. One phrase in
this family that is often heard in English—with something approaching the
French pronunciation—is **enfant terrible** (tay-REEBLə), literally, "terrible
child," but usually translated as "brat" or "unruly child," denoting a child
given to making embarrassing remarks or disclosures. Note that there is no
age limit on being termed an **enfant terrible**. Indeed, it is frequently applied to some grown-ups who have never grown up. Finally, there is **enfant
trouvé** (troo-VAY), translated as "foundling"; literally, "found child."

enfin (ahn-FAN)
finally
   Also translated as "in short," "to conclude," "at last," and, among British
speakers, "in fine," which has the same meanings. Interesting observation:
we often find it necessary to translate English idioms for American readers.

en flagrant délit (ahn flah-GRAHN day-LEE)
red-handed

Also translated as "in the very act." The phrase is a French translation of the Latin *in flagrante delicto* (in flah-GRAHN-tay day-LEE-ktoh), meaning "in the very act of committing the offense"; literally, "while the crime is blazing." Both the French and the Latin phrases are applied broadly, so no actual crime need be involved. Indeed, tabloid newspapers routinely report racy news of men and women being caught in flagrante delicto by snooping reporters and photographers. The acts revealed don't earn brownie points for the contending parties in a divorce court.

engrosser quelqu'un (ahn-groh-SAY kayl-KœN)
knock someone up
  Conventionally translated as "get someone pregnant."

en haut (ahn oh)
on high
  Also translated as "above," "aloft," or "overhead."

en masse (ahn mahss)
all together
  Also translated as "in a mass," "as a group," and "in a body." This phrase appears in English with little change in pronunciation.

en mauvaise odeur (ahn maw-VAYZ aw-DUHR)
in ill repute
  Literally, "in bad odor."

ennui (ahn-NWEE)
boredom
  Another apt word that has been taken into English, without change in pronunciation.

en papillotes (ahn pah-pee-YAWT)
in curlpapers
  Also given in English as "in papillotes" (PAP-ə-lohts). Anyone with access to a restaurant that serves its lamb chops with bone ends encased in curlpapers will know that the extra dollar or so tacked on to the price of the dish covers the pennies of extra expense incurred by this unnecessary fillip. (See also PAPILLOTE for a more rewarding dining experience.)

en passant (ahn pah-SAHN)
by the way
   Also translated as "in passing."

en plein (ahn plan)
fully
   A term introducing several useful phrases: **en plein air** (plan nair), translated as "in the open air"; **en pleine nuit** (playn nwee), translated as "in the middle of the night" and "at dead of night." Then there is **en plein hiver** (plan nee-VAIR), translated as "in the middle of winter" and "in the depths of winter." To close on a brighter note, there are **en plein jour** (plan zhoor), translated as "in broad daylight"; and **en plein soleil** (plan saw-LAYə), translated as "in full sun."

en rapport (ahn rah-POR)
in sympathy or *accord*
   Literally, "in relation." **Rapport** has been taken into English without change in pronunciation, conveying the meaning of "relation" or "connection."

entente (ahn-TAHNT)
agreement
   Also translated as "understanding," the most famous **entente** being that termed the **entente cordiale** (kor-DYAHL), the friendly understanding established between England and France in 1904.

en tête-à-tête (ahn tayt tah tayt)
alone together
   Also translated as "in private," "face-to-face," and, literally, "head to head." Somehow this last translation doesn't convey the sense of intimacy implicit in the others.

entêtement (ahn-taytə-MAHN)
pigheadedness
   Also translated as "stubbornness" or "obstinacy," and as "infatuation." Now what does this last translation have to do with the others? For an answer, consult parents of teenage children.

en tout (ahn too)
wholly
>   Literally, "in all."

entre Charybde et Scylla (ahntrə shah-REEBDə ay see-LAH)
between a rock and a hard place
>   Also translated as "between the devil and the deep blue sea," and, liter-
ally, as "between Scylla and Charybdis." And who or what were Scylla and
Charybdis? In Greek legend, Scylla was a sea monster—with twelve feet
and six heads—that dwelt on a rock in the Straits of Messina, where—with
an act felonious in mind—she lay in wait for sailors who went off their
course. Charybdis, also a monster, lived under a fig tree across the straits
from where Scylla plied her trade. Thus, in trying to avoid death at the
hands of Scylla, ships were driven toward the perils of Charybdis. And so,
ever since, the French and others have used "between Scylla and Charybdis" to refer to hapless people—especially authors—who are caught in a
trap. In trying to avoid one fault, they inevitably fall into another. (See also
ENTRE LE MARTEAU ET L'ENCLUME.)

entre chien et loup (ahntrə shyan ay loo)
at twilight
>   Literally, "between dog and wolf." Also translated as "at dusk," when it
is hard to distinguish one shape from another, just as it may be hard at dusk
to tell a dog from a wolf.

entre deux âges (ahntrə duu zahzh)
middle-aged
>   Literally, "between two ages."

entre deux vins (ahntrə duu van)
tipsy
>   Better translated as "half-drunk"; literally, "between two wines."

entre l'arbre et l'écorce il ne faut pas mettre le doigt (ahntrə lahrbrə ay
lay-KORSS eel nuu foh pah maytrə luu dwah)
don't meddle in other people's affairs
>   Good advice; literally, "don't stick your finger between the tree and its
bark," **écorce** meaning "bark."

entre le marteau et l'enclume (ahntrə luu mahr-TOH ay lahn-KLÜM)
between the devil and the deep blue sea
Also translated as "between a rock and a hard place"; literally, "between the hammer and the anvil." Ouch! (See also ENTRE CHARYBDE ET SCYLLA.)

entre les mains des dieux (ahntrə lay man day dyuu)
in the lap of the gods
Literally, "in the hands of the gods," where everything inevitably rests. The reference is to the unknown chances the future holds for all of us.

entre nous (ahntrə noo)
between ourselves
Also translated as "in confidence" or as "between you and me."

entrepreneur de pompes funèbres (ahn-truu-pruu-NUHR duu pawnpə fü-NAYBRə)
undertaker
By the squeamish among us, called "mortician." The French phrase is more businesslike, literally calling this person "funeral contractor."

entreprise de pompes funèbres (ahn-truu-PREEZ duu pawnpə fü-NAYBRə)
funeral parlor
Again the French call a spade a spade; literally, "funeral firm." Much more to the point than the folksy "funeral parlor," which sounds like a place where one serves tea and biscuits to visitors.

en trois coups de cuillère à pot (ahn trwah koo duu kwee-YAIR rah poh)
in a jiffy
Or, as we say, "in two shakes of a lamb's tail." In the French there is no mention of lambs or their tails. Instead they say, nearly literally, "in three stirrings of a ladle," **cuillère à pot** meaning "ladle."

en vérité (ahn vay-ree-TAY)
truly
Also translated as "indeed"; literally, "in truth."

en vieillissant on devient plus fou et plus sage (ahn vyay-yee-SAHN awn duu-VYAN plü foo ay plü sahzh)
aging is a double-edged sword

At least that's how La Rochefoucauld saw it; literally, "As we grow old, we become more foolish and more wise." Read the newspapers for confirmation of the wisdom of this adage. Or look into your own heart.

en voilà assez! (ahn vwah-LAH ah-SAY)
that'll do!

More literally, "that's enough!"

éperdu d'amour (ay-pair-DÜ dah-MOOR)
madly in love

The adjective **éperdu** can also be translated as "distracted" or "bewildered." It all depends on one's penchant for hyperbole.

escargot (ayss-kahr-GOH)
edible snail

Perhaps the menu item most readily identifiable as uniquely French—adored by devotees, considered repulsive by the uninitiated. (See also AVANCER COMME UN ESCARGOT.)

esprit (ayss-PREE)
spirit

Also translated variously as "mind," "intelligence," "soul," and "wit." Several phrases are introduced by **esprit**. For example, **esprit borné** (bor-NAY) means "narrow mind." Another is **esprit de corps** (duu kor), a term that has been taken into English without change in pronunciation. It may be translated as "team spirit" or "company spirit," depending on context, but the best translation is "esprit de corps," denoting a spirit of comradeship and loyalty to the organization to which one belongs. Less uplifting is **esprit dérangé** (day-rahn-ZHAY), translated as "disordered mind." The next phrase, **esprit d'escalier** (dayss-kah-LYAY), is delightful. It may be translated as "slow on the uptake" or literally as "staircase wit." The allusion is to the plight of a clever person, not too quick on the uptake, who is passing someone going in the opposite direction on a staircase or escalator. By the time our protagonist has thought of an appropriately witty remark to direct at the other person, he is too far away from him. Thus, **esprit d'escalier** refers to a rejoinder that occurs to one too late and therefore loses its pertinency. By contrast, there is **esprit présent** (pray-ZAHN), translated as "ready wit." How the rest of us envy anyone who is quick on the uptake! (See also JEU D'ESPRIT.)

essai raté (ay-SAY rah-TAY)
blown chance
   Also translated as "failed attempt," the kind of effort we all regret.

et l'avare Achéron ne lâche point sa proie (ay lah-VAHR ah-shay-RAWN nuu lahsh pwahn sah prwah)
once you're dead, forget it!
   A line from Racine, literally translated as "and grasping Acheron never lets go of his prey." In classical mythology, Acheron is one of the rivers over which Charon ferried the souls of the dead. No need to buy a round-trip ticket—this is a one-way journey.

et le combat cessa faute de combatants (ay luu kawn-BAH say-SAH foht duu kawn-bah-TAHN)
declare war and nobody shows up
   A line from Corneille in *Le Cid*; literally, "and the combat ceased for lack of soldiers." Thus, we may ask what happens in wartime when no one wants to keep on fighting? The answer is simple: no soldiers, no war.

étouffer quelque chose dans l'oeuf (ay-too-FAY kaylkə shohz dahn luhf)
nip something in the bud
   Also translated as "destroy something before it has time to develop"; literally, "kill something in the egg."

étouffer quelqu'un de baisers (ay-too-FAY kayl-KœN duu bay-ZAY)
smother someone with kisses
   Also translated as "suffocate someone with kisses," conveying a chilling message. Better to stay with "smother."

et pourtant j'avais quelque chose là (ay poor-tahn zhah-VAY kaylkə shohz lah)
and yet I had something there
   The words reported to have been said by the French poet André Chénier (1762–1794) while tapping his forehead, the "there" there. The

date was July 25th—just three days before the end of the Reign of Terror—
and Chénier was on his way from prison for a date with the guillotine.

être à l'agonie (aytrə ah lah-gaw-NEE)
be at death's door
> Also translated as "be at the point of death" or, in Latin, *in extremis.*

être à six pieds sous terre (aytrə ah see pyay soo tair)
be pushing up the daisies
> More nearly literally, "be six feet under."

être à tu et à toi avec quelqu'un (aytrə ah tü ay ah twah ah-VAYK kayl-KœN)
be close to someone
> Better translated as "be on a first-name basis with someone." (See also
> TUTOIEMENT.)

être au septième ciel (aytrə oh sayt-TYAYM syayl)
supremely happy
> While English speakers in recent years have spoken of "being on cloud
> nine," there was a time when we settled for "being in seventh heaven,"
> which is a literal translation of the French idiom. And when did we so de-
> scribe ourselves? Usually when we were in the first, rapturous stages of love.
> Also when a first novel was accepted for publication. But why did we say we
> were in seventh heaven? Why not sixth or fifth heaven? Perhaps because of
> a medieval cabalistic belief that there were seven heavens, the seventh—at
> the top—being the abode of God and the highest class of angels. Beats
> cloud nine, doesn't it? Even beats walking on air!

être aux cent coups (aytrə oh sahn koo)
be at wit's end
> Also translated as "be frantic," "be in deep trouble," or "not know which
> way to turn." The literal translation of this idiom, "be at a hundred blows,"
> is beyond deciphering. Help!

être connu de tout le voisinage (aytrə kaw-NÜ duu too luu vwah-zee-NAHZH)
local celebrity

Translated as "be widely known;" more literally, "be known throughout the neighborhood."

être cousu d'or (aytrə koo-ZÜ dor)
filthy rich
Literally, "be sewn with gold."

être dans la panade (aytrə dahn lah pah-NAHDə)
eat low on the hog
Well translated as "be up against it" and "be down to one's last dollar." After all, **panade** means "bread soup," and if that's all one has to eat. . . .

être dos à dos (aytrə doh zah doh)
be back-to-back
Square dancers will readily see the familiar "do-si-do" in this idiom.

être en . . . (aytrə ahn)
be in . . .
The opening words of a variety of interesting locutions, for example, **être en bisbille avec quelqu'un** (beess-BEEYə ah-VAYK kayl-KœN), translated as "feud with someone," "be at odds with," and "be at loggerheads." The noun **bisbille** means "squabble." Then there is **être en goguette** (gaw-GAYT), translated as "be in a convivial mood" and "be on a spree." And, of course, **être en guerre** (gair), "be at war," and **être en majorité** (mah-zhaw-ree-TAY), "be in the majority." More happily, there is **être en rapport avec quelqu'un** (rah-POR ah-VAYK kayl-KœN), translated as "still talking," "be on good terms," "have dealings with someone," and "be in touch with someone." More earthy is **être en rut** (rüt), "be in heat," the English borrowing "rut" being easily seen in this idiom. To turn to a comfortable situation, we have **être en savates** (sah-VAHT), "be in one's slippers." But lest we close our minds to less pleasant thoughts, we must remember that **savate**, while conveying an image of comfortable slippers, is also the name given to French boxing, a sport that countenances kicking as well as punching one's opponent. Finally, we have **être en terrain mouvant** (tay-RAN moo-VAHN), "be on shaky ground," and **être en vogue** (vawgə), "be fashionable" or "be in style." "Vogue" (pronounced vohg) is familiar in English, of course, conjuring up images of gorgeous models elegantly clothed.

être habillé avec chic (aytrə ah-bee-YAY ah-VAYK sheek)
be stylishly dressed
   In this phrase we find yet another English adoption from the French language, this time without change in pronunciation. While "stylish" and "fashionable" and "with flair" are often used when "chic" will do the job, there is a certain JE NE SAIS QUOI (which see) to chic that epitomizes the quality we are interested in conveying.

être heureux comme un poisson dans l'eau (aytrə uu-RUU kawm œn pwah-SAWN dahn loh)
be happy as a pig in shit
   More conventionally and literally translated as "be happy as a fish in water."

être le jouet du hasard (aytrə luu zhway dü ah-ZAHR)
single is better?
   Translated as "lose control of one's future," "be the plaything of chance," or "be hostage to fortune"—fortune here meaning "fate." English essayist Francis Bacon (1561–1626) took note of man's lot in "He that hath wife and children hath given hostages to fortune; for they are impediments to great enterprises, either of virtue or mischief."

être malade à crever (aytrə mah-LAHD ah kruu-VAY)
feel like death warmed over
   Best translated as "be dreadfully ill" or "feel ghastly," the infinitive **crever** here meaning "die."

être malmené par la critique (aytrə mahl-muu-NAY pahr lah kree-TEEK)
raked over the coals
   By literary critics, that is. Literally, "be maltreated by criticism."

être marron (aytrə mah-RAWN)
be had
   More conventionally translated as "be a sucker"; literally, "be a chestnut."

être mis en préretraite (aytrə mee ahn pray-ruu-TRAYT)
on the shelf at fifty

More conventionally translated as "be retired early" or "be given early retirement." And, as the British are wont to say, "be made redundant." Ugh!

être né (aytrə nay)
be born
Which becomes part of two interesting locutions: **être né sous une bonne étoile** (soo zün bawn nay-TWAHL), "be born under a lucky star," and **être né sous une mauvaise étoile** (soo zün maw-VAYZ zay-TWAHL), "be born under an unlucky star." Consult your neighborhood astrologer.

être noyé (aytrə nwah-YAY)
be all at sea
Also translated as "be out of one's depth," more literally as "fail to understand."

être palpitant d'émotion (aytrə pahl-pee-TAHN day-moh-SYAWN)
throb with emotion
French exaggeration. More literally, "be quivering with emotion." Another exaggeration. Notice the English cognate "palpitate" in **palpitant**.

être plein de courbatures (aytrə plan duu koor-bah-TÜR)
nothing but aches and pains
Well translated as "be aching all over" or "be full of aches."

être savant en . . . (aytrə sah-VAHN ahn)
to be learned in . . .
You supply the field of expertise.

être soigné aux petits oignons (aytrə swah-NYAY oh puu-TEE zaw-NYAWN)
be looked after really well
A masterpiece of culinary idiom, also translated as "be given excellent attention." The implication is that nothing has been overlooked, especially not **les petits oignons**, the desirable miniature pickling onions.

être sur . . . (aytrə sür)
be on . . .
The start of several interesting locutions: **être sur la paille** (lah pīyə), translated as "be stony broke" or "be penniless," suggesting reduced to bed-

ding down on straw (**paille**). No happier is **être sur la sellette** (lah say-LAYT), "be raked over the coals," "be on the carpet," and "be on the hot seat." The literal translation is "be on the stand," not a witness stand, but something more like a plant stand or the stool on which a culprit formerly was made to sit. A useful idiom is **être sur le gril** (luu greel), translated as "be on tenterhooks"; literally, "be on the grill." And a reasonable assumption is that there are hot coals beneath the grill. Ouch! Almost as unhappy is **être sur le retour** (luu ruu-TOOR), translated as "over the hill"; more literally, "be on the trip home," a pleasant enough euphemism until we think carefully about the terminal meaning of "home" in this phrase. Clearly unhappy is **être sur le sable** (luu sahblə), meaning "be unemployed," "be on one's uppers," "be down-and-out," "be on the beach," and "live like a beachcomber," the last two translations appropriately reflecting the use of the noun **sable**, which means "sand." Then there is **être sur les dents** (lay dahn), translated as "be dog tired"; literally, "be on the teeth," possibly suggesting "with nothing to chew." Finally, there is **être sur le trône** (luu trohn), translated as "be on the john"; literally, "be on the throne," which is a common English euphemism for this essential bathroom fixture.

être suspendu aux lèvres de quelqu'un (aytrə süss-pahn-DÜ oh layvrə duu kayl-KœN)
utter fascination

Well translated as "to hang on someone's every word"; more literally, "to hang on someone's lips."

être tordu (aytrə tor-DÜ)
have a screw loose

Also translated as "be off one's rocker" or "be round the bend"; literally, "be twisted."

être tout raplati (aytrə too rah-plah-TEE)
done in

Also translated as "be completely washed out"; literally, "be flattened."

et surtout, pas de zèle! (ay sür-TOO pah duu zayl)
and above all, no zeal!

An instruction attributed to French statesman Charles Maurice de Talleyrand (1754–1838), speaking to his subordinates.

expédier quelqu'un dans l'autre monde (ayks-pay-DYAY kayl-KœN dahn lohtrə mawnd)
rub somebody out
    Also translated as "bump someone off"; literally, "send somebody off to the other world."

explication de texte (ayks-plee-kah-SYAWN duu taykstə)
interpretation of a text
    Also translated as "critical analysis of a text." This French term is commonly used by literary scholars to denote reliance on careful analysis of a text, focusing on style, language, and content.

extirper quelqu'un de son lit (ayks-teer-PAY kayl-KœN duu sawn lee)
drag someone out of bed
    This translation, though accurate, is not as brutal as it sounds. After all, **extirper** may also be translated as "extirpate," "eradicate," and "uproot," any one of which surpasses "drag" in intensity. But if you have no stomach for any of these, you may also translate the phrase as "wake someone up."

F

facile comme bonjour (fah-SEEL kawm bawn-ZHOOR)
easy as pie
    Literally, "easy as saying hello." For men and women of good will, that is.

facilité de parler, c'est impuissance de se taire (fah-see-lee-TAY duu pahr-LAY say tan-pwee-SAHNSS duu suu tair)
why talk when you have nothing to say?
    Easy. Some people can't help running off at the mouth all the time. Racine's words, translated more closely as "fluency of speech is often inability to be silent," put the thought elegantly.

faible d'esprit (fayblə dayss-PREE)
feeble-minded

This adjectival phrase can also be used as a noun, meaning "feeble-minded person."

fainéant (fay-nay-AHN)
idler

As a noun also translated as "loafer" or "do-nothing." As an adjective, **fainéant** is translated as "idle" or "lazy."

faire bonne chère (fair bawn shair)
eat well

The key to this phrase, often translated as "dine well," is the noun **chère**, which means "food," giving the phrase the literal meaning "prepare good food." But we also know the adjective **chère**, the feminine form of **cher**, both of which mean "dear." French, like other languages, has its traps for the unwary. (See also CHER AMI.)

faire bonne mine (fair bawn meen)
put a good face on it

Also translated as "give a good reception to"; literally, "put a good expression on it."

faire claquer son fouet (fair klah-KAY sawn fway)
blow one's own horn

Literally, "crack one's own whip." Suggesting that no one else will do it for you.

faire contre mauvaise fortune bon coeur (fair kawntrə maw-VAYZ for-TÜN bawn kuhr)
keep a stiff upper lip

Also translated as "put a brave face on things"; somewhat more literally as "maintain good spirits in the face of hard luck."

faire dans sa culotte (fair dahn sah kü-LAWT)
wet one's pants

A common reaction when one is scared stiff—ask any soldier who has faced enemy fire for the first time. Thus we may translate the locution as "shake in one's boots"; literally, "make in one's pants."

faire de la lèche à quelqu'un (fair duu lah laysh ah kayl-KœN)
lick someone's boots
   A popular translation, also freely rendered as "suck up to someone."

faire de la prose sans le savoir (fair duu lah prohz sahn luu sah-VWAHR)
make prose without knowing it
   A delicious line from a scene in Molière's *Le Bourgeois gentilhomme* (*The Would-Be Gentleman*, 1671), in which the central character expresses delight on learning that he has been speaking in prose for his entire life.

faire des . . . (fair day)
do or *make some . . .*
   The words that introduce many idioms, including **faire des pompes** (pawnpə), "do push-ups." The contemporary English phrase "pump iron" resonates here. Then there is **faire des progrès** (praw-GRAY), which translates as "improve"; more literally, "make progress." For would-be lady-killers and raving beauties, we have **faire des ravages** (rah-VAHZH), "break hearts." For the rest of us there is **faire des vagues** (vahgə), translated literally as "make waves," more commonly translated as "make trouble" or "cause complications." Finally, there is **faire des yeux de velours à quelqu'un** (zyuu duu vuu-LOOR ah kayl-KœN), translated as "make goo-goo eyes," "make sheep's eyes at someone," and, literally, as "make velvet eyes at someone." Whatever the translation, the meaning is clear: look amorously or longingly at someone.

faire don de sa vie pour sauver quelqu'un (fair dawn duu sah vee poor soh-VAY kayl-KœN)
the ultimate sacrifice
   Best translated as "lay down one's life for another"; literally, "make a gift of one's life in order to save someone."

faire du . . . (fair dü)
do or *make* or *cause . . .*
   These words introduce a great number of idioms, including **faire du bien à** (byan ah), translated as "do good to." On a more pedestrian level, there is **faire du café** (kah-FAY), "make some coffee." Less helpful is **faire du chagrin à quelqu'un** (shah-GRAN ah kayl-KœN), translated as "cause somebody distress." (Although English has adopted the noun **chagrin**, the

English pronunciation is shuu-GRIN.) For a pleasant interlude try **faire du farniente sur la plage** (fahr-NYAHNT sür lah plahzh). This phrase is translated usually as "lounge on the beach" and, with its use of **farniente**, "idleness," is evocative of the Italian *dolce far niente*, "pleasant idleness"; literally, "sweet doing nothing." No need to tell the French and Italians how to make use of their spare time! To return to the everyday world, try **faire du froufrou** (froo-FROO), translated as "show off." (See also FROUFROU.) Moving away from mundane matters, we have **faire du genou à quelqu'un** (zhuu-NOO ah kayl-KœN), translated as "play footsie," "flirt with someone," and "be clandestinely intimate with someone." Note, however, that while some among us may play footsie, the French locution focuses on the surreptitious use of the knee, **genou**. Good to know! And now on to **faire du mal à** (mahl ah), translated as "do harm to." Then, if you are in the mood for work, try **faire du rabiot** (rah-BYOH), translated as "work overtime" or "put in extra hours"; the noun **rabiot** means "extra." If it's noise you or your neighbors want, there are **faire du raffut** (rah-FÜ), translated as "make a racket" or "make a row"; and **faire du tintamarre** (tan-tah-MAHR), with the meaning of "make a racket" or "make a hullabaloo." The particular attraction of **tintamarre** as a word is its onomatopoeic evocation of a clanging bell, akin to that of the English word "tintinnabulation" made famous by Edgar Allan Poe. This discussion closes on a less than encouraging note: **faire du sentiment** (sahn-tee-MAHN), translated as "lay it on thick" or "sentimentalize"; and **faire du zèle** (zayl), translated as "overdo something" and "be overzealous." Both proclivities to be avoided.

faire feu de tout bois (fair fuu duu too bwah)
remember to recycle
That is, "make the most of what one has"; literally, "use all available wood to make fires."

faire la . . . (fair lah)
do or make or play or give or take or cook or sell the . . .
The infinitive **faire** followed by the article **la** introduces many French idioms, including **faire la bête** (bayt), translated as "play the fool" or "act stupid." Then there is **faire la bouche en coeur** (boosh ahn kœr), translated as "play hard to get"; literally, "make your mouth into a heart." Perhaps because mouths so arranged appear ready to return a kiss but do not follow through? A most interesting idiom is **faire la fine bouche** (feenə

boosh), translated as "turn up one's nose"; literally, "make a thin mouth." Whether we're dealing with an Anglo-Saxon nose or a Gallic mouth, if you cannot see the basis for the French idiom, try saying something pleasant while your lips are pressed firmly against each other. A phrase for everyone charitable is **faire la manche** (mah*n*sh), translated as "pass the hat." The French literally say "pass the sleeve," but who can fight idioms? Then there is the reprehensible **faire la mijaurée** (mee-zhaw-RAY), translated as "give oneself airs"; literally, "play the part of an affected woman." Again dealing with personal mannerisms, there is **faire la moue** (moo), translated as "pout"; literally, "make a moue," **moue** having been taken into English with the same meaning, "pouting grimace," and the same pronunciation. Now for some fun: **faire la noce** (nawss) is translated as "live it up," also as "go on a spree" and "have a wild time." The literal meaning of **noce** is "wedding," and no wedding worth its salt is anything less than a great shindig. Turning to the workaday world, there is **faire la semaine anglaise** (suu-MAYN nah*n*-GLAYZ), translated as "work a five-day week"; literally, "work the English week," which gives us some insight into the French perception of British customs. A practical phrase is **faire la soudure entre** (soo-DÜR ah*n*trə), translated as "bridge the gap between"; literally, "make a weld between." Continuing in the practical vein, there is **faire la toilette de son chien** (twah-LAYT duu sawn shya*n*), translated as "groom one's dog." And anyone who has ever enjoyed a fine meal in a French restaurant knows that many locals consider dining out without one's dog—usually a lapdog—robs the experience of some of its pleasure. So, of course, one would surely be certain to groom the little critter before leaving for the restaurant.

faire l'autruche (fair loh-TRÜSH)
bury one's head in the sand

   Also translated as "avoid reality" or "ignore the facts of a situation"; literally, "play the ostrich," showing that Americans are not the only ones who believe that ostriches hide from danger by burying their heads in the sand.

faire le . . . (fair luu)
make or *play* or *do* or *take the . . .*

   Just as **faire la** introduces many idioms, **faire le** contributes its share, including **faire le blasé** (blah-ZAY), translated as "act bored" or "affect indifference toward everything." The adjective **blasé**, of course, has been taken into English without change of spelling or pronunciation. Then there is **faire le chien couchant** (shyan koo-SHAHN), translated as "kowtow"; literally, "play the sleeping dog." On a noisier note, consider **faire le diable à quatre** (dyahblə ah kahtrə), translated as "make a hell of a row," more literally as "make the devil of a row." Continuing on this note, there is **faire le fanfaron** (fahn-fah-RAWN), translated as "blow your own horn," "brag," "boast," and "go around bragging," with **fanfaron** evoking the meaning and spelling of the English word "fanfare." In a display of the French attitude toward foreign nationals, we have **faire le grec** (grayk), translated as "manipulate the cards"; literally, "do the Greek." Then, for unmitigated reprehensibility, we have **faire le mal pour le mal** (mahl poor luu mahl), translated as "do evil for evil's sake." To move on to a more sanguine subject, there is **faire le Père Noël** (pair noh-AYL), translated as "play Santa Claus." On a decisive note, there is **faire le saut** (soh), translated as "take the plunge." Finally, there is **faire le sucré** (sü-KRAY), translated as "butter up" and "turn on the sweetness."

faire l'école buissonière (fair lay-KAWL bwee-saw-NYAIR)
play hooky
   Also translated as "play truant" or "skip school." Note that any unauthorized absence from work or other responsibility can be characterized by using this same French phrase.

faire les premiers pas (fair lay pruu-MYAY pah)
get started
   Also translated as "make the first move," "take the initiative," and, literally, "take the first steps."

faire les présentations (fair lay pray-zahn-tah-SYAWN)
make the introductions
   A social act, in the sense of introducing people to one another.

faire l'homme d'importance (fair lawm dan-por-TAHNSS)
put on airs
   Also translated as "presume" and, literally, "play the man of importance."

faire mauvais accueil à quelqu'un (fair maw-VAY zah-KœYə ah kayl-KœN)
give someone the small hello
More conventionally translated as "make someone feel unwelcome" or as "give someone a poor reception."

faire pareil que (fair pah-RAYə kuu)
to do the same thing as
As someone else, that is.

faire pipi (fair pee-PEE)
go to the john
Translated also as "pee," more formally as "urinate." Both better than "make a wee." (See also next entry.)

faire ses besoins (fair say buu-ZWAHN)
relieve oneself
Also translated as "go to the john," literally as "meet one's needs." The extremes we go to in order to avoid being descriptive! (See also previous entry.)

faire ses choux gras (fair say shoo grah)
feather one's nest
Also translated as "make a profit"; literally, "make one's cabbages fat." Apparently by applying fertilizer and good soil to grow in.

faire son apparition (fair sawn nah-pah-ree-SYAWN)
turn up
Also translated as "appear" or "make one's appearance." **Apparition** shares only spelling and etymology with the English word "apparition."

faire travailler la tête (fair trah-vah-YAY lah tayt)
get your head on straight
More conventionally translated as "make your head work" or "get your head working."

faire trempette (fair trahn-PAYT)
dunk one's bread
Or anything else you care to dunk—for example, a doughnut—but understand that **trempette**, literally, is "piece of bread for dunking." To further

clarify—confuse?—things, this phrase also can be translated as "have a quick dip" in a swimming pool or at the beach.

faire un drôle de nez (fair œn drohl duu nay)
look disgruntled
Literally, "make a funny nose."

faire une cochonnerie à quelqu'un (fair ün kaw-shaw-NəREE ah kayl-KœN)
play a dirty trick on someone
Note that **cochonnerie** translates literally as "pig swill," which shows the French attitude toward dirty tricks.

faire une histoire pour une vétille et passer une énormité (fair ün neess-TWAHR poor rün vay-TEEYə ay pah-SAY ün nay-nor-mee-TAY)
strain at a gnat and swallow a camel
More literally translated as "make a fuss over peccadilloes but commit offenses of real magnitude," **vétille** meaning "triviality."

faire une razzia dans le frigo (fair ün rahz-YAH dahn luu free-GOH)
midnight snack
Best translated as "raid the icebox" or, more precisely, "raid the refrigerator."

faire un faux pas (fair œn foh pah)
goof
Also translated as "stumble" or "make a foolish error" or, best of all, "make a faux pas," since "faux pas" is now a vital term in the English language. This thought is also expressed by **faire un impair** (nan-PAIR), which is translated as "put your foot in your mouth," "make a tactless blunder," or, again, as "make a faux pas." (See also FAUX PAS.)

faire un trou à la lune (fair œn troo ah lah lün)
skip town
Also translated as "flee one's creditors"; literally, "make a hole in the moon." Talk about getting lost!

faire valser l'argent (fair vahl-SAY lahr-ZHAHN)
spend money like water
    Also translated as "throw money around," literally as "waltz money around."

faire vinaigre (fair vee-NAYGRə)
get a move on
    Also translated as "hurry up"; literally, "make vinegar." Instead of wine, which takes longer.

fais ce que dois, advienne que pourra (fay suu kuu dwah ahd-VYAYN kuu poo-RAH)
to thine own self be true
    As Polonius says in Hamlet. And we may also translate the French phrase as "do your duty, come what may."

faiseur de mariages (fuu-ZUHR duu mah-RYAHZH)
matchmaker
    In the interest of fairness, understand that women may also engage in this profession, a female matchmaker being known as **faiseuse** (fuu-ZUHZ) **de mariages**.

fais le, sinon! (fay luu see-NAWN)
do it, or else!
    And the **sinon**, "or else," is understood to be something unpleasant.

fais voir! (fay vwahr)
I'm from Missouri
    Conventionally translated as "show me!" or "let me have a look."

fait accompli (fayt tah-kawn-PLEE)
accomplished fact
    Also translated as "thing already done," and best of all as "fait accompli," pronounced as in French.

faites votre devoir, et laissez faire aux dieux (fayt vawtrə duu-VWAHR ay lay-SAY fair oh dyuu)
don't attempt the impossible

Corneille, in his play *Horace*, gives us this admirable advice, literally "do your duty and leave the rest to the gods." Also translated as "do only what can reasonably be expected of you."

famille monoparentale (fah-MEEYə moh-noh-pah-rahn-TAHL)
single-parent family
　　Yes, Virginia, even in France!

farceur (fahr-SUHR)
joker
　　Also translated as "wag," "droll person," and, literally, "player of farces."

farouche (fah-ROOSH)
savage
　　Also translated as "wild," "unsociable," "sullen," and "shy." An interesting range of meanings.

fausse modestie (fohss maw-dayss-TEE)
false modesty
　　A term close in meaning to **fausse pudeur** (pü-DUHR), which is also translated as "false modesty." For **fausse modestie**, however, additional meanings are "self-effacement" and "absence of vanity," while **fausse pudeur** carries the further meaning of "false sense of decency."

faute avouée est à demi pardonnée (foht tah-VWAY ay tah duu-MEE pahr-daw-NAY)
get it off your chest
　　Literally, "a sin confessed is a sin half pardoned."

faute de grammaire (foht duu grah-MAIR)
solecism
　　More understandably translated as "grammatical error," the term "solecism" being preferred only by those who have little to show off but their English vocabularies.

faute de grives, on mange des merles (foht duu greevə awn mahnzh day mairlə)
beggars cannot be choosers
　　This proverb, literally, "if you don't have thrushes, you eat blackbirds," is also translated as "cut your coat according to your cloth," "half a loaf is

better than none," and "if you don't have steak, you eat potatoes." In short, make the best of what you have.

faute de mieux (foht duu myuu)
for want of something better
   Often used in English and pronounced as in French.

faut te faire soigner! (foh tə fair swah-NYAY)
you're out of your mind!
   Where one might say "have your head examined!" or "you ought to have your head examined," the French say, literally, "you need to be treated."

fauves (fohvə)
wildcats
   Usually translated as "wild beasts," the **fauves** were a group of young French artists early in the twentieth century known for their imaginative use of brilliant color, simplicity, and vitality. Their ranks included Matisse, Braque, Dufy, and Rouault.

faux (foh)
false
   Also translated as "erroneous," "wrong," and "sham," this adjective leads us to several interesting locutions: **faux brave** (brahv), translated as "swaggerer" or "braggart"; **faux bruit** (brwee), "false rumor"; **faux feu** (fuu) translates as "flash in the pan," literally, "false fire" and denoting someone who enjoys brief success; **faux frère** (frair) translates as "false friend," literally as "false brother." Best known of all is **faux pas** (pah), literally, "false step," translated as "social indiscretion," "slip in behavior," "breach of etiquette or propriety," or "misstep." (See also FAIRE UN FAUX PAS and FAIRE UN IMPAIR.) Finally, there is **faux seins** (san), translated as "falsies"; literally, "false breasts."

femme (fahm)
woman
   As one might expect, this noun gives us many interesting phrases, including **femme célibataire** (say-lee-bah-TAIR), "unmarried woman." Then there are **femme couverte** (koo-VAIRT) and **femme mariée** (mahree-AY), both meaning "married woman." It is interesting to note that

couverte, the feminine form of **couvert** (koo-VAIR), "covered," suggests that a woman so described is protected, or covered, by her husband. Moving into modern life, we have **femme d'affaires** (dah-FAIR), translated as "businesswoman," **affaires** here meaning "businesses" or "matters." Then there is **femme de lettres** (duu laytrə), literally, "woman of letters," which is also translated as "literary woman." Departing from this lofty phrase, we have four phrases of dubious character: **femme de mauvaises moeurs** (duu maw-VAYZ muhr), translated as "loose woman," literally, "woman of bad morals"; **femme de moeurs légères** (duu muhr lay-ZHAIR), translated as "woman of easy virtue," literally, "woman with broad morals"; **femme de petite vertu** (duu puu-TEET vair-TÜ), translated as "woman of easy virtue," literally, "woman of little virtue"; and **femme galante** (gah-LAHNT), translated as "prostitute" or "courtesan," the latter being an almost archaic term signifying nothing more than a prostitute who is active in high social or financial circles. The list goes on: **femme fatale** (fah-TAHL), literally, "fatal woman," has been adopted by English and is best translated as "femme fatale," preferably with the French pronunciation, not the English (fem fa-TAL), denoting a real charmer who's not to be trusted. But, back again to more felicitous phrases: **femme sage** (sahzh), literally, "wise woman," is best translated as "virtuous woman" or "well-behaved woman"; and **femme savante** (sah-VAHNT) is translated as "learned woman" or, like **femme de lettres**, "woman of literary interests."

fendre un cheveu en quatre (fahndrə œn shuu-VUU an kahtrə)
split hairs

Also translated as "make overly subtle distinctions"; literally, "split a hair into four parts." Subtle enough for you?

ferme ta gueule! (fairmə tah guhl)
shut your trap!

Also translated literally as "shut your mouth," and as "shut your face"—as we are more apt to say today—with none of these locutions suitable for use on formal occasions. Incidentally, the message conveyed by this slang phrase is frequently given as **ferme ta** or **ferme la**, with **gueule** understood.

feu d'artifice (fuu dahr-tee-FEESS)
firework display

A second meaning of this term is "brilliant display of wit."

feu follet (fuu faw-LAY)
will-o'-the-wisp

Also translated as "ignis fatuus" (IG-niss FACH-oo-əss). This is the flitting phosphorescent light seen sometimes over marshy areas and thus carrying the meaning "something misleading or deluding." The adjective **follet** is best translated as "scatterbrained."

feuille à scandale (fuhyə ah skahn-DAHL)
supermarket tabloid

Best translated as "scandal sheet," the literal meaning of the term.

feu sacré (fuu sah-KRAY)
divine fire of genius

Literally, "sacred fire," construed as "divinely inspired ardor or enthusiasm" and applied to the best of literature.

fiche-moi (feesh-MWAH)
give me

The construction **fiche-moi** appears especially in two common phrases. **Fiche-moi la paix!** (lah pay), **paix** meaning "peace," is best translated as "stop picking on me!" or "get off my back!" **Fiche-moi le camp!** (lə kahn), **camp** meaning "camp," is usually translated as "beat it!" "shove off!" or "clear off!" (See also FOUS-MOI LE CAMP!)

figé par la mort (fee-ZHAY pahr lah mor)
stiff

Literally, "rigid in death." This is the rigor mortis known so well by readers of detective stories and tabloid newspapers.

filer à l'anglaise (fee-LAY ah lahn-GLAYZ)
skip town

Soldiers and aging veterans know this as "go AWOL." The rest of us translate this idiom as "slip away unnoticed," "run away," or "take French leave," ironic because the literal meaning of the phrase is "take English leave."

fille (feeyə)
daughter or girl

This noun is the core of several common phrases used to denote a prostitute, including **fille de joie** (duu zhwah), literally, "girl of joy," translated as "prostitute" or "courtesan"; **fille des rues** (day rü), literally, "woman of the streets," translated as "streetwalker"; and **fille publique** (pü-BLEEK), translated as "prostitute," literally, "public girl." (See also FEMME GALANTE.)

fin de siècle (fan duu syayklə)
decadent
   Also translated as "advanced" and "ultramodern." But how does a simple phrase with the literal meaning of "end of the century" justify such translations? The **siècle** intended originally was the nineteenth. Does that help? Certainly if you recall the mood of the final years of that century, which were marked by distinctive movements in art and society. Thus far, no comparable unrest has emerged as we near the end of the twentieth. At least not sufficient to justify application of this phrase to the end of our century.

flan (flahn)
custard
   A word that appears frequently on the menus of chic restaurants in France and elsewhere. (See also C'EST DU FLAN.)

flâneur (flah-NUHR)
idler
   Also translated as "loafer," "stroller," or "lounger." Not exactly someone determined to make something of his life, in the conventional sense, at least.

fleur-de-lis (fluhr-duu-LEESS)
lily flower
   This, the emblem of the royal family of France, is always given in English as "fleur-de-lis" and usually pronounced fluhr-duu-LEE by those who do not know French.

fleurette (fluh-RAYT)
amorous nonsense
   Literally, "little flower" or "floweret," but translated as "pretty speech" or "gallant speech."

flux de bouche (flü duu boosh)
loquacity

Also, "salivation"; literally, "flow of the mouth." A companion phrase with the translation of "wordiness" or "loquacity" is **flux de paroles** (duu pah-RAWL), literally, "flow of words."

foie gras (fwah grah)
foie gras

A feature of French cuisine that is never translated into English, where it would have to be called "fattened liver" and would never command the high price of foie gras. This specialty is produced usually by force-feeding geese to enlarge the poor creatures' livers. By the way, the French pronunciation is retained in English, even by vegetarians.

force (forssə)
force or *strength*

The **force** phrases of special interest: **force d'âme** (dahm), translated as "moral strength"; literally, "strength of soul"; **force de caractère** (duu kahrahk-TAIR), "strength of character"; and **force majeure** (mah-ZHUHR), literally, "superior force" and also translated as "irresistible compulsion." This last is the only one of the three adopted in English, where "force majeure" regularly appears in certain types of contracts to characterize a disruptive and unexpected event that may prevent one of the parties to the contract from fulfilling contractual responsibilities.

fou (foo)
mad

Also translated as "madly" and "wild," giving us two happy phrases: **fou d'amour** (dah-MOOR), translated as "madly in love"; and **fou de joie** (duu zhwah), "wild with delight." Could anything be better? But then we have **fou d'inquiétude** (dan-kyay-TÜDə), the scourge of parents, translated as "mad with worry." Finally, there is **fou qui se taît passe pour sage** (kee suu tay pahss poor sahzh), translated as "silence can be golden"; literally, "the fool who holds his tongue passes for a wise man."

fourchette d'Adam (foor-SHAYT dah-DAHN)
the fingers

Literally, "Adam's fork." Forks and spoons had not yet been invented. Nor had chopsticks.

fourrer son nez partout (foo-RAY sawn nay pahr-TOO)
busybodies anonymous

Literally, "stick one's nose into everything." (See also SE FOURRER LES DOIGTS DANS LE NEZ.)

fous-moi le camp! (foo-MWAH lə kahn)
fuck off!
  Also translated as "bug off," "beat it!" and "get the hell out of here!" (See also FICHE-MOI LE CAMP, which is not as vulgar.)

fraises des bois (frayz day bwah)
wild strawberries

franchir le Rubicon (frahn-SHEER luu rü-bee-KAWN)
there's no going back
  Literally, "cross the Rubicon"; often translated as "take the decisive step." Thank you, Julius Caesar.

frappé de stupeur (frah-PAY duu stü-PUHR)
bowled over
  Literally, "struck by astonishment *or* amazement"; also translated as "thunderstruck."

frasques de jeunesse (frahskə duu zhuu-NAYSS)
we were just out for a good time, your Honor
  Translated as "youthful indiscretions *or* escapades."

frisson (free-SAWN)
shiver
  Also translated as "shudder" or as "frisson" (pronounced free-SOHN).

frissonnement de volupté (free-sawn-MAHN duu vaw-lüp-TAY)
quiver of sensual delight

froides mains, chaud amour (frwahdə man shoh dah-MOOR)
cold hands, warm heart
  Literally, "cold hands, warm love." A persistent myth.

frotter les oreilles à quelqu'un (fraw-TAY lay zaw-RAYə ah kayl-KœN)
give a few smart ones
  Literally translated as "box someone's ears."

froufrou (froo-FROO)
rustle or *rustling*
> As of a silken skirt, that is. (See also FAIRE DU FROUFROU.)

fuir quelqu'un comme la peste (fweer kayl-KœN kawm lah payst)
steer clear of someone
> Literally, "avoid someone like the plague."

fumer comme un troupier (fü-MAY kawm œn troo-PYAY)
three packs a day
> Translated as "smoke like a chimney"; literally, "smoke like a trooper."

fumer le calumet de la paix (fü-MAY luu kah-lü-MAY duu lah pay)
make nice
> Also translated as "bury the hatchet"; literally, "smoke the peace pipe."

fuyez les dangers de loisir (fwee-YAY lay dahn-ZHAY duu lwah-ZEER)
don't goof off
> Also translated as "avoid the perils of leisure."

G

gâcher sa vie (gah-SHAY sah vee)
waste one's life
> Also translated as "fritter away one's life." (See also IL A MANQUÉ SA VIE.)

gageure est la preuve des sots (gah-ZHUHR ay lah pruhvə day soh)
pari-mutuel insanity
> Best translated as "betting marks the fool"; literally, "a wager is a fool's evidence." For proof, observe the lines of people waiting to buy lottery tickets when the jackpot runs into tens of millions.

gagner (gah-NYAY)
earn or *win*

And what may we earn or win? First there is the discouraging **gagner mé-diocrement sa vie** (may-dyaw-kruu-MAHN sah vee), translated as "scrape by" or, more literally, "earn a poor living." Then there is **gagner sa croûte** (sah kroot), "earn one's bread and butter"; literally, "earn one's crust." Indicating that in some societies, all one can hope for is unbuttered bread. More sanguinely, there is **gagner quelqu'un à sa cause** (kayl-KœN ah sah kohz), translated as "win someone over to one's cause." But back to everyday life: **gagner sa vie** (sah vee), "earn one's living"; and **gagner son pain** (sawn paN), "earn one's bread," which is after all the staff of life. Hold the butter!

galant homme (gah-LAHN tawm)
gentleman

Also translated as "man of honor."

gamin (gah-MAN)
kid or *urchin*

The feminine form, **gamine** (gah-MEEN), is also used, with the same meaning as that of **gamin**.

garce (gahrss)
bitch or *slut*

The French language, like English, has a plethora of pejorative terms.

garçon (gahr-SAWN)
boy

Also translated as "lad," "fellow," "bachelor," "male servant," and "waiter."

garde tes réflexions pour toi (gahrdə tay ray-flaykss-SYAWN poor twah)
be quiet!

Also translated as "keep your mouth shut!" and, more literally, as "keep your thoughts to yourself!"

garder (gahr-DAY)
keep or *remain*

This infinitive finds use in many idioms, including **garder la tête froide** (lah tayt frwahdə), translated as "keep cool"; more literally, "keep a cool head." Then there is **garder le silence** (luu see-LAHNSS), translated as "say nothing" and "keep silent." Usually the right thing to do. But the right thing always is **garder son aplomb** (sawn nah-PLAWN), translated as "keep one's cool"; more formally, "remain composed." This thought can also be put in other words: **garder son sang-froid** (sawn sahn-FRWAH), translated as "keep one's cool"; more formally, "keep one's composure." English borrowed **sang-froid**, literally "cold blood," from French in the eighteenth century, with the meaning of "self-possession," and refuses to return it. Fortunately, "sang-froid" retains the French pronunciation. Try pronouncing this word without suggesting that it is yet another Freudian term, of which we have more than we need.

gardez (gahr-DAY)
take or *keep*

This imperative form of **garder** (see above) serves well in three common locutions. First is **gardez bien** (byan), translated as "take good care." Then there is **gardez la foi** (lah fwah), translated as "keep the faith." Best of all is **gardez le sourire** (luu soo-REER), translated as "keep smiling."

gauche (gohsh)
awkward

Also translated as "clumsy" and "tactless"; literally, "left." Illustrating once again that this is a right-handed world. **Gauche** has been taken into English, with the French pronunciation, and is the adjective of choice for many people when pointing the finger at someone who shows less than perfect manners or consideration for others.

gaucherie (gohsh-REE)
awkwardness

Again a word that has been taken into English, with the French pronunciation intact, to characterize an action labeled "gauche" or "tactless."

gdb (zhay day bay)
hangover

This is the abbreviation of GUEULE DE BOIS (which see), the phrase of choice when speaking of a hangover. (See also MAL AUX CHEVEUX.)

genre (zhahnrə)
genus or *kind*

Also translated as "style" or "sort." The term has been taken into English, with the French pronunciation, and finds special use, as in French, in discussing a painting that portrays scenes from everyday life.

gens (zhahn)
people

As one would expect, there are many types of people who are accommodated in French: **gens d'affaires** (dah-FAIR), translated as "business people." English is no stranger to this type of locution, since we have our "men of affairs," and one day perhaps we will also have "women of affairs." Or maybe we will have to settle for "people *or* persons of affairs." Then there are **gens de lettres** (duu laytrə), translated as "writers" or "authors," literally, "people of letters"; **gens de loi** (duu lwah), translated as "lawyers," literally, "people of law"; **gens de mer** (duu mair), translated as "sailors," literally, "people of the sea"; **gens d'épée** (day-PAY), translated as "professional soldiers," literally, "people of the sword"; **gens de plume** (duu plüm), translated as "writers," literally, "people of the pen"; and **gens de robe** (duu rawb), translated as "lawyers" and "magistrates," literally, "people of the robe," reflecting the customary garb of attorneys and magistrates appearing in French law courts. Two more locutions are noteworthy: **gens de même farine** (duu maym fah-REEN), translated as "birds of a feather," more literally as "people made of the same flour"; and **gens du monde** (dü mawndə), translated as "society people" and "fashionable people"; literally, "people of the world."

gibier (zhee-BYAY)
game

Two locutions employing this term are of interest. One is **gibier à plume** (ah plüm), translated as "feathered game," such as wild turkeys, quail, and partridge. Every schoolchild who has been introduced to instruction in French knows **plume** as "pen," but here it is used in its other principal sense, that of "quill" or "feather," reminding us that bird feathers were formerly used as writing instruments. The other is **gibier de potence** (duu paw-TAHNSS), translated as "gallows bird"; literally, "game for the gibbet," denoting a person who deserves to be hanged for his or her crimes.

gobe-mouches (gawb-MOOSH)
credulous fool

Also translated as "simpleton." This phrase, literally the hungry bird known as "flycatcher," is used to describe a person who swallows, or believes, everything he hears or reads.

gourmand comme un chat (goor-MAHN kawm mœn shah)
greedy but choosy
   Literally, "big eater, like a cat." As ailurophiles know, cats are greedy, but fussy about what they eat. (See also next entry.)

gourmet (goor-MAY)
epicure
   A person, that is, who knows and appreciates fine food. Unlike a **gourmand**, whose only aim in eating is to eat a great deal, no matter what dishes are put before him.

graçe à Dieu (grahss ah dyuu)
thanks be to God

grande chère et beau feu (grahndə shair ay boh fuu)
complete comfort
   Also translated as "all one ever wants"; literally, "ample food and a fine fire," leading to the satisfying rhetorical question "who could ask for anything more?"

grande dame (grahndə dahm)
great lady
   A phrase frequently encountered in American newspaper and television prose dealing with the lives of the rich and famous. The French pronunciation is approximated in English.

grande fortune, grande servitude (grahndə for-TÜN grahndə sair-vee-TÜD)
yes, you can be too rich
   A well-known French proverb, "a great fortune is a great slavery." A comforting thought for those of us who have no fortune to worry about.

grande passion (grahndə pah-SYAWN)
serious love affair
   Literally, "great passion," denoting passionate love for another person.

grandes maisons se font par petite cuisine (grahndə may-ZAWN suu fawn pahr puu-TEET kwee-ZEEN)
save your pennies, the pounds will take care of themselves.

This proverb has been rendered in English since the thirteenth century as "many a little makes a mickle," the archaic word "mickle" meaning "large amount"; since the seventeenth century as "little and often fills the purse" and "penny and penny laid up will be many." All of these make the case for domestic thrift better than "great houses are made by a small kitchen," which is the literal translation of the French proverb. (See also LES PETITS RUISSEAUX FONT LES GRANDES RIVIÈRES.)

Grand-Guignol (grahn gee-NYUHL)
blood and thunder

"Grand Guignol," pronounced as in French, is used in English—like the French **Grand-Guignol**—to characterize plays or movies involving macabre and gruesome incidents. The term took its name from the eighteenth-century **Guignol**, the principal character in a popular puppet show, similar to the ever-popular Punch and Judy show.

grand prix (grahn pree)
a great or extraordinary prize

A name taken into English without change in pronunciation, and familiar to all fans of high-speed automobile races.

gratter quelques dollars (grah-TAY kaylkə daw-LAHR)
make a little on the side

Also translated as "pick up a few bucks"; literally, "scrape a few dollars." The connotation of this term is not that of scrimping to accumulate a nest egg. Rather it suggests activities not quite kosher.

grève (grayvə)
strike

Two kinds of strikes are worth including here: **grève de la faim** (duu lah fan), "hunger strike," and **grève sur le tas** (sür luu tah), "sit-down strike," with **tas** literally meaning "pile" or "heap," making for a more vivid metaphor than "sit-down strike."

grosse tête, peu de sens (grohss tayt puu duu sahnss)
big head, little sense

Telling us that a big head—even when housing a large brain—need not be associated with cleverness or wisdom.

gruyère (grwee-YAIR)
Swiss cheese
   Which, all over the world, also goes under the name "Gruyère" and "Gruyère cheese." Gruyère is the name of the Swiss district where this cheese is produced.

gueule de bois (guhl duu bwah)
hangover
   Literally, "mouth of wood," a metaphor readily understandable by anybody so afflicted. (See also GDB.)

guerre (gair)
war
   As everyone knows, there is more than one type of war, for example, **guerre à mort** (ah mor), translated as "war to the death"; **guerre à outrance** (ah oo-TRAHNSS), also translated as "war to the death" and "war without mercy," literally as "war to the utmost"; **guerre atomique** (ah-taw-MEEK), "atomic war"; **guerre civile** (see-VEEL), "civil war"; and **guerre mondiale** (mawn-DYAHL), "world war."

guillemets (gee-yə-MAY)
quotation marks

H

habiter la banlieue (ah-bee-TAY lah bahn-LYUU)
live in the burbs
   In the suburbs, that is.

habiter la ville (ah-bee-TAY lah veel)
live in a town or *city*

hachis (ah-SHEE)
ground beef

Also translated as "hamburger." (See also BIFTECK HACHÉ.)

harcèlement sexuel (ahr-sayl-MAHN saykss-SWAYL)
sexual harassment

hardi comme un coq sur son fumier (ahr-DEE kawm œn kawk sür sawn fü-MYAY)
bold as a rooster on its own dunghill
A striking simile.

hâtez-vous lentement (ah-TAY voo lahn-TəMAHN)
more haste, less speed
A proverb all of us should take to heart; literally, "make haste slowly," a French translation of the Latin *festina lente*.

haut (oh)
high or *strong*
The start of several interesting idioms, including **haut à la main** (ah lah man), translated as "arrogant" or "high-handed," literally, "high in the hand"; **haut goût** (goo), "strong *or* high flavor," reflecting the use of "high" to describe meat that is slightly tainted; **haut les coeurs!** (lay kuhr), translated as "take heart," literally, "up with your hearts"; **haut ton** (tawn), translated as "high tone," "high fashion," and "high social standing."

heureux au jeu, malheureux en amour (uu-RUU oh zhuu mah-luu-RUU ahn nah-MOOR)
lucky at cards, unlucky in love
Literally, "lucky at gambling, unlucky in love," an untruth designed to cheer up jilted lovers.

heurter quelqu'un de front (uhr-TAY kayl-KœN duu frawn)
clash head-on
Also translated as "offend someone to his face."

histoire sans queue ni tête (eess-TWAHR sahn kuu nee tayt)
cock-and-bull story

Also translated as "absurd, improbable story"; literally, "story without a tail or head."

homme (awm)
man
The French language is rich in its characterizations of men, including: **homme à bonnes fortunes** (ah bawn for-TÜN), "ladykiller," literally, "lucky man"; **homme à femmes** (mah fahm), "ladies' man" or "womanizer"; **homme à tout faire** (mah too fair), "jack of all trades" or "handyman"; **homme comme il faut** (kawm eel foh), "gentleman"; **homme d'affaires** (dah-FAIR), "businessman" or "agent," literally, "man of affairs"; **homme de confiance** (duu kawn-fee-AHNSS), "right-hand man" or "man of trust"; **homme de guerre** (duu gair), "soldier," literally, "man of war"; **homme de lettres** (duu laytrə), "man of letters" or "literary man"; **homme de paille** (duu pīyə), "straw man"; **homme de plume** (duu plüm), "author," "writer," literally, "man of the pen"; **homme de robe** (duu rawb), "lawyer," literally, "man of the robe"; **homme d'esprit** (dayss-PREE), "man of intellect" or "man of wit"; **homme d'état** (day-TAH), "statesman"; and **homme du monde** (dü mawndə), "man of the world."

honi soit qui mal y pense (aw-NEE swah kee mahl ee pahnss)
shame to him who thinks evil of it
Motto of the Most Noble Order of the Garter, the garter being the symbol of the highest order of knighthood in Great Britain, said to have been constituted about 1348.

honneur et patrie (aw-NUHR ay pah-TREE)
honor and fatherland
Motto of the French Legion of Honor.

hors (or)
except or *apart from* or *away from* or *out* or *out of*
A term used in many idioms, including **hors concours** (kawn-KOOR), "not competing for a prize," literally, "out of competition," said, for example, of a picture in an exhibition; **hors de combat** (duu kawn-BAH), "disabled," literally, "out of the fight"; **hors de l'Eglise, point de salut** (duu lay-GLEEZ pwahn duu sah-LÜ), translated as "there's no salvation outside the Church"; **hors de ligne** (duu leenyə), translated as "exceptional" or "uncommon," literally, "out of line"; **hors de pair** (duu pair), translated as

"peerless" or "without equal"; **hors de prise** (duu preez), "out of danger," more literally, "out of reach"; **hors de prix** (duu pree), "extravagantly expensive"; **hors de saison** (duu say-ZAWN), translated as "inopportune," more literally, "out of season"; **hors-d'oeuvre** (DUHVRə), translated as "hors d'oeuvre," and spoken as in French, denoting a side dish served as an appetizer at the beginning of a meal; and **hors la loi** (lah lwah), "outlawed," literally, "outside the law."

hôtel de ville (oh-TAYL duu veel)
city hall or *town hall*

hôtel-Dieu (oh-TEL dyuu)
chief hospital of a town
    Literally, "hotel *or* hospice of God."

huit jours (wee zhoor)
week
    Literally, "eight days."

hurler à la lune (ür-LAY ah lah lün)
go fight city hall!
    Literally, "howl at the moon," an expressive way of saying "raise a futile voice against a person in high position."

hurler avec les loups (ür-LAY ah-VAYK lay loo)
when in Rome, do as the Romans do
    Better translated as "go along with the crowd" or "follow the crowd"; literally, "howl with the wolves."

idée (ee-DAY)
idea

As one might expect, there are several types of ideas, including **idée fixe** (feeks), translated as "obsession" or "monomania," literally, "fixed idea," and often given in English as "idée fixe" and pronounced as in French, denoting an idea obsessing the mind; **idée grossière** (groh-SYAIR), translated as "rough idea"; **idée préconçue** (pray-kawn-SÜ), translated as "preconception" and "preconceived idea"; and finally, **idée reçu** (rə-SÜ), translated as "generally accepted idea" or "received idea."

il a beaucoup de moyens (eel lah boh-KOO duu mwah-YAN)
he has what it takes

An idiomatic way of saying "he's a smart fellow" or "he has plenty of brains"; literally, "he has many means."

il aboie après tout le monde (eel lah-BWAH ah-PRAY too lə mawndə)
he snarls at everybody

So we see that snarling is not restricted to dogs.

il a détalé comme un lapin (eel lah day-tah-LAY kawm œn lah-PAN)
he took off like a bat out of hell

Also translated as "he skedaddled," "he took off," and, more literally, "he bolted like a rabbit."

il a du fric (eel lah dü freek)
he's really loaded

Also translated as "he's rolling in dough" and "he has plenty of cash." Take your choice. **Fric** translates as "cash," as well as "bread" and "dough." And you thought English was the only truly inventive—for which substitute "only true borrower"—language.

il a été rectifié (eel lah ay-TAY rayk-tee-FYAY)
he was bumped off

Also translated as "he got what was coming to him" and "they did away with him"; literally, "he was corrected" or "he was set right."

il a la gâchette facile (eel lah lah gah-SHAYT fah-SEEL)
he's quick on the draw
   Also translated as "he's trigger-happy," with **gâchette** meaning "trigger."

il a l'air très distingué (eel lah lair tray deess-tan-GAY)
a regular Anthony Eden
   More literally, "he looks very distinguished."

il a la mer à boire (eel lah lah mair rah bwahr)
he has a Sisyphean task
   Literally, "he has the sea to drink up."

il a l'échine souple (eel lah lay-SHEEN sooplǝ)
you can walk all over him
   Also translated as "he's a doormat"; literally, "he has a flexible backbone."

il a le diable au corps (eel lah luu dyahblǝ oh kor)
he has the devil in him
   Literally, "he has the devil in his body."

il a les défauts de ses qualités (eel lah lay day-FOH duu say kah-lee-TAY)
he has the faults that go with his virtues
   Literally translated as "he has the flaws of his qualities."

il a le talent de se faire des ennemis (eel lah luu tah-LAHN duu suu fair day zayn-MEE)
attracting enemies like flies
   Also translated as "he's good at making enemies" and "he has a gift for making enemies."

il a manqué sa vie (eel lah mahn-KAY sah vee)
he's wasted his life
   Literally, "he has missed his life." (See also GÂCHER SA VIE.)

il a payé cher son imprudence (eel lah pay-YAY shair sawn nan-prü-DAHNSS)
no such thing as a free lunch
Literally translated as "he paid dearly for his rashness." And who does not?

il a une araignée au plafond (eel lah ün nah-ray-NYAY oh plah-FAWN)
he has a screw loose
This idiom is also translated as "he has a bee in his bonnet"; literally, "he has a spider on the ceiling." Bees, spiders. Spiders, bees.

il a voulu rester en dehors (eel lah voo-LÜ rayss-TAY ahn duu-OR)
he wanted out
Also translated as "he wanted to stay out of things" or "he wanted to remain uninvolved"; more literally, "he wanted to remain outside."

il brode très bien (eel brawdə tray byan)
he spins a good yarn
Literally, "he embroiders very well."

il comprend tout à retardement (eel kawn-PRAHN too tah ruu-tahr-duu-MAHN)
slow on the uptake
Usually translated as "he's slow to understand" or "he catches on slowly," **retardement** being defined as "delayed action."

il conduit bien sa barque (eel kawn-DWEE byan sah bahrkə)
doing fine, thank you
Usually translated as "he's getting on very well"; literally, "he steers his boat well."

il connaît le système (eel kawn-NAY luu seess-TAYM)
he knows his way around
Literally, "he knows the system." This meaning is also conveyed by **il connaît la musique** (lah mü-ZEEK), literally "he knows music." (See also JE CONNAIS LA MUSIQUE.)

il connaît toutes les finesses (eel kawn-NAY toot lay fee-NAYSS)
wise guy

Usually translated as "he knows all the tricks" or "he knows all the ins and outs," **finesses** being defined as "niceties" or "finer points."

il écorche le français (eel lay-KORSH luu frahn-SAY)
he murders the French language
Also translated as "he speaks broken French." One of the fears of travelers visiting France—and a great inhibitor of those who would profit most from attempting to try out their French—is that they will be derided, or worse, for speaking French badly. For them, the best advice is to listen carefully to native speakers of the language and then try their best. No one was ever thrown out of a French taxicab, hotel, or fine restaurant because of poor pronunciation or usage.

il en est bien mordu (eel lahn nay byan mor-DÜ)
mad about her
Usually translated as "he's crazy about her" or "he's wild about her"; literally, "he's madly in love with her." Let's hope everything turns out well.

il est à ma mesure (eel lay tah mah mə-ZÜR)
I think I can, I think I can
Translated as "I can do it," "it's not beyond me," or "it's within my capabilities," **mesure** literally meaning "measurement."

il est assez coureur (eel lay tah-SAY koo-RUHR)
he's a bit of a womanizer
Also translated as "he's a wolf" or "he's a philanderer" or "he's a woman chaser," the last translation perhaps being closest in intent, since **coureur** literally means "runner."

il est bien empoisonné (eel lay byan nahn-pwah-zaw-NAY)
he's in deep trouble
Usually translated as "he's in a real mess" or "he's really in the soup now," **empoisonné** literally meaning "poisoned." Enough to make one shudder.

il est doux comme un agneau (eel lay doo kawm mœn nah-NYOH)
a real sweetheart
Well translated as "he's as gentle as a lamb."

il est encore bleu (eel lay tahn-KOR bluu)
he's still wet behind the ears
　　More literally, "he's still a rookie."

il est fait comme un rat (eel lay fay kawm mœn rah)
his goose is cooked
　　Also translated as "he's in for it now" or, more literally, as "he's cornered like a rat."

il est incontestable qu'elle est la meilleure (eel lay tan-kawn-tayss-TAHBLə kayl lay lah may-YUHR)
she's number one
　　More literally, "she's unquestionably the best."

il est l'artisan de sa propre ruine (eel lay lahr-tee-ZAHN duu sah prawprə rween)
nobody but himself to blame
　　Usually translated as "he brought about his own ruin"; literally, "he's the craftsman of his own destruction."

il est majeur et vacciné (eel lay mah-ZHUHR ay vahkss-see-NAY)
he's a big boy now
　　More conventionally translated as "he's old enough to look after himself"; literally, "he's come of age and has had his vaccinations." What more can we do for him?

il est mort le surlendemain (eel lay mor luu sür-lahn-də-MAN)
on his last legs
　　A dismal thought best translated as "he died two days later."

il est né fatigué (eel lay nay fah-tee-GAY)
lazybones
　　Translated as "he's just plain lazy"; literally, "he was born tired."

il est payé pour le savoir (eel lay pay-YAY poor luu sah-VWAHR)
he's paid his dues
　　Also translated as "he's learned the hard way"; literally, "he paid to learn that."

il est plus aisé d'être sage pour les autres que pour soi-même (eel lay plü zay-ZAY daytrə sahzhə poor lay zohtrə kuu poor swah-MAYM)
we love to give, not receive, advice
Wisdom from La Rochefoucauld: "It's easier to be wise for others than for oneself." Maybe we all should check out our brokers' own accounts before we put ourselves in the broker's hands.

il est plus honteux de se défier de ses amis que d'en être trompé (eel lay ay plü zawn-TUU duu suu day-FYAY duu say zah-MEE kuu dahn naytrə trawn-PAY)
one man's view of friendship and trust
More wisdom from La Rochefoucauld: "It's more shameful to distrust one's friends than to be deceived by them."

il est quelque peu menteur (eel lay kaylkə puu mahn-TUHR)
don't be too trusting
An example of French understatement, translated as "he's a bit of a liar."

il est resté muet comme une carpe (eel lay rayss-TAY mü-AY kawm ün kahrpə)
he never opened his mouth
Better translated as "he said not a word" or "he was struck dumb"; literally, "he was silent as a carp." The fish, that is.

il est susceptible de gagner (eel lay sü-sayp-TEEBLə duu gah-NYAY)
he may well win
Also translated as "he's liable to win." Sounds like an even-money bet, or maybe 6 to 5.

il est trop poli pour être honnête (eel lay troh paw-LEE poor aytrə aw-NAYT)
watch out for this fellow!
Translated as "he's so polite that I smell a rat" or "his politeness makes me suspect his motives"; literally, "he's too polite to be honest." And, therefore, unable to give you an honest opinion.

il était la statue du désespoir (eel lay-TAY lah stah-TÜ dü day-zayss-PWAHR)
he was the epitome of despair
Literally, "he was the statue of despair."

il fait plus de bruit que de mal (eel fay plüss duu brwee kuu duu mahl)
his bark is worse than his bite
   Literally, "he makes more noise than mischief."

il faut cultiver son jardin (eel foh kül-tee-VAY sawn zhahr-DAN)
mind your own business
   A saying attributed to Voltaire, also translated as "attend to your own affairs"; literally, "one must cultivate one's own garden."

il faut de l'argent (eel foh duu lahr-ZHAHN)
money talks
   Translated as "money is essential" or "you must have money." Who can
argue with that?

il faut de tout pour faire un monde (eel foh duu too poor fair œn
mawndə)
variety is the spice of life
   A cliché better translated as "it takes all sorts to make a world."
   But English poet William Cowper (1731–1800), who seems to have believed in variety, expressed his attitude this way:

>   *Variety's the very spice of life*
>   *That gives it all its flavour.*

   And from then on it was all downhill? (See also TOUS LES GOÛTS SONT
DANS LA NATURE.)

il faut laver son linge sale en famille (eel foh lah-VAY sawn lanzh sahl
ahn fah-MEEYə)
don't wash your dirty linen in public
   Literally, "one should wash one's dirty linen in private," a remark attributed to Voltaire but made famous by Napoleon.

il faut manger pour vivre, et non pas vivre pour manger (eel foh mahn-
ZHAY poor veevrə ay nawn pah veevrə poor mahn-ZHAY)
don't be a pig
   Molière, in his play *Amphitryon*, said "one must eat to live, and not live
to eat." Hard to tell from the great number of cookbooks published each
year whether anyone follows this excellent precept today.

il faut partir du bon pied (eel foh pahr-TEER dü bawn pyay)
get off on the right foot
    Literally, "one must set off on the right foot," the adjective "right" meaning "correct."

il faut payer les violons (eel foh pay-YAY lay vyoh-LAWN)
eventually you'll have to pay your bills
    Literally, "the violinists must be paid," which has the same meaning as "the piper must be paid" and is generally considered much better for the ears. (See also QUI PAIE LES VIOLONS CHOISIT LA MUSIQUE.)

il faut que je fonce (eel foh kuu zhə fawnss)
I must dash
    Also translated as "I must leave" or "I must fly"; more literally, "I must tear along."

il faut que jeunesse se passe (eel foh kuu zhuu-NAYSS suu pahss)
youth must have its fling
    Also translated as "wild oats must be sown" and "youth will have its course," a sixteenth-century English proverb. No matter how the thought is expressed, the trouble is that parents have to live through it.

il faut souffrir pour être belle (eel foh soo-FREER poor aytrə bayl)
vanity, vanity!
    Translated as "vain people will do anything to maintain their appearance" or "no indignity is too great for the insufferably vain" and, literally, "to be beautiful, it is necessary to suffer." If you don't believe this, study the protocols of supermodels and weightlifters, or examine the bank accounts of plastic surgeons.

il faut subir et se taire (eel foh sü-BEER ay suu tair)
you must suffer in silence
    Literally, "it's necessary to suffer and be quiet about it." Not exactly what therapists counsel.

il faut vivre dans l'instant (eel foh veevrə dahn lanss-TAHN)
seize the moment

This is the phrase left to us by Roman poet Horace—he expressed it as *carpe diem*, but however expressed, we are counseled that "one must live in the present." And that's not the worst advice ever given.

il faut vous faire soigner! (eel foh voo fair swah-NYAY)
better see a shrink!
   Somewhat closer to a literal translation is "you need to have your head examined!"

il l'a mise dans une situation intéressante (eel lah meez dahn zün see-tü-ah-SYAWN an-tay-ray-SAHNT)
he got her into trouble
   A much better translation than the literal "he got her into an interesting situation." Any way you cut it, someone is pregnant, and we're reluctant to say so.

il les lâche avec des élastiques (eel lay lahsh ah-VAYK day zay-lahss-TEEK)
as stingy as they come
   Well translated as "he's tightfisted," literally as the colorful "he releases them but with rubber bands attached." "Them," of course, are tens and twenties.

il lève bien le coude (eel layvə byan luu koodə)
he drinks too much
   More literally, "he likes to bend the elbow."

il m'aime—un peu—beaucoup—passionnément—à la folie—pas du tout (eel maym—œn puu—boh-KOO—pah-syaw-nay-MAHN—ah lah faw-LEE—pah dü too)
he loves me, he loves me not.
   We all know this surefire way to determine—with the help of daisy petals—whether the boy we're sweet on really loves the petal plucker. What the French say (in translation) is: "he loves me—a little—a lot—passionately—madly—not at all." The good thing about the French chant is that it gives one various shades of adoration. Far better than an all-or-nothing determination.

il m'a taxé d'imbécile (eel mah tahk-SAY dan-bay-SEEL)
he called me an idiot
 And that's plain talk.

il m'a tenu un drôle de langage (eel mah tuu-NÜ œn drohl duu lahn-GAHZH)
I don't understand anything he says
 Also translated as "he sure talks strangely" and "he said some odd things to me."

il me fiche le cafard (eel muu feesh luu kah-FAHR)
he gets me down
 Also translated as "he depresses me"; literally, "he gives me the cockroach." The French sure abhor this lowly creature, but they are not alone.

il m'ennuie au superlatif (eel mahn-NWEE oh sü-pair-lah-TEEF)
he really bugs me
 Also translated as "he's a real pain in the neck," more formally as "I find him extremely trying."

il ment comme un arracheur de dents (eel mahn kawm œn nah-rah-SHUHR duu dahn)
he lies through his teeth
 Also translated as "compulsive liar"; more literally, "he lies like a dentist," especially, one supposes, when he says "this won't hurt." It is worthwhile noting that **arracheur de dents** is literally "tooth puller."

il me prend pour un enfant de choeur (eel muu prahn poor œn nahn-FAHN də kuhr)
he doesn't listen to a word I say
 Also translated as "he gives me no credit for anything" and "he thinks I'm still wet behind the ears"; literally, "he takes me for a choirboy."

il me vient au genou (eel muu vyan toh zhuu-NOO)
he comes up to my knee
 A little fellow.

il n'a aucun savoir-vivre (eel nah oh-KœN sah-VWAHR veevrə)
he has no idea how to behave

Best translated as "he has no savoir faire," showing how big an impression this term has made on the English language. When the French invented **savoir-faire**, literally, "knowing how to do," they threw away the key. No translation has come close to expressing the quality conveyed by "adroitness" or "diplomacy" any better, and Americans have no difficulty in using the French pronunciation for this vital term.

il nage dans la joie (eel nahzh dahn lah zhwah)
happy as can be
   Translated as "he's overjoyed" or "his joy knows no bounds"; literally, "he's swimming in joy." So while speakers of English may jump for joy, the French swim for it. Nothing like an idiom for throwing logic out the window—regardless of what language is being discussed.

il n'a pas desserré les dents (eel nah pah day-say-RAY lay dahn)
he hasn't said a word
   Also translated as "he hasn't opened his mouth" or, literally, "he hasn't unclenched his teeth."

il n'a pas encore de barbe au menton (eel nah pah zahn-KOR duu bahrbə oh mahn-TAWN)
he's still wet behind the ears
   Also translated as "he's immature"; literally, "he has no beard on his chin."

il n'a pas inventé la poudre (eel nah pah an-vahn-TAY lah poodrə)
he'll never set the world on fire
   Also translated as "he's not very bright"; literally, "he has not invented gunpowder." Or, as too many of us say, "he's no rocket scientist."

il n'a pas la loi chez lui (eel nah pah lah lwah shay lwee)
he's not the master of his own house
   A criticism reflecting a nineteenth-century view of domestic felicity.

il n'a plus la tête bien solide (eel nah plü lah tayt byan saw-LEED)
he's getting soft in the head
   More humanely translated as "his mind isn't what it used to be"; literally, "he no longer has a sound head."

il n'appartient qu'aux grands hommes d'avoir de grands défauts (eel nah-pahr-TYAN koh grahn zawm dah-VWAHR duu grahn day-FOH)
great men, great faults

Wisdom from La Rochefoucauld, also translated as "only great men have great defects," which is proven again and again by biographers intent on attracting readers. The literal translation is "it belongs only to great men to have great defects."

il n'a rien dans le buffet (eel nah ryan dahn lə bü-FAY)
he hasn't eaten a thing all day

More literally, "he hasn't a thing in his belly," **buffet** here meaning "belly." Take note that this phrase can also be translated as "he has no guts," and that's an entirely different thought.

il n'a rien fichu de la journée (eel nah ryan fee-SHÜ də lah zhoor-NAY)
a useless so-and-so

Well translated as "he hasn't lifted a finger all day" or "he hasn't done a thing all day."

il ne crache pas sur le caviar (eel nuu krahsh pah sür luu kah-VYAHR)
he doesn't turn up his nose at caviar

Literally, "he doesn't spit on caviar."

il ne faut jamais remettre au lendemain ce qu'on peut faire le jour même (eel nuu foh zhah-MAY ruu-MAYTRə oh lahn-də-MAN suu kawn puu fair luu zhoor maym)
procrastination, thief of time

Literally translated as "never put off until tomorrow what you can do today."

il ne faut pas . . . (eel nuu foh pah)
one should not . . .

This admonitory phrase serves to introduce a number of common locutions, among them **il ne faut pas abuser des meilleures choses** (ah-bü-ZAY day may-YUHR shohz), which may be translated literally as "one must not overindulge in the best things." More colloquial translations are "even the best things can be overdone," "enough is as good as a feast" (an English proverb dating from the fifteenth century), and "there really can be too much of a good thing." In short, skip the rich dessert! Then there are **il ne faut pas défier un fou de faire des folies** (day-FYAY œn foo duu fair day faw-LEE), translated as "one should not challenge a fool to commit follies"; **il ne faut pas dire fontaine je ne boirai pas de ton eau** (deer fawn-TAYN zhuu nuu bwah-RAY pah duu tawn noh), the French equivalent of "don't burn your bridges behind you," also translated as "always make sure you have a fall-back position" and, almost literally, "you don't have to tell a fountain you won't drink all its water"; and **il ne faut pas être sorcier** (zaytrə sor-SYAY), translated as "you don't have to be a molecular biologist"; more literally, "you don't have to be a wizard." To understand something, that is. Common sense is found everywhere, so we are not surprised when the French give us **il ne faut pas éveiller le chat qui dort** (zay-vay-YAY luu shah kee dor), the equivalent of the fourteenth-century English proverb "let sleeping dogs lie"; literally, "don't wake a sleeping cat." Why we cite dogs and the French cite cats is a problem better left to scholars searching for a research grant. This brief introduction to the long list of **il ne faut pas** possibilities concludes with the best advice ever given: **il ne faut pas vendre la peau de l'ours avant de l'avoir tué** (vahndrə lah poh duu loorss ah-VAHN duu lah-VWAHR tway), most often translated as "don't count your chickens before they're hatched." As one might expect, the literal translation is quite different: "don't sell the bearskin before you've killed the bear." Good advice no matter which metaphor you prefer.

il ne manquait plus que ça (eel nuu mahn-KAY plü kə sah)
that's the last straw
  An intemperate observation also translated as "that's all we needed" or "that beats all"; literally, "nothing was lacking but that."

il n'en a pas le premier sou (eel nahn nah pah luu pruu-MYAY soo)
he's dead broke
  Also translated as "he doesn't have two pennies to rub together"; literally, "he doesn't have the first penny."

il n'en fiche pas une ramée (eel nahn feesh pah zün rah-MAY)
he just sits around
  Also translated as "he doesn't do a damned thing." The noun **ramée**, translated as "leafy branches," provides no clue to the meaning of this locution.

il ne rougit de rien (eel nuu roo-ZHEE duu ryan)
he's shameless
   Also translated as "he has no shame"; literally, "nothing makes him blush."

il ne sait pas se commander (eel nuu say pah suu kaw-mahn-DAY)
he's out of control
   Literally, "he can't control himself." Also expressed by **il ne sait pas se maîtriser** (may-tree-ZAY), usually translated as "he has no self-control."

il ne sait rien de rien (eel nuu say ryan duu ryan)
he's totally in the dark
   Also translated as "he hasn't a clue" or "he knows absolutely nothing."

il ne se prend pas pour de la merde (eel nuu suu prahn pah poor də lah mairdə)
he thinks he's hot shit
   This thought may also be translated as "he thinks a lot of himself," but this sanitization misses the spirit of the original French. **Merde**, after all, translates as "shit" and is heard everywhere and often all over France.

il n'est pas . . . (eel nay pah)
he isn't . . .
   Isn't what? Read on. First we must consider **il n'est pas dans son assiette** (dahn sawn nah-SYAYT), translated as "he's not himself" or, more literally, "he's off his feed." But that's not all: **il n'est pas en odeur de sainteté** (zahn naw-DUHR duu san-tuu-TAY), translated as "he's in the doghouse," literally, "he doesn't smell of saintliness"; **il n'est pas méchant au fond** (may-SHAHN oh fawn), translated as "he's basically okay" or, more literally, "basically, he's not really wicked"; and **il n'est pas né d'hier** (nay dee-YAIR), translated as "he's nobody's fool," literally, "he wasn't born yesterday." Finally, and least colorfully, **il n'est pas visible le matin** (vee-ZEEBLə luu mah-TAN), "in the morning he's not in to visitors."

il n'est pire eau que l'eau qui dort (eel nay peer oh kuu loh kee dor)
still waters run deep
   A proverb with at least two possible interpretations: "silent conspirators are the most dangerous" and "deep thinkers are persons of few words." The

literal translation is "no water is worse than still water." So you pays your money and you takes your choice.

il n'est plus dans la course (eel nay plü dahn lah koorss)
he's out of touch
   Also translated as "he's off the track," in the sense of straying from the subject.

il n'est sauce que l'appétit (eel nay sohss kuu lah-pay-TEE)
food tastes best when you're hungry
   Literally, "there's no sauce like appetite."

il n'y a pas à dire (eel nee ah pah zah deer)
the matter is settled
   More closely translated as "there is nothing to be said."

il n'y a pas de fumée sans feu (eel nee ah pah duu fü-MAY sahn fuu)
there's no smoke without fire
   The allusion is to slander and rumor.

il n'y a pas de héros pour son valet de chambre (eel nee ah pah duu ay-ROH poor sawn vah-LAY duu shahnbrə)
no man is a hero to his valet
   And while we all know that valets are a dying breed, we must agree that the persons closest to you know all your shortcomings and defects. As for one's public persona—its fate is in the hands of one's press representatives and public relations firms. (See also PEU D'HOMMES ONT ÉTÉ ADMIRÉS PAR LEURS DOMESTIQUES.)

il n'y a pas de laides amours (eel nee ah pah duu layd zah-MOOR)
beauty is in the eyes of the beholder
   Literally, "there are no homely lovers." Just examine the wedding pictures in your local newspaper. There's someone dear for everyone. And stars in the eyes become rose-colored glasses.

il n'y a pas de quoi (eel nee ah pah də kwah)
don't mention it
   This is the standard response to **merci** (mair-SEE, "thank you"). Also translated as "it's a pleasure" or "it's nothing"; literally, "there's no need for

it." But this phrase introduces at least three longer locutions. One is **il n'y a pas de quoi en faire toute une histoire** (ahn fair too tün neess-TWAHR), translated as "why the song and dance about it?" The phrase may be translated literally as "there's no need to make a fuss about it"; and a sister phrase, **il n'y a pas de quoi en faire tout un fromage** (ahn fair too tœn fraw-MAHZH), has the same meaning, but is literally translated as "there's no need to make a cheese about it." A cheese, of course, is usually the result of sustained, careful effort over a relatively long period of time. A third way of conveying the same meaning is **il n'y a pas de quoi fouetter un chat** (fway-TAY œn shah), translated as "it's nothing to make a fuss about" or "forget it" and, literally, "it's hardly any reason for flogging a cat."

il n'y a pas de sot métier (eel nee ah pah də soh may-TYAY)
don't look down on any form of work
   Translated usually as "every trade has its value," literally as "there's no such thing as a silly job." So get out there and file your résumé with McDonald's.

il n'y a pas le feu! (eel nee ah pah lə fuu)
don't rush!
   Also translated as "take your time!" The literal translation is "there's no fire."

il n'y a pas un chat dans la maison (eel nee ah pah œn shah dahn lah may-ZAWN)
nobody's home
   Also translated as "the house is empty"; literally, "there isn't a cat in the house."

il n'y a plus d'enfants (eel nee ah plü dahn-FAHN)
there are no longer any children
   Molière's words, in *Le Malade imaginaire* (*The Hypochondriac*), indicating that today's children-who-are-not-children are not a new phenomenon.

il n'y a plus de Pyrénées (eel nee ah plü duu pee-ray-NAY)
no obstacles remain
   An elegant way of expressing this thought, literally translated as "there are no longer any Pyrenees." Attributed to Louis XIV of France, who con-

sidered that France in 1700 had become a de facto ally of Spain by virtue of his grandson's departure to ascend the throne of Spain as Philip V. Nothing like having a large, happy family to advance one's territorial or commercial interests!

il n'y a que le premier pas qui coûte (eel nee ah kuu luu pruu-MYAY pah kee koot)
first, get off the dime!
Translated as "the first step is the hardest"; literally, "it is only the first step that costs," in the sense that getting started on any project is the step that requires the greatest strength of character.

il n'y a que les montagnes qui ne se rencontrent pas (eel nee ah kuu lay mawn-TAHNYə kee nuu suu rahn-KAWNTRə pah)
people can always find common ground
As this locution literally tells us, "only mountains can never meet." Thus, we are led to believe that no matter how far people are from one another, fate can bring them together. And people can do much to see that this happens. A romantic thought!

il n'y a que les morts qui ne reviennent pas (eel nee ah kuu lay mor kee nuu ruu-VYAYN pah)
it is only the dead that never return
Attributed to Bertrand Barère (1755–1841), a French revolutionary and regicide, known as the "Anacreon of the guillotine," roughly understandable as the "poet of the guillotine." He knew what he was talking about with regard to the permanence of decapitation.

il parle français comme une vache espagnole (eel pahrl frahn-SAY kawm mün vahsh ayss-pah-NYAWL)
he massacres the French language
Literally, "he speaks French like a Spanish cow." It is not surprising that this French characterization has persisted, since the French so love their language, and Spaniards are a nearby target.

il perd ses plumes (eel pair say plüm)
he's going bald

Conventionally translated as "he's losing his hair"; literally, "he's losing his feathers."

il pleut à verse (eel pluu ah vairss)
it's pouring down rain
   Also translated as "it's raining cats and dogs"; literally, "it's raining in torrents." But this thought is also expressed as **il pleut à seaux** (eel pluu ah soh), literally, "it's raining buckets," and as **il pleut des hallebardes** (eel pluu day zahl-BAHRD), literally, "it's raining halberds," which can be thought of as battle-axes. Ouch! (See also IL TOMBE DES CORDES.)

il porte lanterne à midi (eel port lahn-TAIRN ah mee-DEE)
talk about careful!
   Translated as "he's prudent to a fault"; literally, "he carries a lantern at noon." Of course, you never can tell. A total eclipse may be imminent.

il prend son whisky sec (eel prahn sawn wees-KEE sayk)
he takes his whiskey straight
   Without water or ice cubes, that is. The only proper way. (See also BOIRE LE WHISKY NATURE.)

il ramasse de l'argent comme s'il en pleuvait (eel rah-MAHSS duu lahr-ZHAHN kawm seel lahn pluu-VAY)
he's raking it in
   More literally, "he's picking up money as though it's raining the stuff."

il rit bien qui rit le dernier (eel ree byan kee ree luu dair-NYAY)
don't crow too soon
   Most often translated as "he laughs best who laughs last" or, as Yogi Berra is said to have counseled, "the game ain't over till it's over." An equivalent proverb is **rira bien qui rira le dernier** (ree-RAH byan kee ree-RAH luu dair-NYAY).

il sait se retourner (eel say suu ruu-toor-NAY)
he knows how to cope
   Also translated as "he knows how to land on his feet." The kind of fellow we admire.

il se blesse pour rien (eel suu blayss poor ryan)
he has a thin skin
    Also translated as "he's quick to take offense" or "he's easily offended," literally as "he's wounded by nothing."

il se ferait hacher pour vous (eel suu fuu-RAY ah-SHAY poor voo)
he'd go through hell and high water for you
    Literally, "he'd slash himself to pieces for you." Talk of friendship!

il se laisse dominer par sa femme (eel suu layss daw-mee-NAY pahr sah fahm)
he's henpecked
    Also translated as "he lets himself be pushed around by his wife" or "he allows himself to be dominated by his wife." (See also MARI DOMINÉ PAR SA FEMME.)

il sent le fagot (eel sahn luu fah-GOH)
his days are numbered
    More closely translated as "he's suspected of heresy," meaning there is doubt of his piety or sincerity or reliability. Thus—since heresy was once severely punished—the literal translation of this phrase, "he smells of the fagot," that is, of being burned at the stake. And that's a smell you never get out of your clothes.

il se pique le nez toute la journée (eel suu peek luu nay toot lah zhoor-NAY)
a real drinker
    More closely translated as "he boozes all day long." The literal translation of this locution is something close to "he pricks his nose all day long," which may relate to the changes we often observe in the noses of longtime drinkers.

il se prend pour le nombril du monde (eel suu prahn poor luu nawn-BREEL dü mawndə)
God's gift to the world
    In an earlier time, this would have been translated as "he thinks he's the cat's meow." Today the literal translation is as intriguing as it is descriptive, "he thinks he's the belly button of the world." This thought is also con-

veyed by **il se prend pour quelque chose** (kaylkə shohz), usually translated as "he thinks he's really something" or "he's an egotist." (See also IL NE SE PREND PAS POUR DE LA MERDE.)

il s'est fait renvoyer de son travail (eel say fay rahn-vwah-YAY duu sawn trah-VĪ)
forced retirement
Also translated as "he was fired," "he was thrown out of work," and "he was dismissed from his job." Whatever translation you choose, you're getting the same sad message.

ils ne passeront pas (eel nuu pah-SəRAWN pah)
they shall not pass
The World War I rallying cry originating in the determined stand of the French at Verdun in 1916. The German army had launched a massive offensive that led to almost complete destruction of the city and more than seven hundred thousand casualties in this, the longest battle of the war.

ils n'ont rien appris ni rien oublié (eel nawn ryan nah-PREE nee ryan noo-blee-YAY)
when will they ever learn?
A saying commonly attributed to Talleyrand, the great French statesman (1754–1838); literally, "they have learned nothing and forgotten nothing." "They" were the Bourbons, the French émigrés who returned to France after the Revolution of 1789.

ils se pelotaient (eel suu pə-law-TAY)
lovers' lane activity
    Literally, "they were necking."

ils se ressemblent comme deux gouttes d'eau (eel suu ray-SAHNBLə kawm duu goot doh)
like peas in a pod
    Literally, "they're as alike as two drops of water."

ils sont . . . (eel sawn)
they are . . .
    They are what? To begin, **ils sont copains comme cochons** (kaw-PAN kawm kaw-SHAWN), "they're thick as thieves," more literally translated

as "they're close as pigs," more gently as "they're great pals," **copains** meaning "buddies" or "pals"; **ils sont dans les meilleurs termes** (dahn lay may-
YUHR tairm), "they're on the best of terms"; **ils sont d'un avis opposé**
(dœn nah-VEE aw-poh-ZAY), translated as "they disagree" or, more literally, "they have different opinions"; **ils sont faits l'un pour l'autre** (fay lœn
poor lohtrə), translated as "they're the perfect match," literally, "they were
made for each other"; and, finally, **ils sont très bien installés** (tray byan
nanss-tah-LAY), translated as "they have a comfortable home."

il tombe des cordes (eel tawnbə day kordə)
it's raining cats and dogs
    Literally, "it's raining nooses." People go to extremes in characterizing
heavy rains. (See also IL PLEUT À VERSE.)

il tondrait sur un oeuf (eel tawn-DRAY sür œn nuuf)
talk about misers!
    Best translated as "he's a skinflint"; literally, "he'd shave an egg."

il travaille comme un sabot (eel trah-VĪYə kawm mœn sah-BOH)
talk about low productivity!
    Conventionally translated as "he's a clumsy worker"; literally, "he works
like a clumsy oaf."

il va recevoir des tomates (eel vah ruu-suu-VWAHR day taw-MAHT)
he'll have a hostile reception
    Literally, "he'll be greeted with tomatoes."

il vaut mieux tâcher d'oublier ses malheurs que d'en parler (eel voh
myuu tah-SHAY doo-blee-YAY say mah-LUHR kuu dahn pahr-LAY)
why dwell on your problems?
    Advice that seems to be ignored; literally translated as "it's better to try
to forget one's misfortunes than to talk about them." Easier said than done.
Besides, what would psychotherapists say about this?

**il vaut mieux un danger qu'on connaît qu'un danger qu'on ne connaît
pas** (eel voh myuu œn dahn-ZHAY kawn kawn-NAY kœn dahn-ZHAY
kawn nuu kawn-NAY pah)
be realistic!
    This proverb, warning against being blindsided, is conventionally trans-

lated as "better the devil you know than the devil you don't"; literally, "better the danger you know than the danger you don't know."

il vendrait ses père et mère (eel vahn-DRAY say pair ay mair)
he has no scruples at all
Literally, "he would sell his father and mother."

il vous rit au nez (eel voo ree toh nay)
he's laughing in your face
Literally, "he's laughing in your nose."

il y a anguille sous roche (eel lee yah ahn-GEEYə soo rawsh)
something's wrong here
While we sometimes feel that all is not well, we may frequently be unable to put our finger on the cause of our disquiet. Shakespeare's Hamlet gave us the classic expression for this situation: "something is rotten in the state of Denmark." And while we may say "there's more to it than meets the eye," French here tells us literally, "there's an eel under the rock," which locution is directly translated from a classic Latin metaphor. (See also ÇA SENT LE POISSON ICI.)

il y a de quoi se flinguer (eel lee yah duu kwah suu flan-GAY)
it's more than a body can bear
More closely translated as "it's enough to make you want to end it all"; literally, "it's enough to make you want to shoot yourself."

il y a du louche dans cette affaire (eel lee yah dü loosh dahn sayt tah-FAIR)
I smell a rat
Translated sometimes as "something fishy's going on"; more closely as "this business is a bit shady." (See also C'EST UNE AFFAIRE LOUCHE.)

il y a loin de la coupe aux lèvres (eel lee yah lwan duu lah koop oh layvrə)
there's many a slip between cup and lip
The message is clear: "nothing is certain till you have it in hand"; literally, "it's a long way from the cup to the lips." So maybe it's a good thing to take your stock market profits from time to time.

il y va de sa tête (eel lee vah duu sah tayt)
his life is at stake
      Also translated as "his life hangs in the balance"; literally, "his head depends on it."

impeccable! (an-pay-KAHBLə)
perfect!
      Also translated as "great!" and "smashing!"

impossible n'est pas français (an-paw-SEEBLə nay pah frahn-SAY)
there's no such word as "cannot"
      Attributed to Napoleon. Literally, "'impossible' isn't a French word."

incontinence nocturne (an-kawn-tee-NAHNSS nawk-TÜRN)
the plague of boys
      Translated as "bedwetting" or "enuresis"; literally, "nighttime incontinence."

infortunes conjugales (an-for-TÜN kawn-zhü-GAHL)
see your family counselor
      Translated as "marital problems"; literally, "marital misfortunes."

ingénue (an-zhay-NÜ)
ingénue or ingenue
      Translated also, but infrequently, as "artless young woman." The French word has been taken into English along with its French pronunciation and the narrow meaning of "unworldly young woman as played on the stage."

J

J'accuse (zhah-KÜZ)
I accuse
      This memorable indictment, written by French novelist Emile Zola (1840–1902) in his open letter of 1898, was published in a newspaper and

led to a prison sentence for Zola on a charge of impeachment of French military authorities. He evaded imprisonment by fleeing to England. Addressed to the president of France, the letter denounced the French army's persecution of Captain Alfred Dreyfus, a Jewish artillery officer on the general staff, who had been accused unjustly of delivering defense documents to a foreign government. Dreyfus was court-martialed and sentenced to life imprisonment on Devil's Island. As a consequence, French political life seethed in the chaos of militarism and virulent anti-Semitism. Zola's *J'accuse* did much to move the government toward reopening its investigation, and Dreyfus was retried and found guilty again, but he was pardoned. It was not until 1906 that the verdict was reversed and Dreyfus was restored to his army rank. He fought in World War I and was decorated for his actions in that war.

j'ai les pieds qui fourmillent (zhay lay pyay kee foor-MEEYə)
I have pins and needles in my feet
  Literally, "I have ants swarming in my feet." (See also AVOIR DES FOURMIS DANS LES JAMBES.)

j'ai le ticket avec son amie (zhay luu tee-KAY ah-VAYK sawn nah-MEE)
we hit it off
  Usually translated as "I've made a hit with his girlfriend."

j'ai un poids sur la poitrine (zhay œn pwah sür lah pwah-TREEN)
my chest feels tight
  Also translated as "I have difficulty in breathing"; literally, "I have a weight on my chest." Sounds like a heart attack!

jamais bon coureur ne fut pris (zhah-MAY bawn koo-RUHR nuu fü pree)
experience teaches wisdom
  The French version of the English proverb "old birds are not to be caught with chaff"; literally, "a good runner was never captured."

jargon (zhahr-GAWN)
gibberish
  Also translated as "jargon," another of many adoptions of French words, but in English pronounced JAHR-gən.

je connais la musique (zhuu kawn-NAY lah mü-ZEEK)
tell me something I don't know
   Usually translated as "I've heard it all before" or as "I know my way around"; literally, "I'm acquainted with music."

je connais Marseille comme ma poche (zhuu kawn-NAY mahr-SAYə kum mah pawsh)
I know Marseilles like the back of my hand
   Literally, "I know Marseilles like my pocket."

je crains de gêner (zhuu kran duu zhay-NAY)
am I bothering you?
   Usually translated as "I'm afraid I'm a nuisance" or "I fear I'm putting you out."

je crève de faim (zhuu krayvə duu fan)
food, food!
   Literally translated as "I'm famished" or "I'm starving."

je crois que non (zhuu krwah kuu nawn)
I don't think so
   Also translated as "I think not."

je crois que oui (zhuu krwah kuu wee)
I think so

je l'ai dit et je le maintiens (zhuu lay dee ay zhuu luu man-TYAN)
I said it and I stand by it
   A locution indicating unwavering opinion; literally, "I've said it and I support it."

je le ferai contre vents et marées (zhuu luu fuu-RAY kawntrə vahn zay mah-RAY)
I'll do it come hell or high water
   Literally, "I'll do it against winds and tides." Can't ask for a stronger commitment.

je le vois venir avec ses gros sabots (zhuu luu vwah vuu-NEER ah-VAYK say groh sah-BOH)
I know what he's after

Also translated as "I can see him coming from a mile away"; literally, "I can see him coming with his big wooden shoes." Maybe it would be more appropriate to say "I can hear him coming with his big wooden shoes."

je maintiendrai (zhuu man-tyan-DRAY)
I will maintain
> Motto of the Netherlands.

j'embrasse mon rival, mais c'est pour l'étouffer (zhahn-BRAHSS mawn ree-VAHL may say poor lay-too-FAY)
don't think I've changed my mind!
> A line from Corneille, "I embrace my rival, but only to choke him."

je me moque royalement de ma situation (zhuu muu mawk rwah-yahlə-MAHN duu mah see-tü-ah-SYAWN)
fire me, please!
> Translated as "I don't give two hoots about my job" or "I couldn't care less about my job." Also, with much gratification in the saying, "You can take this job and shove it!"

je m'en contrefiche (zhuu mahn kawn-trə-FEESH)
I couldn't care less
> Also translated as "I don't give a damn about it." Other ways to express the same thought are **je m'en fiche pas mal** (zhuu mahn feesh pah mahl), and **je m'en fous** (zhuu mahn foo).

je m'en vais chercher un grand Peut-être (zhuu mahn vay shair-SHAY œn grahn puu-TAYTRə)
I'm dying
> Literally, "I am going to seek a great perhaps," the deathbed utterance attributed to Rabelais.

je m'en vais voir le soleil pour la dernière fois (zhuu mahn vay vwahr luu saw-LAYə poor lah dair-NYAIR fwah)
I'm dying
> Literally, "I'm going to see the sun for the last time," the deathbed utterance attributed to Jean-Jacques Rousseau (1712–1778).

je n'ai pas beaucoup de liquide (zhuu nay pah boh-KOO duu lee-KEED)
I'm tapped out
Also translated as "I'm short of cash" or "I haven't much ready money"; most literally, "I don't have much by way of liquid assets."

j'en ai soupé de ces histoires (zhahn nay soo-PAY duu say zeess-TWAHR)
I'm sick and tired of all this nonsense
Literally, "I've had a bellyful of all these stories."

je ne cherche qu'un (zhuu nuu shairshə kœn)
I seek but one
That's all it takes.

je ne le connais ni d'Adam ni d'Eve (zhuu nuu luu kawn-NAY nee dah-DAHN nee dayvə)
I don't know him from Adam
Also translated as "I have no idea who he is"; literally, "I don't know him from Adam or Eve."

je n'en peux plus (zhuu nahn puu plü)
that's it!
The phrase of choice to use when you've had it up to there; usually translated as "I can't stand it any longer."

je n'en vois pas la nécessité (zhuu nahn vwah pah lah nay-say-see-TAY)
I don't see the necessity for it
The reply attributed to a French aristocrat before the Revolution, on being reminded that the people must live.

je ne peux pas le gober (zhuu nuu puu pah lə gaw-BAY)
he's too much
Also translated as "I can't stand him"; literally, "I can't swallow him."

je ne sais pas (zhuu nuu say pah)
I don't know

je ne sais quoi (zhuu nuu say kwah)
that indefinable something

The Frenchest of French locutions; literally, "I know not what," and that is why it is lamely translated above as "that indefinable something." Understand, however, that when you encounter someone who can correctly be characterized as having **je ne sais quoi**, you will fully grasp just what the phrase means.

je ne sais trop (zhuu nuu say troh)
I'm not quite sure

Also translated as "I don't know exactly"; literally, "I don't know very much."

j'enlève ma robe pour mettre quelque chose de plus confortable (zhahn-LAYVə mah rawb poor maytrə kaylkə shohz duu plü kawn-for-TAHBLə)
music to a young man's ears

Almost literally translated as "I'll slip out of this dress into something more comfortable."

j'en mettrais ma tête sur le billot (zhahn may-TRAY mah tayt sür luu bee-YOH)
I'd stake my life on it

Literally translated as "I would put my head on the block." And this statement is not to be taken lightly in the land that gave civilization the guillotine.

je n'y toucherais pas avec des pincettes (zhuu nee tooshə-RAY pah ah-VAYK day pan-SAYT)
I wouldn't touch it with a ten-foot pole

Literally, "I wouldn't touch it with tongs."

je pense donc je suis (zhuu pahnss dawnk zhuu swee)
I think, therefore I am

The translation of the indubitably true Latin maxim *cogito, ergo sum*, made famous—in the Latin—by the French philosopher and mathematician René Descartes (1596–1650).

je prends mon bien partout où je le trouve (zhuu prahn mawn byan pahr-TOO oo zhuu lə troovə)
I take what is useful to me where I find it

Also translated as "I take my property wherever I find it." The reply of Molière to those who accused him of plagiarism.

je sais ce que je sais (zhuu say suu kuu zhuu say)
I know what I know
The response of someone whose credibility in giving testimony has been challenged.

je suis drôlement emmerdé (zhuu swee drohlə-MAHN an-mair-DAY)
I'm in deep trouble
Also translated as "I'm really in the soup" and, vulgarly but closely, as "I'm in deep shit."

je suis la cinquième roue du carrosse (zhuu swee lah san-KYAYM roo dü kah-RAWSS)
everyone ignores me
Translated as "I'm treated as though I don't exist"; literally, "I'm the fifth wheel of the coach."

je suis vraiment navré (zhuu swee vray-MAHN nah-VRAY)
forgive me
Literally, "I'm truly sorry."

j'étais rouillé en français (zhay-TAY roo-YAY ahn frahn-SAY)
my French was rusty

je t'en prie (zhuu tahn pree)
please
The familiar form of this civility. (See also JE VOUS EN PRIE.)

jeter (zhuu-TAY)
throw
This infinitive, which is translated in other ways as well, is part of many interesting idioms, including **jeter au panier** (oh pah-NYAY), translated as "throw out," "throw into the wastebasket," "throw into the garbage," and, literally, "throw into the basket"; **jeter de la poudre aux yeux de quelqu'un** (duu lah poodrə oh zyuu duu kayl-KœN), translated as "mislead" and "deliberately deceive someone," literally, "throw dust in someone's eyes"; **jeter des cris** (day kree), translated as "scream" and "cry out"; **jeter le manche après la**

cognée (luu ma*n*sh ah-PRAY lah kaw-NYAY), translated as "throw in your cards," "give up in despair," and, literally, as the ultimate act of the frustrated handyman, "throw the handle after the axe"; **jeter quelqu'un à la rue** (kayl-K*œN* ah lah rü), translated as "throw someone out into the street," warning us to be sure to pay the rent and to stay away from bars that employ bouncers; **jeter son argent par la fenêtre** (saw*n* nahr-ZHAH*N* pahr lah fə-NAYTRə), translated as "speculate wildly," literally, "throw money out the window"; and, finally, **jeter son bonnet par-dessus les moulins** (saw*n* baw*n*-NAY pahr-duu-SÜ lay moo-LA*N*), translated as "act in defiance of public opinion or the proprieties," literally, "throw one's cap over the mills."

jeu (zhuu)
play or *sport* or *game* or *gambling*
   This noun leads us into many idioms, including **jeu de cartes** (duu kahrt), translated as "card game"; **jeu de dupes** (duu düpə), translated as "fool's game," for example, three-card monte; **jeu de hasard** (duu ah-ZAHR), translated as "game of chance"; **jeu de mains** (duu ma*n*), translated as "horseplay" and "rough play," literally, "hand play," not with caresses but with blows; **jeu de mots** (duu moh), translated as "pun," literally, "play on words"; **jeu de puces** (duu püss), translated as "tiddlywinks," literally, "game of fleas"; **jeu d'esprit** (dayss-PREE), translated as "witticism" and "humorous trifle," literally, "play of wit"; **jeu de théâtre**, translated as "claptrap," more literally, "stage trick"; and, finally, **jeu du hasard** (dü ah-ZAHR), translated as "freak of fortune" (see JEU DE HASARD above).

jeux de main, jeux de vilain! (zhuu duu ma*n* zhuu duu vee-LA*N*)
things can take a serious turn
   Literally, "rough play, villain's play." Better translated as "stop fooling around, or the game will end in tears!" (See also JEU DE MAINS.)

je vais rejoindre votre père (zhuu vay ruu-ZHWANDRə vawtrə pair)
I'm going to rejoin your father
   Said to have been Marie Antoinette's parting words to her children, spoken while she was on her way to the guillotine in October 1793. Her husband, Louis XVI, had met the same fate earlier in the year.

je vous en prie (zhuu voo zah*n* pree)
please
   A polite form of this civility. (See also JE T'EN PRIE.)

je vous prie de me pardonner (zhuu voo pree duu muu pahr-daw-NAY)
please forgive me

je vous suis redevable de la vie (zhuu voo swee ruu-duu-VAHBLə duu lah vee)
I'm indebted forever
   Literally, "I owe you my life."

joie de vivre (zhwah duu veevrə)
joy of living
   Often used in English, with the French pronunciation, to denote "delight in being alive."

joie mêlée de remords (zhwah may-LAY duu ruu-MOR)
no undiluted joy
   Literally translated as "pleasure mixed with remorse."

jouer (zhway)
play
   This infinitive leads us into several common locutions, including **jouer aux échecs** (oh zay-SHAYK), translated as "play chess"; **jouer aux gendarmes et aux voleurs** (oh zhahn-DAHRMə ay oh vaw-LUHR), "play cops and robbers"; **jouer avec le feu** (ah-VAYK luu fuu), literally, "play with fire"; **jouer son va-tout** (sawn vah-TOO), translated as "bet the farm" and "risk one's all," literally, "bet everything one has"; and **jouer sur les mots** (sür lay moh), translated as "pun" or "play with words."

jour (zhoor)
day
   We have our choice of days, including **jour de congé** (duu kawn-ZHAY), translated as "holiday," literally, "day's leave"; **jour de fête** (duu fayt), translated as "festival," literally, "fete day"; **jour de jeûne** (duu zhuhn), "fast day"; **jour de l'an** (duu lahn), "New Year's Day"; **jour gras** (grah), translated as "day when meat may be eaten," literally, "fat day"; and **jour maigre** (maygrə), translated as "meatless day," "fish day," or "fast day," literally, "lean day."

journée de repos (zhoor-NAY duu ruu-POH)
TGIS

For those who may not be up on the latest jargon, "thank God it's Saturday"; better translated as "day off," literally, "day of rest."

joyeux Noël (zhwah-YUU noh-AYL)
Merry Christmas

jurer comme un troupier (zhü-RAY kawm mœn troo-PYAY)
swear like a trooper

jusqu'à la gauche (zhüss-KAH lah gohsh)
to the bitter end
    Literally, "to the left side."

jusqu'à perpète (zhüss-KAH pair-PAYT)
forever
    Also translated as "till doomsday" or "till the cows come home"; literally, "to perpetuity," **perpète** being prison slang for **perpétuité** (pair-pay-twee-TAY). Another, more colorful way of expressing the same thought is **jusqu'au jour où les poules auront des dents** (zhüss-KOH zhoor oo lay pool oh-RAWN day dahn), literally, "till the day when hens have teeth." (See also ATTENDRE LA SEMAINE DES QUATRE JEUDIS.)

j'y suis, j'y reste (zhee swee zhee rayst)
here I am, here I stay
    Also translated as "I will not budge." This asseveration is attributed to the French soldier and statesman Marshal MacMahon (1808–1893), made when he was urged to abandon the Malakoff Tower in 1855, which had been taken by his forces during the Crimean War.

képi (kay-PEE)
kepi
    This is the familiar French military hat with a circular flat top and a visor.

kermesse (kair-MAYSS)
fair or *bazaar*

kil de rouge (keel duu roozh)
bottle of cheap red wine

la beauté n'est pas tout (lah boh-TAY nay pah too)
beauty's only skin-deep
    Literally, "beauty isn't everything." In fact, that's not the entire story: **la beauté sans vertu est une fleur sans parfum** (lah boh-TAY sahn vair-TÜ ay tün fluhr sahn pahr-FœN), literally, "beauty without virtue is a flower without fragrance."

la belle dame sans merci (lah bayl dahm sahn mair-SEE)
the beautiful but merciless lady
    Every student of English literature knows this phrase as the title of a haunting and mysterious ballad, "La Belle Dame Sans Merci," by John Keats (1795–1821).

la Belle Epoque (lah bayl lay-PAWK)
the Edwardian Age

la belle France (lah bayl frahnss)
fair France
   An appellation frequently applied by the French to their beloved country; literally, "beautiful France."

la bourse ou la vie! (lah boorssə oo lah vee)
your money or your life!
   More literally, "your purse or your life!" **La Bourse**, incidentally, is the Parisian stock exchange, equivalent to Wall Street.

la bride sur le cou (lah breed sür luu koo)
unchecked or *unrestrained*
   Also translated as "with free rein"; literally, "bridle on the neck." When a rider allows the reins to remain slack on a horse's neck, the horse feels free to act as a healthy horse will, that is, gallop as fast as it wishes.

l'absence est à l'amour ce que le vent est au feu; il éteint le petit, il allume le grand (lahb-SAHNSS ay tah lah-MOOR suu kuu luu vahn ay toh fuu eel lay-TAN luu puu-TEE eel ah-LÜM luu grahn)
absence tests love
   Literally, "absence is to love what wind is to fire; it extinguishes the small, it inflames the great." A metaphor attributed to Count Bussy-Rabutin (1618–1693), a French soldier, adventurer, and writer, who published a book recounting court scandals, not all of them factual.

l'absence fait le larron (lahb-SAHNSS fay luu lah-RAWN)
don't lose your credit cards
   Translated as "opportunity makes the thief"; literally, "absence makes the thief." (See also L'OCCASION FAIT LE LARRON.)

l'Académie française (lah-kah-day-MEE frahn-SAYZ)
the French Academy
   One of the world-famous French institutions, established in 1635. It comprises forty members, considered the most distinguished men of French letters—the first woman elected, in 1980, was the Belgian-born French

novelist Marguerite Yourcenar. The prime goal of the academy is preservation of the purity of the French language. To this end, in 1639, the academy began compiling a definitive dictionary of the French language. It is almost unnecessary to point out that the task has yet to be completed, but most scholars consider that this effort—along with the scholarly writings of the academicians on grammar, rhetoric, and poetry—has had a salubrious effect on French cultural life and on the development of the precious French language.

la caque sent toujours le hareng (lah kahk s*ahn* too-ZHOOR luu ah-RAH*N*)
the acorn doesn't fall far from the tree
    Also given by the proverb "what's bred in the bone will come out in the flesh"; literally, "the herring barrel always smells of herring." And try as one may, there's little one can do about it.

lâcher la rampe (lah-SHAY lah rah*n*pə)
kick the bucket
    Literally, "loosen the slope." Since many of life's slopes are slippery, one may consider this a most appropriate metaphor for the inevitable final journey of life.

lâcher le morceau (lah-SHAY luu mor-SOH)
come clean
    Also translated as "spill the beans"; literally, "release the morsel."

lâcher un vent (lah-SHAY œn vahn)
break wind
    The widely used euphemism for one of life's embarrassing moments; literally, "release wind."

la chute (lah shüt)
the Fall
    Of Man, that is, because of Adam's disobedience.

la cigarette du condamné (lah see-gah-RAYT dü kawn-dah-NAY)
a condemned man's last smoke
    By the time one faces a firing squad, there's little use in worrying over the ill effects of the weed.

La Comédie humaine (lah kaw-may-DEE ü-MAYN)
The Human Comedy
  The title given by the French novelist Honoré de Balzac (1799–1850) to his masterpiece, a series of novels in which he undertook to depict the various sides of human life, organized in three main areas: manners, philosophy, and marriage.

la Côte d'Azur (lah kohtə dah-ZÜR)
the French Riviera
  Literally, "the azure coast," but in English always called by its French name, pronounced as nearly as possible in the French way.

la critique est aisée et l'art est difficile (lah kree-TEEK ay tay-ZAY ay lahr ay dee-fee-SEEL)
anybody can be a critic
  A truth that anyone but a critic will accept. This observation of the French playwright Philippe Destouches (1680–1754), literally "criticism is easy and art is difficult," cannot be denied. Or can it?

la douceur exquise du succès (lah doo-SUHR ayk-SKEEZ dü sük-SAY)
the sweet smell of success
  Literally, "the exquisite sweetness of success." However you say it, you surely know it or hope to know it.

l'adversité fait les hommes, et le bonheur les monstres (lahd-vair-see-TAY fay lay zawm ay luu bawn-NUHR lay mawnstrə)
adversity makes men, and prosperity monsters
  The first claim cannot be denied; the second is too often true, alas.

la façon de donner vaut mieux que ce qu'on donne (lah fah-SAWN duu daw-NAY voh myuu kuu suu kawn dawn)
it's how you give that counts
  Literally, "the manner of giving is worth more than that which is given." Within limits, of course.

la faim chasse le loup du bois (lah fan shahss luu loo dü bwah)
you can stand just so much
  A proverb translated as "when the going gets really tough, most of us give up"; literally, "hunger will drive even a wolf out of the woods."

l'affaire lui a pété dans la main (lah-FAIR lwee ah pay-TAY dahn lah man)
the deal fell through
    Also translated as "the scheme never got off the ground" or "the scheme never got to first base"; literally, "the scheme farted in his hand." The French really have a way with words.

l'affaire marche (lah-FAIR mahrsh)
things are going well
    Literally, "the affair *or* deal progresses." This thought is also expressed by **l'affaire s'achemine** (sah-shuu-MEEN). It's when one moves on to **l'affaire est dans le sac** (ay dahn lə sahk), translated as "not to worry!" or "it's in the bag," that we begin to worry. Or should begin to worry.

la fin justifie les moyens (lah fan zhüss-tee-FEE lay mwah-YAN)
the end justifies the means
    More accurately, but not expressed in French here, the end is used as a justification for the means.

la gaffe est de taille (lah gahf ay duu tīyə)
it's no small blunder
    The noun **gaffe** is often used in English (pronounced gaf), with the meaning of "social blunder," and **taille** means "size." (See also FAUX PAS.)

l'âge critique (lahzh kree-TEEK)
change of life

l'âge d'or (lahzh dor)
the golden age

la hâte est l'ennemie de la précision (lah ahtə ay laynə-MEE duu lah pray-see-ZYAWN)
haste makes waste
    More closely, "speed and accuracy don't mix"; literally, "speed is the enemy of precision."

laid comme un singe (lay kawm mœn sanzh)
ugly as sin
    Literally, "ugly as a monkey."

laisse faire! (layss fair)
never mind!
 Also translated as "don't bother!"

laisser (lay-SAY)
leave
 The infinitive **laisser** gives us several common words and phrases, including **laisser-aller** (ah-LAY), translated as "casualness," "unlimited freedom," "unconstraint," or "a letting go," literally, "let go"; **laisser en rade** (ahn rahd), translated as "leave in the lurch," "leave high and dry," and "leave stranded," **rade** meaning "harbor"; **laisser-faire** (fair), "noninterference," also translated as "a letting go." This term, literally translated as "let go," is applied particularly to a policy of government that espouses noninterference with commerce and industry. There follow now a string of idioms, including **laisser quelqu'un mijoter dans son jus** (kayl-KœN mee-zhaw-TAY dahn sawn zhü), translated as "let him suffer" and "let him stew in his own juice," meaning that a poor fellow so treated is reaping the consequences of his own actions. The infinitive **mijoter** has the literal meaning of "simmer." And one wonders whether it is worse to simmer or to stew. Less dramatic is **laisser quelqu'un tranquille** (kayl-KœN trahn-KEEL), translated as "stop bugging someone"; more literally, "leave somebody alone" or "leave someone in peace." Finally, there is **laisser une affaire en suspens** (ün nah-FAIR ahn süss-PAHN), translated as "leave an affair in abeyance."

laissez (lay-SAY)
let
 This is an imperative form of the verb **laisser** (see above), so we are not surprised when we encounter it in a number of practical suggestions, including **laissez dire les sots, le savoir a son prix** (deer lay soh luu sah-VWAHR ah sawn pree), an insight from La Fontaine telling us not to pay attention to what the uninformed say and translated as "let fools talk, knowledge has its value"; **laissez faire, laissez passer** (fair lay-SAY pah-SAY), translated as "let them do as they please." This is the maxim of eighteenth-century economists—still followed today by some politicians—counseling a hands-off policy with regard to production and trade. Then there is **laissez-moi tranquille avec vos questions** (mwah trahn-KEEL ah-VAYK voh kayss-TYAWN), translated as "stop pestering me with your questions"; finally, there is **laissez tomber!** (tawn-BAY), translated as "forget it!" and "give it a rest!"; literally, "let it fall!"

la lecture nourrit l'esprit (lah layk-TÜR noo-REE layss-PREE)
read, read, read!
   Translated as "reading improves the mind." And support Literacy Volunteers of America!

la maladie sans maladie (lah mah-lah-DEE sahn mah-lah-DEE)
hypochondria
   Literally, "the disease without disease."

la minute de vérité (lah mee-NÜT duu vay-ree-TAY)
the moment of truth

la misère est un tyran implacable (lah mee-ZAIR ay tœn tee-RAHN anplah-KAHBLə)
poverty is a stern taskmaster
   Literally translated as "poverty is an implacable tyrant." Couldn't be said better.

l'amitié est l'amour sans ailes (lah-mee-TYAY ay lah-MOOR sahn zayl)
friendship is love without its wings

la mort a toujours tort (lah mor ah too-ZHOOR tor)
death is always at fault
   Never the doctor or the health maintenance organization?

la mort égale tous les êtres (lah mor ay-GAHL too lay zaytrə)
the great leveler
   Translated as "death makes all of us equal." Undeniable.

l'amour enchaîne les coeurs (lah-MOOR ahn-SHAYN lay kuhr)
when two hearts beat as one
   Translated as "love binds hearts together." And divorce rips them apart?

l'amour et la fumée ne peuvent se cacher (lah-MOOR ay lah fü-MAY nuu puhvə suu kah-SHAY)
love and smoke cannot be hidden
   But only one of them can give you cancer.

l'amour finit toujours par triompher (lah-MOOR fee-NEE too-ZHOOR pahr tree-yawn-FAY)
the power of true love
   This proverb, translated as "in the end love conquers all"—all obstacles, that is—appears in English as "love will find a way," dating from the sixteenth century, and in other languages as well.

l'amour ne se raisonne pas (lah-MOOR nuu suu ray-ZAWN pah)
love knows no reason
   Literally translated as "there's no reasoning with love." And that's why we say "crazy in love."

l'amour-propre est le plus grand de tous les flatteurs (lah-moor-PRAWPRə ay luu plü grahn duu too lay flah-TUHR)
self-love is the greatest of all flatterers
   La Rochefoucauld, who never hated a maxim he wrote, scored a bull's-eye with this one.

la moutarde me monta au nez (lah moo-TAHRDə muu mawn-TAH oh nay)
I blew my cool
   Usually translated as "I lost my temper"; literally, "the mustard went up my nose." Could it have been Grey Poupon? Or was I eating in a Chinese restaurant?

la nation boutiquière (lah nah-SYAWN boo-tee-KYAIR)
England
   Literally, "the nation of shopkeepers," the epithet used by Napoleon Bonaparte in one of his speeches to refer to England.

lancer une idée en l'air (lahn-SAY ün nee-DAY ahn lair)
brainstorm
   Also translated as "toss out an idea"—for discussion, that is. Literally, "toss an idea into the air." And see whether it lands in Silicon Valley?

langage des dieux (lahn-GAHZH day dyuu)
poetry
   Literally, "language of the gods."

langage des halles (lahn-GAHZH day ahlə)
billingsgate
Also translated as "coarse, abusive language"; literally, "language of the markets." (See also LES HALLES.)

langue maternelle (lahngə mah-tair-NAYL)
mother tongue
One's native language.

langue véhiculaire (lahngə vay-ee-kü-LAIR)
common language
In the sense of the Italian *lingua franca*; literally, "Frankish language," a common language spoken in Mediterranean ports. Lingua franca has come into English as well as into French and now is used to denote any language that serves as a common tongue among people of diverse speech. But where does **véhiculaire** come into the picture? Well, the Franks are long gone, and truck traffic today is, of course, the primary means of transporting goods among countries bordering on the Mediterranean, so **langue véhiculaire** may be seen as the "truck driver's language." And since lingua franca is a mixture of Italian, French, Spanish, and German, we may presume that **langue véhiculaire**, a recent coinage, has merely built upon that base and added English words as well—a logical assumption, considering the universal influence of the English language.

la nuit porte conseil (lah nwee portə kawn-SAYə)
better sleep on it
Also translated as "go to bed with a problem, wake up with the solution," literally as "night brings counsel."

la nuit tous les chats sont gris (lah nwee too lay shah sawn gree)
in the dark they are all the same
Literally, "at night all cats are gray." The allusion is to a man and a woman sharing a bed at night, when questions of personal beauty are moot.

la parole est d'argent, le silence est d'or (lah pah-RUHL ay dahr-ZHAHN luu see-LAHNSS ay dor)
know when to hold your tongue!

Also translated as "try keeping your own counsel!" Literally, "speech is silver but silence is golden," which is, in translation, an old Persian proverb.

la patience est amère, mais son fruit est doux (lah pah-SYAHNSS ay tah-MAIR may sawn frwee ay doo)
patience is bitter, but its reward is sweet
    A saying attributed to Jean-Jacques Rousseau (1712–1778); more literally translated as "patience is bitter, but its fruit is sweet."

la peine n'est pas toujours proportionnée au délit (lah payn nay pah too-ZHOOR praw-por-syaw-NAY oh day-LEE)
the punishment does not always fit the crime
    As is evident to anyone who follows news reports of the sentences and financial penalties meted out in our courts.

la peur a bon pas (lah puhr ah bawn pah)
fear turns people into Olympic sprinters
    Also translated as "there's nothing like fear to get you moving"; literally, "fear has a good pace." The same thought is conveyed by **la peur lui donnait des ailes** (lwee daw-NAY day zayl), best translated as "fear gave him wings."

l'appétit vient en mangeant (lah-pay-TEE vyan tahn mahn-ZHAHN)
the more you have, the more you want
    This saying of Rabelais, literally "appetite comes with eating," applies not only to food—but to money, conquests, the writing of books, and more.

L'Apprenti-sorcier (lah-prahn-TEE sor-SYAY)
The Sorcerer's Apprentice
    The most widely known composition of the French composer Paul Dukas (1865–1935).

la presse à sensation (lah prayss ah sahn-sah-SYAWN)
the tabloid press
    Also translated as "the gutter press"; literally, "the sensational press." For examples of this phenomenon, check the racks in your local supermarket.

la propreté du corps est parente de propreté de l'âme (lah praw-pruu-
TAY dü kor ay pah-RAHNT duu praw-pruu-TAY duu lahm)
remember to wash your hands!
    Translated as "cleanliness is next to godliness"; literally, "bodily cleanli-
ness is the parent of cleanliness of the soul."

la propriété c'est le vol (lah praw-pree-yay-TAY say luu vawl)
property is theft
    Specifically, "rent is the appropriation of the labor of others," the asser-
tion of French journalist Pierre Proudhon (1809–1865).

la raison du plus fort est toujours la meilleure (lah ray-ZAWN dü plü
for ay too-ZHOOR lah may-YUHR)
might makes right
    More literally, "the reason of the strongest is always a winner."

l'arbre de la liberté ne croît qu'arrosé par le sang des tyrans (lahrbrə
duu lah lee-bair-TAY nuu krwah kah-raw-ZAY pahr luu sahn day tee-
RAHN)
liberty does not come easily
    Literally, "the tree of liberty grows only when sprinkled with the blood
of tyrants."

l'arbre ne tombe pas du premier coup (lahrbrə nuu tawnbə pah dü pruu-
MYAY koo)
persistence, persistence!
    Translated as "the tree does not fall at the first blow," telling us that we
have to be prepared to work hard to gain any desired end.

la reine le veut (lah raynə luu vuu)
the queen wills it
    A formula of royal assent. (See also LE ROI LE VEUT.)

l'argent (lahr-ZHAHN)
money
    A natural lead-in to many observations, including **l'argent coule à flots**
(kool lah floh), meaning "spend money like it's going out of style," more

closely translated as "money flows like water," and literally, "money runs like waves"; **l'argent est la racine de tous nos maux** (ay lah rah-SEEN duu too noh moh), translated as "money is the root of all evil"; **l'argent est le nerf de la guerre** (ay luu nair duu lah gair), translated as "money is the sinews of war" (see also LES NERFS DES BATAILLES SONT LES PÉCUNES). Then there are **l'argent est roi** (ay rwah), translated as "money talks," literally, "money is king"; **l'argent est un bon passe-partout** (ay tœn bawn pahss-pahr-TOO), translated as "money opens all doors," literally, "money is a good master key"; **l'argent est un puissant levier** (ay tœn pwee-SAHN luu-VYAY), another way of saying "money talks," literally, "money is a powerful lever"; **l'argent leur fond dans les mains** (luhr fawn dahn lay man), another way of characterizing profligate spenders, translated as "they spend money like water," literally, "money melts in their hands"; **l'argent n'a pas d'odeur** (nah pah daw-DUHR) stands up for acquiring wealth, translated as "money doesn't smell"; but then we have a word of caution: **l'argent ne fait pas le bonheur** (nuu fay pah luu bawn-NUHR), translated as "money can't buy happiness"; after all, **l'argent ne tombe pas du ciel** (nuu tawnbə pah dü syayl), taken as "money doesn't grow on trees," literally translated as "money doesn't fall from the sky"; and finally, **l'argent va où est l'argent** (vah oo ay lahr-ZHAHN), telling us "money makes money," literally, "money goes where money is," an observation grounded in a realistic understanding of how the capitalist system works. Indeed, all other systems as well.

la Rive gauche (lah reev gohsh)
the Left Bank
   Of the Seine, that is. The Parisian district known for its intellectual and student life.

la roue de la Fortune (lah roo duu lah for-TÜN)
the wheel of fortune
   A metaphor used long before the advent of television.

l'artifice est une nécessité de l'art (lahr-tee-FEESS ay tün nay-say-see-TAY duu lahr)
art depends on make-believe
   Also translated as "art depends on pretense"; literally, "art cannot exist without artifice."

l'art pour l'art (lahr poor lahr)
art for art's sake

la santé est une richesse (lah sahn-TAY ay tün ree-SHAYSS)
good health is a blessing
Literally translated as "good health is wealth."

l'as de l'école (lahss duu lay-KAWL)
he's number one
Translated as "the school's star pupil"; literally, "the school's ace."

la Toison d'or (lah twah-ZAWN dor)
the Golden Fleece
In mythology the fleece of Chrysomallus, the winged ram on which Phrixus, son of Athamas, successfully made his escape. Ino, the wife of Athamas, had told her husband that Chrysomallus had caused a devastating famine, which led Athamas to decide to sacrifice his son. The Golden Fleece, of course, was later the object of the well-known—and successful—search launched by Jason and his Argonauts. Nothing like a good story.

lavage de cerveau (lah-VAHZH duu sair-VOH)
a brainwashing
Not to be taken literally, of course.

la vengeance est un plat qui se mange froid (lah vahn-ZHAHNSS ay tœn plah kee suu mahnzh frwah)
don't act on the spur of the moment
Also translated as "never take revenge in the heat of the moment"; literally, and more appealingly, "revenge is a dish that is eaten cold."

l'avenir appartient à qui se lève tôt (lah-vuu-NEER ah-pahr-TYAN ah kee suu layvə toh)
the early bird catches the worm
Literally, "the future belongs to the early riser." As long as we put in a full day.

la vérité (lah vay-ree-TAY)
truth
As one would expect, there are some interesting locutions that begin with these words, including **la vérité finira par se savoir** (fee-nee-RAH

pahr suu sah-VWAHR), translated as "truth will out"; literally, "in the end the truth will make itself known." At least that's what we're told. Then there is **la vérité n'est pas toujours bonne à dire** (nay pah too-ZHOOR bawn nah deer), translated as "sometimes it's better to keep quiet"; literally, "the truth is sometimes better left unsaid." And finally, **la vérité sort de la bouche des enfants** (sor duu lah boosh day zahn-FAHN), translated as "out of the mouths of babes" from Psalms—suggesting that children speak the truth—and literally translated as "truth comes out of the mouths of little children."

laver la tête à quelqu'un (lah-VAY lah tayt ah kayl-KœN)
give 'em hell
Variously translated as "reprimand," "haul someone over the coals," "give someone hell," and "give someone a dressing down"; literally, "wash someone's head."

la vertu n'irait pas si loin si la vanité ne lui tenait compagnie (lah vair-TÜ nee-RAY pah see lwan see lah vah-nee-TAY nəlwee tuu-NAY kawn-pah-NYEE)
virtue alone will not take you far
A sardonic maxim from La Rochefoucauld, translated literally as "virtue would not go so far if vanity did not keep it company."

la vie (lah vee)
life
Not unexpectedly, many pedestrian and not-so-pedestrian locutions are introduced by this phrase, including **la vie commune** (kaw-MÜN), translated as "conjugal life" and "life together"; **la vie est un combat de tous les jours** (ay tœn kawn-BAH duu too lay zhoor), translated as "life is a daily struggle" and, as the American writer Elbert Hubbard (1856–1915) put it, "life is just one damned thing after another"; less insightful is **la vie est une loterie** (ay tün law-TəREE), translated as "no one knows how life will turn out," "life is a game of chance," and, literally, "life is a lottery." And we all know how long the odds are against winning. The same thought is expressed by **la vie est une vallée de larmes** (ay tün vah-LAY duu lahrm), literally, "life is a vale of tears"; more poignant is **la vie m'est odieuse** (may toh-DYUHZ), translated as "life's not worth living," "I find life unbearable," and, literally, "life is hateful for

me." Finally, there is **la vie n'est pas drôle** (nay pah drohl), translated as "life is not a joke." Consider Henry Wadsworth Longfellow (1807–1882), who could always be counted on for an obvious thought, in "A Psalm of Life":

> *Life is real! Life is earnest!*
>   *And the grave is not its goal;*
> *Dust thou art, to dust returnest,*
>   *Was not spoken of the soul.*

l'eau va à la rivière (loh vah ah lah ree-VYAIR)
money goes to money
    Also translated, in a paraphrase of Matthew, as "to him that has shall more be given," and as "money makes money"; literally, "water flows to the river."

le beau monde (luu boh mawndə)
high society
    Also translated as "the fashionable world."

le bébé a fait son rot (luu bay-BAY ah fay sawn roh)
the baby has burped
    Finally!

le bonheur semble fait pour être partagé (luu bawn-NUHR sahnblə fay poor aytrə pahr-tah-ZHAY)
spread happiness wherever you go!
    A goody-two-shoes line from Racine, translated as "happiness seems made to be shared." Hallmark Cards, are you listening?

Le Bourgeois gentilhomme (luu boor-ZHWAH zhahn-tee-YUM)
commoner turned nobleman
    The title of a Molière play, in English called *The Would-be Gentleman*, usually translated as "the tradesman turned gentleman."

le champ est libre (luu shahn ay leebrə)
the coast is clear
    Literally, "the field is free."

le chantre d'Avon (luu chahntrə dah-VAWN)
the Bard of Avon
  Shakespeare himself.

l'échéance fatale (lay-shay-AHNSS fah-TAHL)
the day of reckoning
  Also translated as "the fatal date." Note that **échéance** also is translated as "expiration date" when discussing a driver's license and the like, but **l'échéance fatale** cannot be renewed.

le chemin de la gloire (luu shuu-MAN duu lah glwahr)
the path to glory
  But remember, as the English poet Thomas Gray (1716–1771) told us in his "Elegy Written in a Country Churchyard," "the paths of glory lead but to the grave." (See also AUCUN CHEMIN DE FLEURS NE CONDUIT À LA GLOIRE.)

le chemin de la ruine (luu shuu-MAN duu lah rween)
the road to ruin
  Unlike **chemin** in the previous entry, it is here translated as "road." Perhaps it's easier to travel the road to ruin than the path to glory.

le cheval de Troie (luu shuu-VAHL duu trwah)
the Trojan horse
  The horse celebrated by Virgil that held within it a contingent of Greek soldiers. When the Trojan guards of Troy dragged the horse through the city gates, the Greek soldiers were able to set fire to the city.

le chevalier de la Triste Figure (luu shuu-vah-LYAY duu lah treest fee-GÜR)
Don Quixote
  Literally, "knight of the woeful countenance," in Cervantes's great novel.

le chien a fait ses saletés dans la cuisine (luu shyan ah fay say sahlə-TAY dahn lah kwee-ZEEN)
the dog has done it again
  Euphemistically translated as "the dog has done its business in the kitchen." Literally, "the dog has made its dirt in the kitchen."

le coût (luu koo)
the cost

Two sayings, both expressing the same thought—don't look at the price if you want to enjoy something you buy or are about to dine at a fine restaurant—begin with these words: **le coût en ôte le goût** (ahn noht luu goo), translated as "the cost takes away the taste," and **le coût fait perdre le goût** (fay pairdrə luu goo), translated as "the cost makes one lose the taste."

le crime fait la honte, et non pas l'échafaud (luu kreem fay lah awntə ay nawn pah lay-shah-FOH)
the crime is the disgrace, not the punishment

These words by Corneille—literally "the crime makes the shame, not the scaffold"—were made famous when they were quoted in a letter written by Charlotte Corday, slayer of Marat, on the eve of her execution in July 1793. Jean-Paul Marat (1743–1793) was a French revolutionary and ally of Robespierre and Danton. Corday was one of the moderate Girondists who opposed Marat. She assassinated Marat by stabbing him while he was in his bath.

l'écume de la société (lay-KÜM duu lah saw-syay-TAY)
the bottom of the barrel

Also translated as "the dregs of society"; more literally, "the scum of society."

le dindon de la farce (luu dan-DAWN duu lah fahrss)
the patsy

Also translated as "the fool"; literally, "the turkey in the farce." In both French and English, the poor bird is either eaten with great gusto or used, as here, to derogate someone.

le fruit du travail est le plus doux plaisir (luu frwee dü trah-VĪYə ay luu plü doo play-ZEER)
hard work provides its own reward

A maxim of a French moralist and soldier, the marquis de Vauvenargues (1715–1747), telling us literally that "the fruit of toil is the sweetest pleasure."

le génie de la langue française (luu zhay-NEE duu lah lahngə frahn-SAYZ)
the genius of the French language

Who would disagree?

le génie est une longue patience (luu zhay-NEE ay tün lawngə pah-SYAHNSS)
genius is continuing patience
　　Close in meaning to the insight attributed to Thomas Edison, who defined genius as "one percent inspiration, ninety-nine percent perspiration."

le jeu n'en vaut pas la chandelle (luu zhuu nahn voh pah lah shahn-DAYL)
it's not worth the effort
　　Literally translated as "the game is not worth the candle," that is, the cost of the candle that provides light for the players.

Le Malade imaginaire (luu mah-LAHD ee-mah-zhee-NAIR)
The Hypochondriac
　　The title of Molière's last play, literally called "The Imaginary Invalid."

le mariage n'a pas été consommé (luu mah-RYAZH nah pah zay-TAY kawn-saw-MAY)
how about an annulment?
　　Literally translated as "the marriage hasn't been consummated."

le meilleur vin a sa lie (luu may-YUHR van ah sah lee)
all of us have faults
　　Literally translated as "even the best wine has its dregs." It's a fact.

le mieux est l'ennemi du bien (luu myuu ay laynə-MEE dü byan)
enough already!
　　Well translated as "leave well enough alone," literally as "better is the enemy of good." Sound advice for those inclined to rewrite, rewrite, and rewrite—send the manuscript off to your publisher!

le moi est haïssable (luu mwah ay ah-ee-SAHBLə)
egoism is odious
　　A saying attributed to the French mathematician Blaise Pascal (1623–1662); literally, "the word 'I' is hateful." The editorial "we" is worse.

le monde (luu mawndə)
world

At least three locutions begin with these words: **le monde est le livre des femmes** (ay luu leevrə day fahm), a saying attributed to Jean-Jacques Rousseau (1712–1778), and translated as "society is woman's book," literally, "the world is women's book"; **le monde récompense plus souvent les apparences du mérite que le mérite même** (ray-kawn-PAHNSS plü soo-VAHN lay zah-pah-RAHNSS dü may-REET kuu luu may-REET maym), a saying attributed to La Rochefoucauld, literally translated as "the world more often rewards the appearance of merit than merit itself"; and **le monde savant** (sah-VAHN), literally, "the learned world."

le mot juste (luu moh zhüst)
the appropriate expression
An expression so apt, literally "the exact word," that it has been adopted in English, with the French pronunciation. And why not? The appropriate expression is something to be sought after by writers everywhere and in any language.

l'empire c'est la paix (lahn-PEER say lah pay)
the empire is peace
Better translated as "the empire stands for peace," words used by Louis Napoleon, later Napoleon III, in a speech in 1852.

l'enfer est pavé de bonnes intentions (lahn-FAIR ay pah-VAY duu bawn zan-tahn-SYAWN)
the road to hell is paved with good intentions
In the English translation, a proverb dating from the eighteenth century. In Latin, in a somewhat different form, it can be found in Virgil. No matter the language used, we are being told to get busy and fulfill our obligations while we still are able.

le paradis (luu pah-rah-DEE)
the peanut gallery
In a theater, of course. Also given as **le dernier balcon** (luu dair-NYAY bahl-KAWN); literally, "the last balcony." Film devotees know the noun **paradis**, literally "heaven," in the classic *Les Enfants du paradis*, translated as *Children of Paradise*, but known everywhere by its French name.

le petit caporal (luu puu-TEE kah-paw-RAHL)
Napoleon

Literally translated as "the little corporal." Napoleon was a bit less than five feet two inches tall, proving that you don't have to be tall to be a giant among men.

le Petit Chaperon Rouge (luu puu-TEE shah-puu-RAWN roozh)
Little Red Riding Hood
The noun **chaperon**, it must be noted, means "chaperon" as well as "hood." So maybe if the girl had been properly chaperoned, she wouldn't have gotten into all that trouble.

le petit gain rempli la bourse (luu puu-TEE gan rahn-PLEE lah boorss)
penny by penny
The equivalent of the seventeenth-century English proverb "penny and penny laid up will be many" and translated as "small savings fill the purse"; literally, "a small gain fills the purse."

le petit oiseau va sortir (luu puu-TEE twah-ZOH vah sor-TEER)
watch the birdie
The classic advice given by amateur photographers; literally, "the little bird will appear."

le quartier latin (luu kahr-TYAY lah-TAN)
the Latin Quarter
Now considered a bohemian quarter, **le quartier latin** at first was the university area of Paris, explaining the origin of its name. Latin was the common language for the students who, beginning in about 1257, came to the Sorbonne, the University of Paris, from many countries in Europe.

le remède est pire que le mal (luu ruu-MAYD ay peer kuu luu mahl)
if it ain't broke, don't fix it
Translated as "the solution is worse than the problem"; literally, "the cure is worse than the disease."

le ridicule ne tue pas (luu ree-dee-KÜL nuu tü pah)
sticks and stones can break my bones
But "words can never harm me," also translated as "ridicule never killed anyone" and, nearly literally, as "ridicule is never fatal."

le roi (luu rwah)
the king

Giving us several interesting locutions, including **le roi est mort, vive le roi!** (ay mor veev luu rwah), translated as "the king is dead, long live the king!" Which tells us that as soon as a king dies, there's another monarch to take his place. To illustrate how powerful a king is, consider **le roi le veut** (luu vuu), translated as "the king wills it," a formula of royal assent—the argument is over. (See also LA REINE LE VEUT.) Then there is **le roi ne meurt pas** (nuu muhr pah), translated as "the king does not die," which takes us back to **le roi est mort, vive le roi!** indicating in a real way that the king does not die. Finally, there is the sardonic comment **le roi règne et ne gouverne pas** (raynyə ay nuu goo-VAIRNə pah), literally "the king reigns and does not govern," an observation attributed to French statesman Louis Thiers (1797–1877).

l'erreur est humaine (lay-RUHR ay tü-MAYN)
to err is human

This is the French translation of a Latin proverb, *humanum est errare*. The English poet Alexander Pope (1688–1744) picked up this thought in "An Essay on Criticism": "to err is human, to forgive divine."

les absents ont toujours tort (lay zahp-SAHN awn too-ZHOOR tor)
never miss an important meeting!

Literally translated as "the absent are always wrong," telling us that when finger-pointing time is at hand, the likeliest targets are those who are not present to defend themselves.

les affaires font les hommes (lay zah-FAIR fawn lay zawm)
business experience makes men

At least that is what we are led to believe.

le sage entend à demi mot (luu sahzh ahn-TAHN ah duu-MEE moh)
you don't have to explain things to a wise person

Literally, "the wise man understands at half a word."

les aristocrates à la lanterne! (lay zah-rees-taw-KRAHT ah lah lahn-TAIRN)
hang them all!

Better translated as "string the aristocrats up!"; literally, as "to the lamp-post with the aristocrats!" (See À LA LANTERNE! for the historical context of this cry.)

les beaux yeux de ma cassette (lay boh zyuu duu mah kah-SAYT)
money, money
    Literally, "the beautiful eyes of my cashbox," a line from Molière's play of 1668, *L'Avare* (*The Miser*).

les bons comptes font les bons amis (lay bawn kawntə fawn lay bawn zah-MEE)
good accounts make good friends

Les Bons Mots (lay bawn moh)
witticisms
    Written here with initial letters capitalized because this phrase is the title of the book you are reading. And all the intended witticisms of this book that fall flat may properly be blamed on the author.

les chiens aboient, la caravane passe (lay shyan ah-BWAH lah kah-rah-VAHN pahss)
let the world say what it will
    Literally, "the dogs bark, the procession moves on," a way of expressing scorn for opinions aired by others. Anyone who expresses this thought had better recall that dogs are also known to bite.

lèse-majesté (layz-mah-zhayss-TAY)
high treason
    In the good old days, when most people were ruled by monarchs, **lèse-majesté**—literally "injured majesty," and adopted in English as "lese (leez) majesty"—was a crime against the sovereign. Today this locution, in French and in English, may be applied to conduct seen as an attack on the customs, beliefs, or practices of an institution or person held in high esteem by most people.

le sens commun n'est pas si commun (luu sahnss kaw-MœN nay pah see kaw-MœN)
common sense is not so common
    An aphorism attributed to Molière.

le service est compris (luu sair-VEESS ay kawn-PREE)
no tip needed
   Translated as "the waiter's tip is included in the bill," usually abbreviated on French restaurant menus as **service compris.**

les événements n'attendent personne (lay zay-vaynə-MAHN nah-TAHNDə pair-SAWN)
time and tide wait for no man
   Literally translated as "events don't wait for anyone." The English proverb given above dates from the sixteenth century.

les extrêmes se touchent (lay zaykss-TRAYM suu toosh)
the extremes meet
   Suggesting that radical political or philosophical positions carried to extremes eventually coincide.

les fils d'une affaire (lay feel dün nah-FAIR)
all the gory details
   Also translated as "the ins and outs of a matter"; literally, "the threads of an affair." The noun **affaire** should not be interpreted here as "affair," as in "love affair." **Fils** here is the plural of **fil**, "thread," and is not to be confused with the singular noun **fils** (feess), meaning "son."

les grandes douleurs sont muettes (lay grahndə doo-LUHR sawn mü-AYT)
distrust public displays of grief
   Literally, "great sorrows are often silent." And, by implication, those given to loud wailing may not actually feel much grief.

les Halles (lay ahl)
Les Halles
   The noun **halle** means "market," and **les Halles**, never given in translation, was formerly the celebrated central wholesale food market of Paris. There, fresh produce, great slabs of beef, as well as other meats and foodstuffs arrived each night from all over France for display in great numbers before redistribution in the trucks of food merchants and restaurateurs. The nightly display also attracted visitors, especially tourists, interested in observing the brilliantly lighted bustle of this great market.

les humanités (lay zü-mah-nee-TAY)
the classics

Also translated as "the humanities."

les ides de mars (lay zeed duu mahrss)
the ides of March

In the ancient Roman calendar, the ides of March, May, July, and October were the fifteenth day of the month; the ides of the remaining months were the thirteenth of the month. The warning "beware the ides of March" achieved immortality when Shakespeare, in his play *Julius Caesar*—also reported in Plutarch—put these words into the mouth of a soothsayer attempting to warn Caesar of big trouble that lay ahead. That trouble, of course, proved to be the assassination that awaited him.

les jeux sont faits (lay zhuu sawn fay)
no more bets, please

Better translated as "the bets have been placed," but always spoken in French by the croupier at any classy roulette table to signal that action has begun and further bets will be refused—until the next turn of the wheel, of course. **Les jeux sont faits** is also taken to mean "the die is cast," in its figurative sense. Thus, when **les jeux sont faits**, there is no turning back.

les jours se suivent et ne se ressemblent pas (lay zhoor suu sweevə ay nuu suu rə-SAHNBLə pah)
tomorrow is a new day

Also translated as "every tomorrow will bring something new" and, almost literally, as "the days go by and each is different from the last."

les loups ne se mangent pas entre eux (lay loo nuu suu mahnzh pah ahntrə uu)
there is honor among thieves

A wry observation; literally, "wolves don't eat one another." Suggesting, of course, that people do—not literally, perhaps. Also given as **les loups ne se dévorent** (day-VOR) **pas entre eux**, with the same meaning.

les mauvais ouvriers ont toujours de mauvais outils (lay maw-VAY zoo-vree-YAY awn too-ZHOOR duu maw-VAY zoo-TEE)
blame yourself!

Better translated in the seventeenth-century English proverb "a bad workman quarrels with his tools," literally as "bad workmen always have bad tools."

Les Misérables (lay mee-zay-RAHBLə)
Les Misérables
Title of the panoramic novel published in 1862 by French novelist Victor Hugo (1802–1885). The title is never used in translation, literally "The Miserable Ones"—not even by the producers of the Broadway dramatization called *Les Misérables*.

les miséreux (lay mee-zay-RUU)
the destitute
Also translated as "the down-and-outs." The phrase is identical in meaning with **les misérables**. (See above.)

les murs ont des oreilles (lay mür awn day zaw-RAYə)
walls have ears
So, especially in this era of electronic bugs, be discreet.

les nerfs des batailles sont les pécunes (lay nair day bah-TĪYə sawn lay pay-KÜN)
money makes war possible
More literally translated as "money makes the sinews of war," a locution attributed to Rabelais. (Also given as L'ARGENT EST LE NERF DE LA GUERRE, which see.)

le soleil brille pour tout le monde (luu saw-LAYə breeyə poor too lə mawndə)
even the poor can enjoy sunshine
Better translated as the sixteenth-century English proverb "the sun shines upon all alike" or, literally, "the sun shines for everybody."

les oreilles ont dû vous tinter (lay zaw-RAYə awn dü voo tan-TAY)
someone's talking about you
Translated as "your ears must have been burning"; literally, "your ears must have been ringing." The infinitive **tinter**, "ring," strikes a familiar

chord—no pun intended—with devotees of Edgar Allan Poe, whose poem "The Bells" almost made "tintinnabulation" a household word.

les outrages du temps (lay zoo-TRAHZH dü tahn)
we all grow old
   Literally, "the ravages of time."

les paroles s'envolent, les écrits restent (lay pah-RAWL sahn-VAWL lay zay-KREE raystə)
think twice before putting anything in writing!
   Literally, "spoken words vanish into thin air, written ones remain forever." Unless a tape recorder is handy.

les petits ruisseaux font les grandes rivières (lay puu-TEE rwee-SOH fawn lay grahndə ree-VYAIR)
every little bit helps
   This proverb, given in English as "take care of the pennies and the dollars will take care of themselves," has the literal meaning "small streams make big rivers." And you can't argue with that. (See also GRANDES MAISONS SE FONT PAR PETITE CUISINE.)

les plaisanteries les plus courtes sont les meilleures (lay play-zahn-TəREE lay plü koort sawn lay may-YUHR)
keep it short, stupid
   Usually translated as Shakespeare put it in *Hamlet*: "brevity is the soul of wit," literally, "the shortest jokes are the best."

les plus sages ne le sont pas toujours (lay plü sahzh nuu luu sawn pah too-ZHOOR)
even the best of us make mistakes
   More literally translated as "the wisest are not always wise."

Les Précieuses ridicules (lay pray-SYUHZ ree-dee-KÜL)
The Ridiculous Snobs
   The title of Molière's one-act play satirizing the pretensions of admirers of the affectations of Parisian society.

les sanitaires (lay sah-nee-TAIR)
the bathroom
   An essential term for tourists in France.

les sept péchés capitaux (lay sayt pay-SHAY kah-pee-TOH)
the seven deadly sins
   Just to remind you, the seven deadly sins are pride, wrath, envy, lust, gluttony, avarice, and sloth. And, to quote from John, in the New Testament, "he that is without sin among you, let him first cast a stone at her."

le style est l'homme même (luu steel ay lawm maym)
the style is the man
   Popularly given as **le style, c'est** (say) **l'homme**, both translated literally as "the style is the man himself." So said French naturalist the comte de Buffon (1707–1788) on his election to the French Academy. (See also L'A-CADÉMIE FRANÇAISE.)

les vaches (lay vahsh)
the fuzz
   Choose your own favorite term for "policemen": "the bulls," "the cops," etc.; literally translated here as "the cows."

l'état, c'est moi (lay-TAH say mwah)
I'm in charge here
   Translated as "I am the government"; literally, "the state, it is I," a saying formerly attributed to French King Louis XIV (1638–1715).

l'état vous a à l'oeil (lay-TAH voo zah ah lœyə)
Big Brother is watching you
   The English novelist George Orwell (1903–1950) gave us this memorable catch phrase for government surveillance of citizens' every activity in *Nineteen Eighty-Four*. The French locution is translated as "the state has its eye on you."

le temps (luu tahn)
time
   Many locutions that begin with these two words are so well known that we may safely describe most of them as clichés. But that does not mean they are to be ignored. Consider **le temps c'est de l'argent** (say duu lahr-ZHAHN), usually translated as "time is money." This bit of wisdom, in English, is attributed to Benjamin Franklin, in the form "remember that time is money." A similar locution is **le temps perdu ne se rattrape jamais** (pair-DÜ nuu suu rah-TRAHPə zhah-MAY), translated as "time and tide

wait for no man," a sixteenth-century English proverb, and translated literally as "time lost is never regained." French novelist Marcel Proust
(1871–1922) tried anyway in his multivolume work *A la recherche du
temps perdu*, in French by no means a cliché; in English titled *Remembrance of Things Past*, literally "in search of lost time"—and far from a
cliché. The next three share a single meaning: **le temps console** (kawn-
SAWL), translated as "time heals all wounds," literally "time consoles,"
and given in a seventeenth-century English proverb as "time and thinking
tame the strongest grief"; **le temps efface tout** (ay-FAHSS too), translated
as "time heals all," literally "everything fades with time"; finally, there is **le
temps panse les blessures** (pahnss lay blay-SÜR), translated as "time heals
all wounds," literally, "time bandages wounds."

l'éternelle situation de trio (lay-tair-NAYL see-tü-ah-SYAWN duu tree-
YOH)
the eternal triangle
   This is the widely known situation of the amorous involvement of one
member of a married couple with another person of the opposite (or same?)
sex. (See also MÉNAGE À TROIS.)

l'étoile du nord (lay-TWAHL dü nor)
the North Star
   Literally, "the star of the north," motto of the state of Minnesota.

lettre de cachet (laytrə duu kah-SHAY)
letter under the seal of the sovereign
   Best translated as "unjust arrest warrant," a letter from the French king
ordering imprisonment, frequently without trial, of the person named in
the letter.

levée de boucliers (lə-VAY duu boo-klee-YAY)
hue and cry
   Also translated as "general outcry"; literally, "the raising of riot shields,"
alluding to a tactic seen to this day in France when police officers are
preparing to deal with rioters.

le ver est dans le fruit (luu vair ay dahn luu frwee)
the rot has already set in

Literally, "the worm is in the fruit." Shakespeare, in *Hamlet*, put it this way: "something is rotten in the state of Denmark."

Le véritable Amphitryon
Est l'Amphitryon où l'on dîne
(luu vay-ree-TAHBLə ahn-fee-tree-YAWN
ay lahn-fee-tree-YAWN oo lawn deen)
will the real host please stand up?

Molière's lines from his play *Amphitryon*, translated as "he who gives the feast is the real host" or "the provider of the feast is the real host"; literally, "the real Amphitryon is the Amphitryon where one dines." In Greek mythology, Amphitryon, husband of Alcmene, was away from home, giving Zeus the idea of assuming the likeness of Amphitryon in order to cuckold Amphitryon. When the Amphitryon impersonator gave a banquet, the real Amphitryon showed up and claimed the honor of being master of the house—in all respects. The dispute was settled when everyone present agreed that he who provided the feast was to them the host. Alcmene in due time gave birth to a son fathered by Zeus. The boy's name? Hercules. The moral? Always take your wife with you when you go on business trips.

le vin obscurcit les idées (luu van awb-skür-SEE lay zee-DAY)
drink muddles the brain
Literally, "wine obscures ideas."

l'exactitude est la politesse des rois (layg-zahk-tee-TÜDə ay lah paw-lee-TAYSS day rwah)
punctuality is the courtesy of kings
A statement attributed to French King Louis XVIII (1755–1824).

l'habit ne fait pas le moine (lah-BEE nuu fay pah lə mwahnə)
don't judge by appearances
Better translated as "clothes don't make the man"; literally, "the habit doesn't make the monk." In John, in the New Testament, we read "judge not according to the appearance, but judge righteous judgment." Couldn't have said it better.

l'homme (lawm)
man

As one might expect, with **l'homme** French gives us insight into human behavior, including: **l'homme est un loup pour l'homme** (ay tœn loo poor lawm), translated as "brother will turn on brother"; literally, "man is a wolf for man." Doesn't say much for the human race. Then we have two additional realistic locutions: **l'homme n'est ni ange ni bête** (nay nee ahnzh nee bayt), an observation attributed to Pascal and translated as "man is neither an angel nor a beast" (see also LE MOI EST HAÏSSABLE); and **l'homme ne vit pas seulement de pain** (nuu vee pah suhlə-MAHN duu pan), broadly translated as "there's more to life than ambition and commerce," literally as "man does not live by bread alone," and in Matthew, in the New Testament: "Man shall not live by bread alone, but by every word that proceedeth out of the mouth of God." Finally, there is **l'homme propose et Dieu dispose** (praw-POHZ ay dyuu dees-POHZ), translated as "man proposes, God disposes," a proverb attributed to many writers, among them Blaise de Montluc, a sixteenth-century French soldier.

l'homme doit se dépasser (lawm dwah suu day-pah-SAY)
so what have you done lately?

Literally, "man must try to surpass himself." The English poet Robert Browning (1812–1889) put it better in "Andrea del Sarto": "Ah, but a man's reach should exceed his grasp, Or what's a heaven for?"

liberté! égalité! fraternité! (lee-bair-TAY ay-gah-lee-TAY frah-tair-nee-TAY)
liberty! equality! fraternity!

Rallying cry of the French Republic. Although it is usually translated as given above, "fraternity" is better translated as "brotherhood."

liens d'amitié (lyan dah-mee-TYAY)
bonds of friendship

Liens is not to be confused with the English noun "lien," which is the legal claim of one person upon the property of another. Incidentally, the English noun "lien" is pronounced leen.

lire en diagonale (leer rahn dyah-gaw-NAHL)
skim through

A marvelous description, literally "read on the diagonal," of how some readers get through material they do not wish to read thoroughly.

lit (lee)
bed

As one might expect, the French have many types of beds, for example, **lit conjugal** (kawn-zhü-GAHL), translated as "marriage bed" or "conjugal bed" and carries the meaning of the bed a couple will occupy throughout their marriage; **lit de noces** (duu nawss), translated as "wedding bed," conveys the meaning of the bed in which a marriage is consummated. Then there is **lit de douleur** (duu doo-LUHR), translated as "bed of pain," which is not the type of bed one orders from a furniture catalog. A related term is **lit de mort** (duu mor), translated as "deathbed," which may or may not be a bed of pain. Then there is **lit de justice** (duu zhüss-TEESS), literally translated as "bed of justice" and better translated as "seat of justice," originally the bed on which the French king reclined during a formal session of **le parlement** (luu pahr-lə-MAHN), which was a judicial body and later became the term given to the session itself. When the king was present, he was considered the fount of justice. Finally, we have **lits superposés** (sü-pair-paw-ZAY), translated as "bunk beds"—and now we're really in a page of our furniture catalog.

littérature d'anticipation (lee-tay-rah-TÜR dahn-tee-see-pah-SYAWN)
science fiction
Literally, "literature of foreseeing."

l'occasion fait le larron (law-kah-ZYAWN fay luu lah-RAWN)
remember to lock your car door
Usually and quite literally translated as "opportunity makes the thief." (See also L'ABSENCE FAIT LE LARRON.)

loin des yeux loin du coeur (lwan day zyuu lwan dü kuhr)
out of sight, out of mind
Literally, "far from the eyes, far from the heart." (Before you become too unhappy over the absence of someone you love, see EN AMOUR L'ÉLOIGNEMENT RAPPROCHE.)

l'oreille basse (law-RAYə bahss)
crestfallen
Also translated as "dejected" and "downcast"; literally, "with lowered ear." The best translation of all, "with one's tail between one's legs," alludes to the canine response of a lowered tail as an indication of defeat or of un-

willingness to enter into a fight. The literal translation, "with lowered ear," recognizes a typical canine response—in a dog that is fixing to fight, its ears rise.

loup de mer (loo duu mair)
old salt
  Also translated as "old sea dog"; literally, "sea wolf." Shades of Jack London.

l'union fait la force (lü-NYAWN fay lah forss)
united we stand
  Literally, "union makes strength." Motto of Belgium.

M

macédoine de fruits (mah-say-DWAHN duu frwee)
medley
  Also translated as "hodgepodge" and, literally, "fruit salad." The literal meaning must not be overlooked. The noun "macédoine," borrowed from French, appears in English with something approximating the French pronunciation. Consult your favorite cookbook or a genial headwaiter for further elucidation.

macérer dans son ignorance (mah-say-RAY dahn sawn nee-nyaw-RAHNSS)
wallow in one's ignorance
  Literally, "soak in one's ignorance." The English verb "macerate," meaning "steep," is cognate with **macérer**.

ma chère (mah shair)
my dear
  The feminine form of MON CHER (which see).

ma chère amie (mah shair rah-MEE)
my dear friend
The feminine form of MON CHER AMI (which see).

ma chérie (mah shay-REE)
my darling
Also translated as "my dearest" and "my beloved." Feminine form of MON CHÉRI (which see).

ma foi! (mah fwah)
indeed!
Also translated as "upon my word!" Literally, "my faith!"

maigre comme un clou (maygrə kawm mœn kloo)
skinny
Also translated as "thin as a rail"; literally, "thin as a nail."

maillot de bain (mah-YOH də ban)
bathing suit
Also translated as "swimsuit." English has adopted "maillot," with the French pronunciation, to mean "tights" and "pullover" as well as "woman's swimsuit."

maison (may-ZAWN)
house or home
It is interesting to see the various types of houses or homes that arise from **maison**, for example, **maison close** (klohz), translated as "brothel," literally, "closed house"; **maison de campagne** (duu kahn-PAHNYə), translated as "country house"; **maison de jeu** (duu zhuu), literally translated as "house of play," best translated as "gambling house" or "casino." French also has the noun **casino** (ka-zee-NOH). Then there are **maison de passe** (duu pahss), translated as "hotel used as a brothel," and **maison de rendez-vous** (duu rahn-day-VOO), translated as "roadhouse," more literally, "discreet meeting place for lovers." The English noun "rendezvous," of course, has been borrowed from the French **rendez-vous**, with the French pronunciation preserved. But there are more uses of **maison**, including **maison de re-traite** (duu ruu-TRAYTə), translated as "old people's home," and **maison de santé** (duu sahn-TAY), translated as "nursing home" or "asylum." Fi-

nally, there is **maison de ville** (duu veel), translated as "town hall" and as "town house *or* residence."

maison grevée d'hypothèques (may-ZAWN gruu-VAY dee-paw-TAYK)
house mortgaged from top to bottom

Literally, "house put under strain by mortgages." In fact, it is the owners of the house that are put under considerable strain.

maître (maytrə)
master

This noun, sometimes an adjective, gives us several interesting phrases, including **maître chanteur** (shahn-TUHR), translated as "blackmailer," literally as "master singer"; **maître de cérémonie** (duu say-ray-maw-NEE), translated as "master of ceremonies"; **maître d'école** (day-KAWL), translated as "schoolmaster" and "teacher." A more sinister phrase is **maître des hautes oeuvres** (day ohtə zuhvrə), translated as "executioner," literally, "master of the high works," an allusion to the height of the guillotine before the blade's descent toward the neck of the person about to die. To close on a happier note, there is **maître Jacques** (zhahk), translated as "factotum" or "jack-of-all-trades," from a character in Molière's 1668 comedy *L'Avare* (*The Miser*), who served both as coachman and cook.

mal (mahl)
bad or *badly* or *with difficulty*

As might be expected, there are many less-than-positive phrases that begin with **mal**, including **mal à propos** (lah praw-POH), translated as "ill-timed," "out of place," "at the wrong moment," "inappropriately," and "inopportunely." Then there is **mal aux cheveux** (loh shə-VUU), translated as "hangover," more literally, "aching hair." (See also GUEULE DE BOIS.) Less devastating—sometimes—are **mal aux dents** (oh dahn), translated as "toothache," and **mal de dents** (duu dahn), with the same meaning. Just as bothersome are **mal de mer** (duu mair), translated as "seasickness," and **mal de tête** (duu tet), "headache." Then there is **mal du pays** (dü pay-EE), translated as "homesickness," which can range from severe to relatively mild in its manifestations. A pejorative way to describe someone is found in **mal éduqué** (lay-dü-KAY), translated as "badly brought up," "ill-bred," and "ill-mannered"; literally, "badly educated." (See also SANS ÉDUCATION.) Finally, there is a phrase that can lead to all sorts of dire consequences **mal entendu** (lahn-tahn-DÜ), translated as "ill-conceived," "ill-managed," and "misunderstood." (See also MALENTENDU.)

malaise (mah-LAYZ)
uneasiness
    Translated as "indisposition." English uses the noun "malaise," with the French pronunciation, to mean "vague, premonitory feeling of discomfort."

malentendu (mah-lahn-tahn-DÜ)
misunderstanding
    Also translated as "misconception" and "mistake." (See also MAL ENTENDU.)

malgré (mahl-GRAY)
despite or *in spite of*
    This preposition is used to introduce several common phrases, including **malgré lui et ses dents** (lwee ay say dahn), translated as "despite his opposition"; literally, "in spite of him and his teeth," which evokes an image of teeth clenched in determination or in obstinacy. Then there are **malgré nous** (noo), translated as "in spite of us," and **malgré soi** (swah), "in spite of oneself." Finally, all-inclusive is **malgré tout** (too), translated as "despite everything" or "in spite of everything."

malheur (mah-LUHR)
bad luck
    Also translated as "misfortune" or "calamity."

malin comme un singe (mah-LAN kum mœn sanzh)
mischievous as a barrel of monkeys
    Literally, "cunning as a monkey."

manger (mahn-ZHAY)
eat
    The metaphors and idioms stemming from this vital verb include **manger comme un cochon** (kawm mœn kaw-SHAWN), literally, "eat like a pig"; **manger comme un ogre** (kawm mœn awgrə), translated as "eat like a horse," literally, "eat like an ogre"; and **manger goulûment** (goo-lü-MAHN), translated as "wolf down food," literally, "eat gluttonously." By

contrast there is **manger comme un oiseau** (kawm mœn nwah-ZOH), literally, "eat like a bird." This metaphor overlooks the sloppiness shown by birds at a feeder, which almost seem to take delight in making a terrible mess. Now for **manger les pissenlits par la racine** (lay pee-sahn-LEE pahr lah rah-SEEN), translated as "push up the daisies"; literally, "eat dandelions by the roots." Whether you prefer the French or the English metaphor, both amount to "die and be buried." Less fatal is **manger ses mots** (say moh), best translated as "mumble" or "swallow one's words"; literally, "eat one's words." As every reader of this book knows, the meaning of the last translation is quite different from that of the identical English idiom. Two especially interesting idioms are **manger son blé en herbe** (sawn blay ahn nairbə), translated as "spend money one doesn't have" or "spend money before one has it," literally—and this is where it gets hairy—"eat one's wheat when it's unripe"; and, finally, **manger sur le pouce** (sür luu pooss), translated as "eat on the run" and "have a snack." The literal translation of this phrase is both "eat on the big toe" and "eat on the thumb." Figure that one out.

maniéré (mah-nyay-RAY)
affected or *having mannerisms*

manière (mah-NYAIR)
manner
Leading to several locutions, including **manière de parler** (duu pahr-LAY), translated as "manner of speaking," and as "mode *or* turn of expression." Then there is **manière de vivre** (duu veevrə), translated as "way of life"; literally, "way of living." Finally, there is **manière de voir les choses** (duu vwahr lay shohz), translated as "outlook," "opinion of things," and "view of things."

marais (mah-RAY)
swamp or *marsh*
A district of Paris favored by tourists is known as *le Marais*.

marcher à la voile et à la vapeur (mahr-SHAY ah lah vwahl ay ah lah vah-PUHR)
AC/DC
A fascinating idiom, translated usually as "be bisexual" and, literally, "proceed under sail and under steam."

mardi gras (mahr-DEE grah)
Shrove Tuesday

Literally, "fat Tuesday," in France the day before the fast of Lent. Formerly, a fat ox was paraded through the streets of Paris, accompanied by men masquerading as priests and by a band of musicians. In New Orleans, "Mardi Gras," pronounced as in French, is a day of merrymaking and carnival that makes any other traditional celebration look as tame as a child's first birthday party.

mariage (mah-RYAHZH)
marriage

A word that leads to many common phrases, including **mariage blanc** (blahn), translated as "unconsummated marriage," literally, "white marriage," the color white suggesting the intact virginity of the bride; **mariage d'amour** (dah-MOOR), translated—happily—as "love match," as is **mariage d'inclination** (dan-klee-nah-SYAWN), literally, "marriage of inclination"; the contrasting phrase **mariage d'argent** (dahr-ZHAHN) is translated as "money match," literally, "marriage for money"; now, getting quite serious about types of marriages, we have **mariage de conscience** (duu kawn-SYAHNSS), translated as "making it legal," literally, "marriage of conscience," denoting a marriage of persons who've been living together extralegally as man and wife; and **mariage de convenance** (duu kawn-VəNAHNSS), literally translated as "marriage of convenience," that is, a marriage contracted from motives of interest, usually financial and presumably satisfying both parties. Going back into history, we have **mariage de la main gauche** (duu lah man gohsh), translated as "morganatic marriage," literally, "a left-handed marriage." In a morganatic marriage—one between a man of high, usually royal, rank and a woman of lower station—the wife gave up any claim to her husband's rank or possessions. In addition, the children resulting from the marriage were not entitled to inherit their father's title or possessions. Such a marriage was called a left-handed marriage because the groom customarily pledged his fidelity with his left hand rather than his right. Something like crossing one's fingers while taking an oath. (See also SE MARIER DE LA MAIN GAUCHE.) Finally, we have the conventional **mariage religieux** (ruu-lee-ZHYUU), translated as "church wedding"; literally, "religious marriage."

mari dominé par sa femme (mah-REE daw-mee-NAY pahr sah fahm)
henpecked husband

Literally, "husband dominated by his wife." (See also IL SE LAISSE DOMINER PAR SA FEMME.)

marmite surveillée ne bout jamais (mahr-MEET sür-vay-YAY nuu boo zhah-MAY)
don't be impatient!
Good advice, well translated as "watching and anxiety won't hasten matters," literally as in the nineteenth-century English proverb "a watched pot never boils." It should be noted that English children are fond of a proprietary product named Marmite, which is made from fresh brewer's yeast. This brown spread, like our own jelly or jam, is eaten on bread or toast but lacks the sweetness we find so palatable.

marraine de guerre (mahr-RAYN duu gair)
pen pal
Literally, "a wartime godmother," that is, a woman who writes to a soldier on active duty—often one she hasn't even met.

marron glacé (mahr-RAWN glah-SAY)
marron glacé
A delicious confection, literally, "glazed chestnut," but never called anything but "marron glacé" and pronounced as in French.

m'as-tu vu? (mah-TÜ vü)
a show-off
An interesting locution, also translated as "egocentric person"; literally, "have you seen me?" The equivalent of "ain't I great?"

ma tante (mah tahnt)
pawnshop
Literally, "my aunt." In English and American slang, a pawnbroker is often called "uncle." Family, after all, can be counted on to help when a small loan is needed. (See also MONT-DE-PIÉTÉ.)

matériel de guerre (mah-tay-RYAYL duu gair)
weaponry
Literally, "war equipment." The noun **matériel** has been taken into English, with the meaning of **matériel de guerre**, as "matériel" or "materiel"

(both pronounced mə-teer-ee-EL), giving sadistic spelling masters ammunition for use in a spelling bee.

mauvais (maw-VAY)
bad

This adjective and its feminine form **mauvaise** (maw-VAYZ) introduce many common expressions, including **mauvais goût** (maw-VAY goo), translated as "bad taste"; **mauvaise herbe** (maw-VAYZ zehrb), translated as "weed"; **mauvaise honte** (maw-VAYZ awnt), translated as "bashfulness" or "diffidence," literally, "false shame"; **mauvaise langue** (maw-VAYZ lahngə), translated as "gossip" or "scandalmonger," literally, "evil tongue"; **mauvaise odeur** (maw-VAYZ zaw-DUHR), translated as "bad or unpleasant smell"; **mauvaise plaisanterie** (maw-VAYZ play-zahn-TəREE), translated as "dirty trick" or "ill-timed jest"; **mauvais esprit** (maw-VAY zayss-PREE), translated as "troublemaker," literally, "bad mind"; **mauvais garçon** (maw-VAY gahr-SAWN), translated as "tough" or "ruffian," literally, "bad boy"; **mauvais lieu** (maw-VAY lyuu), translated as "dive" or "place of ill repute"; **mauvais pas** (maw-VAY pah), translated as "bad situation" or "tight spot," literally, "bad step"; **mauvais présage** (maw-VAY pray-ZAHZH), translated as "bad vibes," "ill omen," or "evil portent"; **mauvais quart d'heure** (maw-VAY kahr duhr), describing a brief but unpleasant time or experience, and translated as "bad spell," literally, "bad quarter of an hour"; **mauvais renom** (maw-VAY ruu-NAWN), translated as "bad reputation"; **mauvais rêve** (maw-VAY rayvə), translated as "nightmare," literally, "bad dream"; **mauvais sang** (maw-VAY sahn), translated as "ill feeling," literally, "bad blood"; **mauvais sujet** (maw-VAY sü-ZHAY), translated as "black sheep," "ne'er-do-well," "bad lot," or "worthless fellow," literally, "bad subject"; **mauvais ton** (maw-VAY tawn), translated as "vulgarity," "bad taste," or "ill breeding," literally, "bad tone"; **mauvais traitements à enfants** (maw-VAY traytə-MAHN ah ahn-FAHN), translated as "child abuse" or "child battering," literally, "bad treatment of children"; finally, **mauvais vouloir** (maw-VAY voo-LWAHR), translated as "ill will."

médecin, guéris-toi toi-même (maydə-SAN gay-ree-TWAH twah-MAYM)
physician, heal thyself

A proverb intended to convey a message to the rest of us, as well as to doctors. Luke, in the New Testament, here tells us to take care of our own problems before daring to tell others how they should behave. Talk-show hosts: heed this message!

méfiez-vous des contrefaçons (may-fyay-VOO day kawn-trə-fah-SAWN)
don't buy a Rolex from a street vendor
Literally, "distrust forgeries."

mélange (may-LAHNZH)
mixture
Also translated as "miscellany" or "medley." **Mélange** has been taken into English with its meaning and pronunciation unchanged.

melon d'eau (muu-LAWN doh)
watermelon
Included here only to point out that this great fruit is not exclusively American.

mémoire (may-MWAHR)
memoir
Also translated as "personal narrative" or "short autobiography."

mémoire de lièvre (may-MWAHR duu lyayvrə)
treacherous memory
Literally, "hare's memory."

ménage (may-NAHZH)
household
Also translated as "housekeeping" and "household management," leading to a well-known phrase that has been taken into English but is pronounced as in French: **ménage à trois** (may-NAHZH ah trwah), literally, "household of three," but never translated in English. This phrase denotes an arrangement in which three adults having sexual relations share living quarters, for example, husband, wife, and wife's lover; and husband, wife, and husband's lover. (See also L'ÉTERNELLE SITUATION DE TRIO.)

ménager la chèvre et le chou (may-nah-ZHAY lah shayvrə ay luu shoo)
sit on the fence
The ultimate in objectivity—indecisiveness?—also translated as "refuse to take sides"; literally, "treat both goat and cabbage with care." The allusion is to the legendary proclivity of goats to eat almost anything in sight.

mener (muu-NAY)
lead

Several common phrases begin with this infinitive: **mener quelqu'un par le bout du nez** (kayl-KœN pahr luu boo dü nay), translated as "lead someone around by the nose," literally, "lead someone by the end of the nose"; **mener une vie cachée** (ün vee kah-SHAY), translated as "lead a secret life," literally, "lead a hidden life"; **mener une vie de désordre** (ün vee duu day-ZORDRə), translated as "lead a dissolute life"; and, finally, **mener une vie de pacha** (ün vee duu pah-SHAH), translated as "live high off the hog," "live it up," or "live like a king," literally, "live like a pasha." You pays your money and you chooses your metaphor.

menteur patenté (mahn-TUHR pah-tahn-TAY)
thoroughgoing liar

Also translated as "congenital liar," literally and colorfully translated as "licensed liar."

menu (muu-NÜ)
petty or *trifling*

This adjective and its feminine form, **menue**, pronounced identically, as are their plural forms, give us several interesting phrases, including **menue monnaie** (maw-NAY), translated as "loose change" and "small change"; **menu gibier** (zhee-BYAY), translated as "small game," referring to animals that are hunted for food; and, finally, two related phrases, **menus frais** (fray), translated as "incidental expenses" or "minor expenses," and **menus plaisirs** (play-ZEER), translated as "incidental expenditures for personal use," literally, "little pleasures."

mère (mair)
mother

The first word of several phrases, including **mère célibataire** (say-lee-bah-TAIR), translated as "unmarried mother"; **mère patrie** (pah-TREE), translated as "motherland"; **mère porteuse** (por-TUHZ), translated as "surrogate mother," which is also given as **mère de substitution** (duu süb-stee-tüss-YAWN), literally, "substitute mother"; and, finally, **mère poule** (pool), translated as "motherly type," literally, "mother hen."

mésalliance (may-zah-LYAHNSS)
misalliance

The term used to denote a marriage with someone considered to be of lower social standing.

mesurer le châtiment à l'offense (muu-zü-RAY luu shah-tee-MAHN ah law-FAHNSS)
make the punishment fit the crime
Evocative of the Mikado's resolve in Gilbert and Sullivan's *Mikado*:

> My *object all sublime*
> *I shall achieve in time* —
> *To let the punishment fit the crime* —
> *The punishment fit the crime.*

(See also OEIL POUR OEIL, DENT POUR DENT.)

mettre (maytrə)
put
An infinitive that leads us into several idiomatic expressions, including **mettre de l'eau dans son vin** (duu loh dahn sawn van), translated as "settle for less" and "lower one's pretensions"; literally, "put water in one's wine." And everyone knows that the result will be a drink less powerful than the undiluted offering. Then there are **mettre en question** (ahn kayss-TYAWN), translated as "doubt," more literally, "call into question"; **mettre en vente** (ahn vahntə), translated as "offer for sale" and "put up for sale"; **mettre la charrue avant les boeufs** (lah shah-RÜ ah-VAHN lay buu), idiomatically translated as "put the cart before the horse"—even though **boeufs** translates literally as "oxen"—and conventionally translated as "reverse the natural order of things" in argument, work, and the like; **mettre le loup dans la bergerie** (luu loo dahn lah bair-zhuu-REE), translated as "set the fox to guard the henhouse," literally, "put the wolf inside the sheep enclosure"; **mettre les pieds dans le plat** (lay pyay dahn luu plah), translated as "put one's foot down," almost literally as "put both feet in the dish"; **mettre les points sur les i** (lay pwahn sür lay zee), translated as "be meticulous," "spell everything out," and "dot the i's and cross the t's," even though the French speak only of dotting the i's; **mettre le verrou** (luu vay-ROO), translated as "lock the door," more literally, "bolt the door"; **mettre quelque chose sous haute surveillance** (kaylkə shohz soo ohtə sür-vay-YAHNSS), translated as "keep your eyes peeled" or "maintain a close watch on something"; **mettre quelqu'un au supplice** (kayl-KœN oh sü-

PLEESS), translated as "torture someone," more literally, "subject someone to torture"; **mettre quelqu'un dans le secret** (kayl-KœN dahn luu suu-KRAY), translated as "blab," "spill the beans" or, literally, "let somebody in on the secret"; **mettre quelqu'un dans sa poche** (kayl-KœN dahn sah pawsh), translated as "twist someone around one's little finger," "have complete influence over someone" or, more literally, "have someone in one's pocket," which turns out to be entirely idiomatic English; **mettre quelqu'un en boîte** (kayl-KœN ahn bwahtə), translated as "put someone on," "pull someone's leg" or, literally, "put someone in a box"; **mettre quelqu'un en colère** (kayl-KœN ahn kaw-LAIR), translated as "make someone angry"; **mettre quelqu'un sous les verrous** (kayl-KœN soo lay vay-ROO), translated as "put someone in the pokey," "lock someone up," "put someone behind bars," "put someone under lock and key," and, literally, "put someone under bolts"; **mettre sens dessus dessous** (sahn dəsü dəsoo), translated as "turn upside down," literally, "turn above below"; and, finally, **mettre sur le tapis** (sür luu tah-PEE), translated as "put on the table," literally, "put on the tablecloth."

mieux (myuu)
better

Better than what? See the following: **mieux que jamais** (kuu zhah-MAY), translated as "better than ever"; **mieux vaut prévenir que guérir** (voh pray-VəNEER kuu gay-REER), translated as "prevention is better than cure," literally, "prevention is worth more than cure"; **mieux vaut tard que jamais** (voh tahr kuu zhah-MAY), translated as "better late than never"; and, finally, **mieux vaut tenir que courir** (voh tuu-NEER kuu koo-REER), translated as "a bird in the hand is worth two in the bush," much more literally as "it's better to hold something than to run after something."

miné par la jalousie (mee-NAY pahr lah zhah-loo-ZEE)
consumed with jealousy

A trite metaphor, perhaps better translated literally as "eroded by jealousy."

mise en scène (meez zahn sayn)
stage setting

Also translated as "production" and, by extension, "the surroundings against which anything is seen."

misère (mee-ZAIR)
poverty
 While poverty is always poverty, we may distinguish at least two important types: **misère dorée** (daw-RAY), literally, "splendid poverty," which
suggests a certain dignity achieved by virtue of the character of a person so
afflicted; and **misère noire** (nwahr), "utter destitution." So while poverty
may always be poverty, we should examine the situations of those so entrapped.

miser sur le mauvais cheval (mee-ZAY sür luu maw-VAY shə-VAHL)
back the wrong horse
 Also translated as "bet on a loser."

mistral (meess-TRAHL)
mistral
 The cold, dry, northerly wind experienced from the Rhône
Valley down into southern France; in English also called "mistral," without change in pronunciation.

mitrailler quelqu'un de questions (mee-trah-YAY kayl-
KœN duu kayss-TYAWN)
bombard with questions
 Also translated as "fire questions at someone." Literally, "machine-gun
someone with questions." The French are better at describing what goes on
at some press conferences.

moins on en dit mieux on se porte (mwan awn nahn dee myuu awn sə
portə)
the less said, the better
 A fifteenth-century English proverb put the thought this way: "least
said, soonest mended."

mon ami (mawn nah-MEE)
my friend
 The feminine form is **mon amie**, pronounced identically.

mon cher (mawn shair)
my dear
 This is the masculine form. (For the feminine form see MA CHÈRE.)

mon cher ami (mawn shair rah-MEE)
my dear friend
This is the masculine form. The feminine form is MA CHÈRE AMIE (which see).

mon chéri (mawn shay-REE)
my beloved
Also translated as "my darling" and "my dearest." (See also MA CHÉRIE.)

mon Dieu! (mawn dyuu)
heavens!
Also translated as "good heavens!" or "my goodness!" and, literally, "my God!"

mon oncle est un minus (mawn nawnklə ay tœn mee-NÜSS)
he's a dead loss
Better translated as "my uncle's a useless specimen," literally as "my uncle's a minus."

mon père, je m'accuse d'avoir péché (mawn pair zhuu mah-KÜZ dah-VWAHR pay-SHAY)
Father, I have sinned
Words heard in the confessional.

mon petit chou (mawn pətee shoo)
my little darling
Literally, "my little cabbage." What's with the French obsession with cabbages?

mon petit lapin (mawn pətee lah-PAN)
my sweetheart
Also translated as "my little lamb," even though the literal translation is "my little rabbit." A small difference between two cultures.

mont-de-piété (mawn duu pyay-TAY)
pawnshop
Literally, "mount of piety," called in Italian *monte di pietà*, literally, "mount of compassion" or "mount of piety." The Italian term reflects the

establishment of municipal pawnshops in sixteenth-century Rome as an act of charity by the sponsors, who helped the poverty-stricken escape from usury by enabling them to borrow at low interest rates.

monter en amazone (mawn-TAY ahn nah-mah-ZOHN)
ride sidesaddle

An interesting idiom, literally translated as "ride in the style of an Amazon." The noun **amazone** is variously translated as "horsewoman" or "athlete" or "virago," the last being a pejorative term. The proper noun **Amazone** means "Amazon"—the mythical female warrior as well as the South American river.

morceau (mor-SOH)
bit or *piece* or *morsel*

A noun that is part of several interesting idioms, including **morceau de roi** (duu rwah), translated as "a bit fit for a king," literally, "king's morsel"; **morceau honteux** (awn-TUU), translated as "last piece," literally, "shameful morsel," indicating the last bit of food on a dish at table, which customarily is left untouched to show good manners; **morceau pour violon** (poor vyoh-LAWN), translated as "piece for the violin"; and a plural phrase, **morceaux choisis** (mor-SOH shwah-ZEE), translated as "selected extracts or passages."

mordre la poussière (mordrə lah poo-SYAIR)
bite the dust

Could the Hollywood Western, long favored by Parisian moviegoers, have left its mark on the French language in this idiomatic way of saying "die"?

mort aux vaches! (mor roh vahsh)
down with the cops!

Literally, "death to the cows!" We, of course, prefer to call police officers "cops" and, pejoratively, "pigs" or "bulls."

mort volontaire (mor vaw-lawn-TAIR)
suicide

Literally, "voluntary death."

morue (maw-RÜ)
whore
Also translated as "cod"—the fish, that is.

mot (moh)
word
This noun leads us into several useful expressions, including **mot à mot** (moh tah moh) and **mot pour mot** (moh poor moh), both translated as "literally" or "word for word"; also **mot corrompu par l'usage** (moh kor-rawn-PÜ pahr lü-ZAHZH), literally "word corrupted by usage"—a verbal handwringer's idea. (You and I, not words, are susceptible to corruption. But what would William Safire and other popular commentators on language do if they were denied the pleasure of decrying trends in usage?) On to three more expressions: **mot grossier** (moh graw-SYAY), translated as "dirty word," more literally, "coarse word"; **mots croisés** (moh krwah-ZAY), translated as "crossword puzzle," literally, "crosswords"; and, finally, **mot-valise** (moh vah-LEEZ), translated as "portmanteau word" or "blend," both meaning a word made by putting together parts of other words, as in the English word "motel," which is a blend of "motor" and "hotel." Incidentally, the French word **portemanteau** (port-mahn-TOH) means "coatrack" or "coat hanger," literally, "carries the cloak." And from it we have the English word "portmanteau"—literally "valise." Does all this increase your sense of well-being?

moules marinières (mool mah-ree-NYAIR)
moules marinières
Restaurant menus and cookbooks offer no English translation for this example of French cookery, literally translated as "mussels in smocks." The term appears to allude to the fact that in preparing this dish, the mussels are not removed from their shells—thought to resemble smocks—thus making use of their natural juice, to which wine and shallots are added.

moulin à paroles (moo-LAN ah pah-RUHL)
chatterbox
Literally, "word mill," giving us a vivid mental image of words being ground up and ejected rapidly and incessantly.

mourir (moo-REER)
die

How many ways can one die? Read on. First there is **mourir à la tâche** (ah lah tahsh), translated as "die in harness," literally, "die at one's work"; **mourir debout** (duu-BOO), translated as "die with one's boots on," literally, "die standing," and this, according to some historians, is the actual way in which Elizabeth I, queen of England, died; **mourir de malemort** (duu mahlə-MOR), translated as "die a violent death," literally, "die a cruel death"; **mourir d'ennui** (dahn-NWEE)—only a figurative death—translated as "be bored to death," literally, "die of boredom"; **mourir de vieillesse** (duu vyay-YAYSS), translated as "die of old age"; **mourir en héros** (ahn ay-ROH), translated as "die a hero's death"; **mourir sans postérité** (sahn pawss-tay-ree-TAY), a sad way to die, translated as "die childless" or "die without issue"; finally, another sad way to die, **mourir sur la paille** (sür lah pīyə), translated as "die dead broke," "die without a penny to one's name," and "die penniless," literally, "die on the straw." Not a pleasant bed to lie or die in.

muet (mü-AY)
silent

A word that lends itself to metaphor, for example, **muet comme un poisson** (kawm œn pwah-SAWN), translated as "silent as a fish"; **muet comme une tombe** (kawm ün tawnbə), translated as "silent as the grave"; and **muet de peur** (duu puhr), translated as "struck dumb with fear," more literally, "silent because of fear."

nager entre deux eaux (nah-ZHAY ahntrə duu zoh)
keep a foot in both camps
    Literally, "swim between two bodies of water," and also translated as "swim underwater."

nécessité fait loi (nay-say-see-TAY fay lwah)
beggars can't be choosers
    Also translated as "any port in a storm" and "necessity knows no law"; more literally, "necessity makes its own law." The message is, when you're up against it, accept whatever price or terms are offered. Better yet, take steps in timely fashion to make sure you don't get into such a fix.

ne pas avoir deux sous de jugeote (nuu pah zah-VWAHR duu soo duu zhü-ZHAWT)
not have an ounce of common sense
    Literally, "not have two cents' worth of common sense." Take your choice: either weigh or count common sense.

ne réveillez pas le chat qui dort (nuu ray-vay-YAY pah luu shah kee dor)
let well enough alone
    Best translated as the fourteenth-century English proverb "let sleeping dogs lie"; literally, "don't wake up a sleeping cat." Why a French cat? For that matter, why an English dog?

n'est-ce pas? (nayss pah)
isn't it?
    An idiomatic phrase that appears frequently in French. Also translated as "doesn't it?" and as similar rhetorical questions.

nez retroussé (nay ruu-troo-SAY)
turned-up nose
    Literally. Not as a sign of disdain.

noblesse oblige (naw-BLAYSS aw-BLEEZH)
rank imposes obligations
This French maxim, often used in English and pronounced almost as in French, is literally translated as "nobility obliges." It usually is expanded to "nobility *or* rank imposes its own obligations," and the obligations are to conduct oneself honorably, be magnanimous, show courtesy, and the like.

nom (nawn)
name
As you might expect, there are various types of names, including **nom de demoiselle** (duu də-mwah-ZAYL), translated as "maiden name," literally, "young lady's name"; **nom de famille** (duu fah-MEEYə), translated as "surname," literally, "family name"; **nom de guerre** (duu gair), translated as "pseudonym," literally, "war name"; **nom de plume** (duu plüm), translated as "pen name," but often used in English as "nom de plume" and pronounced nom duu PLOOM; **nom de théâtre** (duu tay-AHTRə), translated as "stage name," literally, "theater name"; and **nom emprunté** (awn-pruhn-TAY), translated as "assumed name," literally, "borrowed name."

nos vertus ne sont le plus souvent que des vices déguisés (noh vair-TÜ nuu sawn luu plü soo-VAHN kuu day veess day-gee-ZAY)
our virtues often are only vices in disguise
Irony from La Rochefoucauld.

nous avons tous assez de force pour supporter les maux d'autrui (noo zah-VAWN tooss ah-SAY duu forss poor sü-por-TAY lay moh doh-TRWEE)
as long as we're not suffering!
An ironic maxim of La Rochefoucauld, literally translated as "we all have strength enough to bear the misfortunes of others."

nous dansons sur un volcan (noo dahn-SAWN sür rœn vawl-KAHN)
we're rearranging the deck chairs on the Titanic
An aphorism, literally, "we are dancing on a volcano," that comes to mind whenever serious social unrest appears imminent or, more often in our troubled times, when family problems threaten to get out of hand. **Nous dansons sur un volcan** is reported to have been uttered at a ball in

Paris just before the revolution of 1830, which brought about street riots and the abdication of Charles X, last of the Bourbon rulers. Volcano indeed! (See also next entry.)

nous sommes assis sur un volcan (noo sawm zah-SEE sür rœn vawl-KAHN)
we're sitting on a powder keg
Literally, "we're sitting on a volcano." Either way, someone prescient sees trouble brewing. (See also previous entry.)

nous sommes tous dans la même galère (noo sawm tooss dahn lah maym gah-LAIR)
we're in this together
Literally, "we're all in the same galley *or* boat." The same thought is conveyed by **nous sommes tous dans le même bain** (noo sawm tooss dahn luu maym ban); literally, "we're all in the same bath." And you can bet that when either of these statements is made, the outlook is not at all good.

nous verrons ce que nous verrons (noo vay-RAWN suu kuu noo vay-RAWN)
what will be will be
Literally, "we shall see what we shall see." The future, that is, cannot reliably be foreseen.

nous voguons, frêle esquifs au gré du hasard (noo vaw-GAWN frayl layss-KEEF oh gray dü ah-ZAHR)
we drift along, fragile skiffs on the waters of fate
Poetic recognition of human frailty.

nouveau riche (noo-VOH reesh)
upstart
A phrase often used in English, with French pronunciation, to denote "one newly rich" or "a wealthy parvenu." (See also PARVENU.)

nouvelle vague (noo-VAYL vahgə)
the latest thing
Literally, "new wave," used especially to denote the film and literary phenomenon that flourished during the 1950s.

noyer le poisson (nwah-YAY luu pwah-SAWN)
duck the question
Also translated as "sidestep the question"; literally, "drown the fish," meaning introduce a red herring into a discussion.

nuit blanche (nwee blahnsh)
sleepless night
Literally, "white night." Another way of conveying the meaning of "sleepless night" is **nuit sans sommeil** (nwee sahn saw-MAYə, literally, "night without sleep."

nul bien sans peine (nül byan sahn payn)
no gain without pain
We must be prepared to work hard if we wish to succeed in any field. Also given as "no pain, no gain."

nul n'est censé ignorer la loi (nül nay sahn-SAY ee-nyaw-RAY lah lwah)
ignorance of the law is no excuse
The verb form **être censé** translates literally as "be supposed to." Yet another demonstration of how frustrating it is to take a French idiom apart.

nul n'est prophète en son pays (nül nay praw-FAYT ahn sawn pay-EE)
no man is a prophet in his own country
See Matthew, in the New Testament, "A prophet is not without honor, save in his own country, and in his own house."

O

objet d'art (awb-ZHAY dahr)
art object
Also translated as "object of artistic value," but often given in English as "objet d'art," with the French pronunciation approximated as best as one can manage.

objet sans prix (awb-ZHAY sahn pree)
priceless object

occupe-toi de tes affaires (aw-küp-TWAH duu tay zah-FAIR)
mind your own business
   Also given as **occupe-toi de tes oignons** (tay zaw-NYAWN), literally, "mind your own onions."

odalisque (aw-dah-LEESK)
concubine
   This term is included because so many painters have painted attractive models posed as **odalisques**—with the same word used in English without change, but pronounced OHD-ə-lisks—female slaves or concubines in a sultan's seraglio.

oeil pour oeil, dent pour dent (œyə poor œyə dahn poor dahn)
let the punishment fit the crime
   Almost literally, "an eye for an eye, a tooth for a tooth," a truncation of the line from Exodus, in the Old Testament: "thou shalt give life for life, eye for eye, tooth for tooth, hand for hand, foot for foot." (See also MESURER LE CHÂTIMENT À L'OFFENSE.)

oeuf (uhf)
egg
   In the plural, **oeufs**, the pronunciation changes, as you will see. But no matter how the word is pronounced, how do you take your eggs? Try **oeufs au lard** (uu oh lahr), "bacon and eggs"; **oeufs brouillés** (uu broo-YAY), "scrambled eggs"; or **oeufs pochés** (uu paw-SHAY), "poached eggs." No matter what style is your favorite, try to make sure you get **oeufs frais** (uu fray), "new-laid eggs."

oeuvre (uhvrə)
work
   Especially work of art or literature, also taken to denote a substantial body of work constituting the lifework of a writer, composer, or artist. (See also CHEF-D'OEUVRE.)

oisiveté forcée (wah-zee-VəTAY for-SAY)
forced idleness or *inactivity*
   Two euphemisms for "layoff." Ugh!

on aurait entendu voler une mouche (awn naw-RAY ahn-tahn-DÜ vaw-LAY ün moosh)
you could have heard a pin drop
> Literally, "you could have heard a fly fly." Which language says it better?

on commence par être dupe, on finit par être fripon (awn kaw-MAHNSS pahr aytrə düpə awn fee-NEE pahr aytrə free-PAWN)
you begin as a dupe and end up as a rogue
> So steer clear of unsavory schemes.

on connaît le véritable ami dans le besoin (awn kawn-NAY luu vay-ree-TAHBLə ah-MEE dahn luu buu-ZWAN)
a friend in need is a friend indeed
> Literally, "you know a true friend in time of need." The other friends, so-called, avoid you completely.

on dit (awn dee)
they say
> Also translated as "people say." (See also ON-DIT.)

on-dit (awn-DEE)
rumor
> This noun is also translated as "piece of hearsay."

on dit que Dieu est toujours pour les gros bataillons (awn dee kuu dyuu ay too-ZHOOR poor lay groh bah-tah-YAWN)
be prepared!
> Voltaire's cynical observation; literally, "they say God is always on the side of the big battalions."

on est dans la merde (awn nay dahn lah mairdə)
up the creek without a paddle
> Also translated as "we're in an awful mess," more literally as "we're in deep shit."

on lui a fait un lavage d'estomac (awn lwee ah fay œn lah-VAHZH dayss-taw-MAH)
he had his stomach pumped out

Literally, "he had his stomach washed out." Sounds better than "pumped out," but don't let this fool you.

on n'apprend pas à un vieux singe à faire des grimaces (awn nah-PRAHN pah zah œn vyuu sanzh ah fair day gree-MAHSS)
some people never learn
   Also translated as "you can't teach an old dog new tricks"; literally, "you can't teach an old monkey to make funny faces."

on n'a rien sans risque (awn nah ryan sahn reesk)
there's no free lunch
   Also translated as "nothing ventured, nothing gained" or, as in a fifteenth-century English proverb, "nothing venture, nothing win"; more literally, "nothing is free of risk." (See also QUI NE RISQUE RIEN N'A RIEN.)

on n'attrappe pas les mouches avec du vinaigre (awn nah-TRAHPə pah lay moosh ah-VAYK dü vee-NAYGRə)
sweet talk can be effective
   Literally, "you don't catch flies with vinegar."

on ne fait pas d'omelette sans casser les oeufs (awn nuu fay pah daw-MəLAYT sahn kah-SAY lay zuu)
you can't get something for nothing
   This French wisdom has made its literal way into English, with the familiar "you can't make an omelet without breaking eggs." Anyone who wants to accomplish something must be willing to make whatever sacrifices are called for. This same thought is given by **on ne fait rien pour rien** (awn nuu fay ryan poor ryan), translated as "you can't get anything for nothing," literally, "one does nothing for nothing."

on ne m'y prend plus (awn nuu mee prahn plü)
you won't fool me again
   Also translated as "I won't be taken in anymore." Let's hope so.

on ne peut pas . . . (awn nuu puu pah)
you can't . . .
   And, of course, one asks you can't do what? To answer the question we have several interesting expressions, including **on ne peut pas forcer les**

gens (for-SAY lay zhahn), translated as "you may lead a horse to water but you can't make it drink," also translated as "you can provide opportunity, but you can't force people to take it," more literally, "you can't compel people"; and **on ne peut pas plaire à tout le monde** (plair rah too lə mawndə), translated as "you can't please everybody," literally, "you can't be liked by everyone." Then there is **on ne peut pas sonner et aller à la procession** (sawn-NAY ay ah-LAY ah lah praw-say-SYAWN), translated as "make up your mind!" The literal translation is "you can't ring bells and march in the parade." One thing or the other! Finally, another bit of sound advice: **on ne peut pas tout avoir** (too tah-VWAHR), translated as "be realistic!" but better translated as "you can't have your cake and eat it too"; literally, "you can't have everything."

on ne peut vivre seul (awn nuu puu veevrə suhl)
one cannot live alone
   The most convincing reason for getting married—or for doing whatever modern people do to find companionship.

on ne répare pas une injustice par une autre (awn nuu ray-PAHR pah zün nan-zhüss-TEESS pahr rün nohtrə)
two wrongs don't make a right
   Literally, "you can't remedy a bad situation by replacing it with another." Another equally bad one, that is.

on ne sait jamais (awn nuu say zhah-MAY)
you never know
   So keep on trying. As the New York State lottery motto puts it, "Hey, you never know." But keep the ridiculously long odds in mind when you risk another dollar.

on ne se moque pas impunément de moi (awn nuu suu mawk pah an-pü-nay-MAHN duu mwah)
don't tread on me
   Also translated as "don't fool with me" or "you can't mock me and get away with it"; literally, "you can't make fun of me with impunity."

on n'est jamais si bien servi que par soi-même (awn nay zhah-MAY see byan sair-VEE kuu pahr swah-MAYM)
don't depend on others!

Well translated by the seventeenth-century proverb "if you want a thing done well, do it yourself."

on ne va pas remonter au déluge (awn nuu vah pah ruu-mawn-TAY oh day-LÜZH)
that's ancient history!
Well translated as "we're not going to dredge up the past again"; literally, "we're not going back over the flood again." The biblical flood, that is.

on parle français (awn pahrl frahn-SAY)
French is spoken
Here, that is. A message sometimes seen in store windows outside France—and Quebec—that is intended to attract customers who speak French.

os à ronger (awss sah rawn-ZHAY)
a bone to pick
In the sense of something to keep one alive or active, not as a subject of disagreement or disapproval.

oublier je ne puis (oo-blee-YAY zhuu nuu pwee)
I can never forget
The attitude that guarantees perpetual hostility within families and between nations.

où il y a de la gêne, il n'y a pas de plaisir (oo eel lee yah də lah zhayn eel nee yah pah də play-ZEER)
comfort comes first
Also translated as "some people think only of their own comfort"; more literally, "where there is discomfort, there's no pleasure."

où sont les neiges d'antan? (oo sawn lay nayzh dahn-TAHN)
where are the snows of yesteryear?
The best-known line written by fifteenth-century French poet François Villon. The English translation given above, itself known widely, was the work of English poet Dante Gabriel Rossetti (1828–1882).

paix et peu (pay ay puu)
a peaceful life on a modest income
What many of us yearn for, literally, "peace and little."

pâle comme la mort (pahl kawm lah mor)
deathly pale
Also conveyed by **pâle comme un linge** (pahl kawm mœn lanzh), literally, "white as a sheet."

panier à salade (pah-NYAY ah sah-LAHD)
paddy wagon
A beautiful idiom, literally, "salad basket," better translated as "police van" and, for those with substantial memories, as "Black Maria." Any way you cut it, better to stay out of it.

panier percé (pah-NYAY pair-SAY)
spendthrift
Literally, "pierced basket," suggesting that for many of us money and possessions go unguarded, slipping away silently and continuously.

papa gâteau (pah-PAH gah-TOH)
doting grandfather
Literally, "cake father," perhaps suggesting that a doting grandfather can always be counted on to bring sweets or other gifts when visiting his grandchildren.

papier cul (pah-PYAY kü)
toilet paper
This essential of modern life is also given as **papier hygiénique** (ee-zhyay-NEEK), but **papier cul** is more colorful as well as functional, since **cul** means "backside." And that's somewhat closer to calling a spade a spade.

papilles gustatives (pah-PEEYə güss-tah-TEEVə)
taste buds
Once again, the beautiful sounds of French!

papillon (pah-pee-YAWN)
butterfly
A noun that leads to several interesting locutions, including **papillons noirs** (pah-pee-YAWN nwahr), translated as "gloomy thoughts," literally, "black butterflies"; as a verb, **papillonner** (pah-pee-yaw-NAY), translated as "flit about," which describes what a butterfly habitually does; **papillonner autour d'une femme** (pah-pee-yaw-NAY oh-TOOR dün fahm), translated as "hover round a woman," another mode of butterfly flight, perhaps that of social butterflies; **papillonner d'une femme à l'autre** (pah-pee-yaw-NAY dün fahm ah lohtrə), translated as "flit from one woman to another," which is the activity of a man who is not intent on finding a mate; and, finally, **papillonner d'un sujet à l'autre** (pah-pee-yaw-NAY dœn sü-ZHAY ah lohtrə), translated as "flit from one subject to another," which is the type of human activity we may compare with that of a butterfly disporting itself in a garden rich in flowers.

papillote (pah-pee-YAWT)
curlpaper
This is the term used for the paper—called this because of its suggestion of the shape of a butterfly—in which hair used to be wrapped to create curls. In French cookery it is the term used for the paper employed in preparing certain fish or meat dishes, for example, **côtelette en papillote** (koh-TLAYT ahn pah-pee-YAWT), in which a cutlet is prepared in a greased or buttered paper wrapper. On American restaurant menus, we sometimes see pompano en papillote. Yum.

parbleu! (pahr-BLUU)
by Jove!
Also translated as "egad!" **Parbleu** is a mild oath, a corruption of **par Dieu** (pahr dyuu), literally translated as "by God!"

parc à bébé (pahrk kah bay-BAY)
playpen
Literally, "baby's park," showing that the French have more regard for a child than the rest of us do. Pens are for pigs.

parfum de scandale (pahr-FUHN duu skahn-DAHL)
whiff of scandal
Not as glamorous as the literal translation, "perfume *or* scent of scandal."

Paris vaut bien une messe (pah-REE voh byan ün mayss)
Paris is well worth a mass
A locution attributed to Henri IV, king of France, upon becoming a convert to Catholicism in 1593.

par le fer et par le feu (pahr luu fair ay pahr luu fuu)
by fire and by sword
That's how we will have our own way, literally, "by arms and by fire."

parler (pahr-LAY)
talk
As you would expect, this infinitive and the form **parlez**, with the same pronunciation, introduce many locutions, including: **parler à découvert** (ah day-koo-VAIR), translated as "talk straight," "speak frankly," and "speak openly," literally, "speak uncovered"; **parler à tort et à travers** (ah tor ay ah trah-VAIR), translated as "talk nonsense," "blab," "speak thoughtlessly," and "talk through one's hat," literally, "talk wrongly and askew"; **parler avec hauteur** (ah-VAYK oh-TUHR), translated as "speak haughtily"; **parler discrètement à l'oreille de quelqu'un** (deess-kraytə-MAHN ah law-RAYə duu kayl-KœN), translated as "leak information," more literally, "put a quiet word in someone's ear"; **parler du nez** (dü nay), translated as "talk through one's hat," literally, "talk through one's nose"; **parler français comme une vache enragée** (frahn-SAY kawm mün vahsh ahn-rah-ZHAY), translated as "butcher the French language," literally, "speak French like an irate cow"; for an even more condemnatory way to express the same thought, there is **parler français comme une vache espagnole** (frahn-SAY kawm mün vahsh ayss-pah-NYAWL), translated as "speak French like a Spanish cow"; **parler la bouche pleine** (lah boosh playn), translated as "mumble," literally, "speak with one's mouth full"; **parler pour ne rien dire** (poor nuu ryan deer), a marvelous way to say "obfuscate" or "say nothing at great length" or "talk for the sake of talking," literally, "talk in order to say nothing"; **parler sans réticence** (sahn ray-tee-SAHNSS), translated as "hold nothing back" or "speak openly" or "be frank," more literally, "speak without reservation"; **parler seul** (suhl), translated as "talk to oneself," literally, "talk alone"; **parlez du loup et vous**

en verrez la queue (dü loo ay voo zah*n* vay-RAY lah kuu), translated as the familiar "speak of the devil" and the fuller "speak of the devil and he will appear," as well as the literal translation "speak of the wolf and you will see his tail," said of a person who has been the subject of conversation—more usually of gossip—and who appears unexpectedly; **parlez-en au futur** (zah*n* oh fü-TÜR), translated as "don't count your chickens before they're hatched," literally, "speak of it in the future tense" (see also VENDRE LA PEAU DE L'OURS AVANT DE L'AVOIR TUÉ). Finally, there is the useful question **parlez-vous français?** (voo frah*n*-SAY), "do you speak French?" With the help of the book you now are consulting, you may be able to answer *Oui, monsieur.*

parole d'honneur (pah-RUHL daw-NUHR)
word of honor

But this is not the only use of **parole**. Consider **paroles de consolation** (pah-RUHL duu kaw*n*-saw-lah-SYAW*N*), translated as "comforting words," literally, "words of consolation," offered to those who are bereaved; and **paroles en l'air** (pah-RUHL zah*n* lair), translated as "idle words" or "vain words," literally, "words in the air," suggesting that the words strike no ears.

partagé entre l'amour et la haine (pahr-tah-ZHAY ah*n*trə lah-MOOR ay lah aynə)
torn between love and hatred

A striking phrase indicating, alas, a condition too often found in troubled human relations.

partager le gâteau (pahr-tah-ZHAY luu gah-TOH)
go halves

On anything. Literally, "share the cake."

partir, c'est mourir un peu (pahr-TEER say moo-REER œn puu)
every time we say good-bye, I die a little

The lugubrious metaphor, literally, "to leave is to die a little," said—not sung—by any lover who faces temporary absence from a loved one.

parvenu (pahr-vuu-NÜ)
upstart

The term, frequently used in English with the same pronunciation, employed to characterize a person who has forced his way into a higher social class. (See also NOUVEAU RICHE.)

pas (pah)
not

A word that also means "step," as three of the following locutions will reveal. First, there is **pas à ma connaissance** (pah zah mah kaw-nay-SAHNSS), translated as "not as far as I know" or "not to my knowledge." Now for three idioms employing **pas** to mean "step": **pas à pas** (pah zah pah), "step-by-step"; **pas glissant** (pah glee-SAHN), translated as "ticklish affair," literally, "slippery step"; and **pas à pas on va loin** (pah zah pah awn vah lwan), translated as "slowly does it," literally, "step-by-step one goes far." Now back to **pas** meaning "not": **pas de nouvelles, bonnes nouvelles** (pah də noo-VAYL bawn noo-VAYL), translated as "no news is good news"; **pas de roses sans épines** (pah duu rohz sahn zay-PEEN), translated as "life is not a bowl of cherries" or "there's no rose without a thorn," literally, "no roses without thorns"; **pas de zèle!** (pah də zayl), a well-known French phrase meaning "don't overdo it!" more literally, "don't be too zealous!" (For more information on this injunction, see ET SURTOUT, PAS DE ZÈLE!) Two common pleas are **pas d'histoires!** (pah deess-TWAHR), literally, "no stories!" better translated as "no fuss, please!" or "much ado about nothing!"; and **pas d'observations je vous prie** (pah dawb-sair-vah-SYAWN zhuu voo pree), best translated as "no comments, please," more literally, "keep your ideas to yourself"; and, finally, there is the evaluation **pas mal** (pah mahl), translated as "not bad *or* not badly" or "good *or* well enough."

passer (pah-SAY)
pass

This infinitive ends up with various meanings when it becomes the focus of various idiomatic constructions, as you will soon see: **passer aux aveux** (oh zah-VUU), translated as "make a confession," whether as an admission of criminality or a penitential avowal of sins; **passer la corde au cou de quelqu'un** (lah kord doh koo duu kayl-KœN), translated as "entrap someone," literally, "put the rope around someone's neck" (see also SI ON LE LAISSE FAIRE IL SE PASSERA LUI-MÊME LA CORDE AU COU); **passer la nuit au dépôt** (lah nwee oh day-POH), translated as "spend a night in the hoosegow," more conventionally, "spend the night in jail"; **passer l'arme à gauche** (lahrm ah gohsh), translated as "cash in one's chips" or "kick the bucket," literally, "pass the weapon to the left hand," where it presumably will no longer be a threat; **passer quelqu'un à tabac** (kayl-KœN ah tah-BAH), an idiom translated as "thrash someone" or "beat the living daylights out of someone" or "beat someone up," literally, "pass someone to the cigar store," stopping cold any attempt at understanding the origin of this idiom; **passer une nuit blanche** (ün nwee blahnsh), translated as "pass a sleepless night," literally, "pass a white night"; **passer une visite médicale** (ün vee-ZEET may-dee-KAHL), translated as "go for a checkup" or "have a checkup," more literally, "have a physical examination"; and, finally, **pas touche!** (toosh), translated as "hands off!" literally, "don't touch!"

pâté (pah-TAY)
paste or *spread*

This noun denotes a remarkable culinary achievement. It is based on chopped or puréed meat, liver, fish, or game and comes in several forms. On restaurant menus outside as well as inside France, it is given in French: **pâté de campagne** (duu kahn-PAHNYə), literally, "farmhouse pâté"; **pâté de foie** (də fwah), translated as "liver pâté" (see also FOIE GRAS); **pâté en croûte** (ahn kroot), translated as "meat pie" or "meat patty"; and, finally, **pâté maison** (may-ZAWN), translated as "house pâté," that is, the chef's own pâté, not one prepared by someone else and brought to the kitchen. All usually delicious.

patience passe science (pah-SYAHNSS pahss syahnss)
patience surpasses science

Or knowledge. Notice the wordplay of the French aphorism.

pattes de mouche (paht duu moosh)
chicken tracks

Literally, "fly tracks," also translated as "spidery scrawl" and "difficult handwriting."

pauvreté n'est pas vice (poh-vruu-TAY nay pah veess)
poverty is no vice

Or, as a seventeenth-century English proverb has it, "poverty is no sin," telling us, as we have known for a long time, that there is no shame in being poor.

payer (pay-YAY)
pay

This infinitive leads us to at least three common locutions: **payer la course** (lah koorss), translated as "pay the fare," literally, "pay the trip"—for a taxi ride, that is; **payer quelqu'un en monnaie de singe** (kayl-KœN ahn maw-NAY də sanzh), translated as "put someone off with empty promises" or, in current terms, "say that the check is in the mail," literally, "pay someone with monkey money"; and, finally, **payer tribut à la nature** (tree-BÜ ah lah nah-TÜR), literally, "pay the debt of nature," more commonly given as "kick the bucket."

pêche (paysh)
peach
Included here only to introduce the famous **pêche Melba** (mayl-BAH), translated as "peach Melba," a delicious dessert of cooked peach, vanilla ice cream, and clear raspberry sauce. The dessert was named in tribute to Dame Nellie Melba (1861–1931), a celebrated Australian soprano.

péché (pay-SHAY)
sin
There is space here only for a few of the many types of sins to which flesh is heir: **péché capital** (kah-pee-TAHL), translated as "capital sin" or "deadly sin," one of seven such sins (see LES SEPT PÉCHÉS CAPITAUX); **péché de jeunesse** (duu zhuu-NAYSS), translated as "youthful indiscretion" or, more literally, "sin of youth"; **péché d'orgueil ne va pas sans danger** (dor-GœYə nuu vah pah sahn dahn-ZHAY), translated as "pride goes before a fall," literally, "the sin of pride is fraught with peril"; and, finally, **péché mortel** (mor-TAYL), translated as "mortal sin," which is distinct from **péché véniel** (vay-NYAYL), translated as "venial sin."

peigner la girafe (pay-NYAY lah zhee-RAHF)
be unproductive
Also translated as "pass time"; literally, "comb the giraffe." No stretch of the imagination is required to understand this idiom.

pensez à moi (pahn-SAY ah mwah)
think of me
Also translated as "remember me." Often used as a tombstone inscription.

pension (pah*n*-SYAW*N*)
boardinghouse
A term that is also used in English and pronounced as in French.

perdre (pairdrə)
lose
And, of course, there are several phrases that employ this infinitive, including **perdre avec élégance** (ah-VAYK ay-lay-GAHNSS), translated as "be a good loser," "lose with class," and, more literally, "be a graceful loser"; **perdre de vue** (duu vü), translated as "lose sight of"; two phrases that mean "blow one's cool" are **perdre son aplomb** (saw*n* nah-PLAW*N*) and **perdre son sang-froid** (saw*n* sah*n*-FRWAH), and both may also be translated as "become flustered"; and, finally, there is **perdre son temps en flâneries** (saw*n* tah*n* ah*n* flah-NəREE), which translates as "lounge around" and "waste one's time in lolling about," literally, "waste one's time in taking strolls."

perfide Albion (pair-FEED ahl-BYAW*N*)
perfidious Albion
Also translated as "deceitful England" or "deceitful Great Britain." Albion (in English pronounced AL-bee-yən) is an ancient name for Great Britain, and the phrase **perfide Albion** was popularized in the anti-British Napoleonic recruiting drive of 1813.

petit (puu-TEE)
little or *small*
Many things and many people in this world may properly be described as "little" or "small," among them **petit ami** (puu-TEET tah-MEE), literally, "little friend," better translated as "boyfriend," and **petite amie**, with the same pronunciation and the same literal meaning, but better translated as "girlfriend" or "mistress"; then there is a proverb using **petit** as an adverb, **petit à petit l'oiseau fait son nid** (puu-TEE tah puu-TEE lwah-ZOH fay saw*n* nee), best translated as "persistence pays off," literally, "little by little the bird makes its nest." Back to the adjectival use: **petit-bourgeois** (pə-tee-boor-ZHWAH), translated as "the middle class" and used in English as "petit bourgeois" and "petty bourgeois" with the French pronunciation, or pronounced PET-tee boor-ZHWAH, and taken to mean "member of the lower-middle class"; an amusing sobriquet applied to Napoleon when he

was a young soldier and said to have been less than five feet two inches tall is **petit caporal** (pə-TEE kah-paw-RAHL), literally, "the little corporal"; **petit chaudron, grandes oreilles** (puu-TEE shoh-DRAWN grahnd zaw-RAYə), translated as "little pitchers have big ears," literally, "small cauldron, big handles"; **petit déjeuner** (pə-TEE day-zhuu-NAY), translated as "breakfast," literally, "small lunch"; **petite-enfant** (pə-teet-tahn-FAHN), translated as "granddaughter," literally, "little child," has as its male counterpart **petit-fils** (pə-tee-FEESS), translated as "grandson," literally, "little son"; **petit monde** (pə-TEE mawnd), translated as "common people," literally, "the little world"; and, to end on a bibulous note, **petit verre** (pə-TEE vair), translated as "quick shot," more conventionally, "small glass of brandy or liqueur," literally, "little glass." Of spirits, that is.

peu (puu)
little

This adverb, sometimes a noun, gives us several interesting locutions, including **peu à peu** (puu ah puu), translated as "in dribs and drabs" and "bit by bit" and "gradually," literally, "little by little"; **peu commune** (puu kaw-MÜN), translated as "uncommon" and "out of the ordinary"; the proverb **peu de bien, peu de soin** (puu duu byan puu duu swan), translated as "few wares, few cares," "nothing's plenty for me," and, almost literally, "little wealth, little care"; **peu de chose** (puu duu shohz), translated as "trifle" and "small matter" and "it's nothing"; **peu de gens savent être vieux** (puu duu zhahn sahvə aytrə vyuu), a maxim of La Rochefoucauld, translated as "few people know how to be old"; **peu d'hommes ont été admirés par leurs domestiques** (puu dawm awn ay-TAY ahd-mee-RAY pahr luhr daw-mayss-TEEK), translated as "few men have been admired by their servants" (see also IL N'Y A PAS DE HÉROS POUR SON VALET DE CHAMBRE); **peu reluisant** (puu ruu-lwee-ZAHN), a phrase with two meanings: when said of a situation or result, "far from brilliant," of a person, "despicable"; and, finally, **peu soigné** (puu swah-NYAY), translated as "careless," "badly kept," and "badly prepared." (See also SOIGNÉ.)

picoler dur (pee-kaw-LAY dür)
candidate for AA

Translated as "hit the bottle hard"; literally, "tipple hard."

pièce de résistance (pyayss duu ray-zeess-TAHNSS)
the main event

More conventionally translated as "the best part of a show" or "the principal dish at a meal." And *pièce de résistance* has found its way into English, with the French pronunciation preserved or approximated.

pièce d'identité (pyayss dee-dahn-tee-TAY)
ID

More properly translated as "identification card." Also given as **carte** (kahrt) **d'identité** .

pied (pyay)
foot

This noun gives us three interesting locutions: **pied à pied** (pyay ah pyay), translated as "every inch of the way," "step-by-step," and, literally, "foot by foot"; **pied-à-terre** (pyay-tah-TAIR), translated as "resting place" or "temporary lodging," literally, "foot on the ground," and used untranslated in English as "pied-à-terre," with the meaning "apartment for occasional use" and the French pronunciation approximated; and, finally, **pied poudreux** (pyay poo-DRUU), translated as "tramp" or "hobo," literally, "dusty foot," a characterization easily understandable when we think back to the condition of unpaved roads in summertime.

pierre qui roule n'amasse pas mousse (pyair kee rool nah-MAHSS pah mooss)
settle down!

This French proverb, literally translated in the familiar sixteenth-century English proverb "a rolling stone gathers no moss," also appears in other languages.

pieux mensonge (pyuu mahn-SAWNZH)
white lie

A lie told for good purpose; literally, "a pious lie."

piquer une crise (pee-KAY ün kreez)
blow one's top

Also translated as "fly off the handle" and "throw a tantrum," **crise** here being translated not as "crisis," but as "rage" or "tantrum."

placer ses affaires bien en ordre (plah-SAY say zah-FAIR byan nahn nordrə)
set one's things in order

And we're talking here not about straightening out an apartment, but about preparing for the inevitable final act of life.

plaider le faux pour savoir le vrai (play-DAY luu foh poor sah-VWAHR luu vray)
entrap someone
A favorite ploy of schoolteachers and police officers, better translated as "tell a lie to get at the truth."

plaie d'argent n'est pas mortelle (play dahr-ZHAHN nay pah mor-TAYL)
money isn't everything
Also translated as "money never killed anyone," literally "a plague of money isn't deadly."

pleins pouvoirs (plan poo-VWAHR)
full powers
A capacity we all hope to retain as we age and fight decay.

plus (plü)
more
A common word that sometimes has the power to get some of us into deep trouble—but not always. Consider the following locutions: **plus ça change, plus c'est la même chose** (plü sah shahnzh plü say lah maym shohz), a dismal commentary on human history telling us that hard as we try, things never improve, and translated as "people and their institutions never change," literally, "the more it changes, the more it is the same thing"; **plus fait douceur que violence** (plüss fay doo-SUHR kuu vyaw-LAHNSS), advising us to try a little tenderness, better translated as "kindness succeeds where force will fail," literally, "kindness accomplishes more than violence"; **plus il en a, plus il en vaut** (plü zeel ahn ah plü zeel ahn voh), translated as "the more one has, the more one desires," and ain't it the truth? On a happier note there is **plus on est de fous, plus on rit** (plü zawn nay də foo plü zawn ree), translated as "the more the merrier," literally, "the more merrymakers, the more fun," so invite everybody; **plus ou moins** (plü zoo mwan), translated as "more or less"; **plus que jamais** (plü kuu zhah-MAY), translated as "more than ever"; **plus royaliste que le roi** (plü rwah-yah-LEEST kuu luu rwah), a commentary on carrying things to extremes, literally translated as "more royalist than

the king," a characterization of zealous reformers who, perhaps unwittingly, pursue their programs too far; and, finally, **plus sage que les sages** (plü sahzh kuu lay sahzh), translated as "wiser than the wise," a commentary on fools.

point d'argent, point de Suisse (pwan dahr-ZHAHN pwan duu sweess)
no money, no Swiss
Recognition that for centuries Swiss professional soldiers were the mercenaries of Europe, willing to serve any state for pay. **Point** in this sense is the equivalent of **pas**, with the meaning of "not."

poisson d'avril (pwah-SAWN dah-VREEL)
April fool's joke
Literally, "fish of April." And don't we often say of a hapless individual, "poor fish"?

pomme (pawm)
apple
This noun leads us to several common terms: **pomme d'Adam** (dah-DAHN), translated as "Adam's apple"; **pomme de discorde** (duu deess-KORD), translated as "bone of contention," literally "apple of discord"; **pomme de terre** (duu tair), translated as "potato," literally, "apple of the earth"; **pomme sauvage** (soh-VAHZH), translated as "crab apple," literally, "wild apple"; and, finally, but by no means the least common term, **pommes frites** (pawm freet), translated as "French fries," the glorious deep-fried delicacy that complements the truly American hamburger—composed of a poor excuse for a soft roll and a German chopped meat patty. Incidentally, the French are known to use the word **hamburger** (ahn-boor-GUHR) when ordering a hamburger.

porte cochère (portə kaw-SHAIR)
carriage entrance
Called "porte cochere" in English, with the French pronunciation preserved almost intact, this appendage to a stately home serves on a rainy day to protect visitors going from their cars to the front door of a house.

porter de l'eau à la rivière (por-TAY duu loh ah lah ree-VYAIR)
carry coals to Newcastle
If this metaphor didn't exist, with the meaning "do something unneces-

sary," we would have to invent it. In French it translates literally as "carry water to the river." Unnecessary enough for you?

poser pour la galerie (poh-ZAY poor lah gah-LəREE)
play to the gallery
    Attempt, that is, to appeal to the popular taste.

poseur (poh-ZUHR)
poseur
    The French **poseur** has been adopted by English without change in pronunciation to mean, as in French, "show-off" or "affected person."

possession vaut loi (paw-say-SYAWN voh lwah)
possession is nine points of the law
    Literally, "possession is worth law," suggesting every advantage any defendant can have in court. The nine points of the law are jocularly given as (1) deep pockets, (2) infinite patience, (3) a kind press, (4) a high-priced lawyer, (5) friendly witnesses, (6) a bought jury, (7) a crooked judge, (8) an iron-clad alibi, and (9) good luck—if you have overlooked anything.

poste restante (pawstə rayss-TAHNT)
general delivery
    Literally, "remaining post *or* mail." "Poste restante," as it is also called in English, is a department at a post office to which mail may be addressed for recipients, and where it will remain until called for—for a specified period of time, that is.

pot-au-feu (poh-toh-FUU)
stew
    Especially "beef stew," a thick soup or stew of meat and vegetables, delicious when properly prepared.

pot-pourri (poh-poo-REE)
potpourri
    A cookery term, literally "rotten pot," also translated as "medley," meaning a combination of incongruous elements.

poudre aux yeux (poodrə oh zyuu)
dust in the eyes
    Something, that is, that blinds one to the facts of a situation.

poulet fermier (poo-LAY fair-MYAY)
free-range chicken
   Literally, "farm chicken," differentiating a chicken that walks about and scratches for its sustenance from a chicken that spends its short life resting cooped up alone within a commercial feeding facility.

pour ainsi dire (poor ran-SEE deer)
so to speak
   Also translated as "as it were."

pourboire (poor-BWAHR)
tip or *gratuity*
   Which leads to **pourboire interdit** (an-tair-DEE), translated as "tipping not allowed." (See also LE SERVICE EST COMPRIS.)

pour couper court (poor koo-PAY koor)
to get to the point
   Also translated as "to be brief"; literally, "to cut the matter short"—often heard near the end of an overly long discourse.

pour marier leur fille ils n'ont pas mégoté (poor mah-RYAY luhr feeyə eel nawn pah may-gaw-TAY)
gave their daughter a really big send-off
   Better translated as "they spared nothing for their daughter's wedding" or "they went all out for their daughter's wedding"; literally, "they didn't skimp on their daughter's wedding."

pourri de fric (poo-REE də freek)
loaded
   Also translated as "filthy rich" and "lousy with money"; literally, "rotten with money."

pour tout dire (poor too deer)
in a word
   Literally, "to say everything." Want to bet?

pour tout potage (poor too paw-TAHZH)
in all
   Also translated as "all told"; literally, "for every soup."

pour un plat de lentilles (poor rœn plah duu lahn-TEEYə)
for a mess of pottage
Literally, "for a dish of lentils," a wonderful way of indicating "a bad bargain," in which one gains something of small value by giving away something of great value. The French phrase derives from Genesis, in which Esau sold his birthright to Jacob "for a mess of pottage."

pousse-café (pooss-kah-FAY)
liqueur taken after coffee
Literally, "it pushes on the coffee." **Pousse-café** is especially a varicolored drink of several liqueurs appearing in layers.

prêcher un converti (pray-SHAY œn kawn-vair-TEE)
preach to the converted
A locution, sometimes given as "you are preaching to the choir," telling people that in arguing with you they are wasting their time, since you already agree with them.

précieux (pray-SYUU)
precious or *overrefined*
This adjective, with the feminine form **précieuse** (pray-SYUHZ), is also used as a noun, meaning a person affecting excessive refinement of taste, language, etc. (See also LES PRÉCIEUSES RIDICULES.)

précis (pray-SEE)
abstract or *summary*
Literally, "cut short." Every student knows "précis" as an English term, pronounced PRAY-see.

prendre (prahndrə)
take or *have* or *put on* or *grab* or *take on* or *the like*
As one might expect, this infinitive leads us into many locutions. Some of them are listed here, for example, **prendre au sérieux** (oh say-RYUU), translated as "take seriously"; and **prendre de la brioche** (duu lah bree-YAWSH), translated as "put on weight," "acquire a corporation," and "develop a paunch," literally, "put on a brioche." The beloved **brioche** led to the so-called brioche created by American so-called bakers in pallid imitation of the real McCoy, described inadequately as a light, sweet roll or bun. But we do talk about "fat buns," don't we? In the same vein we have **pren-**

dre de la graisse (duu lah grayss), translated as "put on fat," and **prendre de l'embonpoint** (duu lahn-bawn-PWAN), translated as "put on weight" or "get stout"; **prendre du poids** (dü pwah), translated as "put on weight," literally, "put on pounds"; and **prendre du ventre** (dü vahntrə), translated as "get fat" and "put on weight," literally, "acquire a belly." Leaving this uncomfortable topic, we have **prendre des précautions après coup** (day pray-koh-SYAWN ah-PRAY koo), translated as "lock the stable door after the horse has bolted," more literally, "take precautions after the mischief has happened," in other words, "too late!" Then there are two happy phrases: **prendre femme** (fahm), translated as "take a wife," and **prendre la balle au bond** (lah bahl oh bawn), translated as "grasp opportunity" and "take time by the forelock," literally, "take the ball on the rebound." On a fleeting note, we have **prendre la fuite** (lah fweet), translated as "take to one's heels" and "take flight." And on an uplifting note we have **prendre la lune avec les dents** (lah lün ah-VAYK lay dahn), translated as "set your sights high," "attempt the impossible," and "there is nothing beyond your reach," literally, "seize the moon in your teeth." Turning to mundane matters, we have **prendre la pilule** (lah pee-LÜL), translated as "on the pill," more literally, "take the (contraceptive) pill." It is of interest that this same **prendre la pilule** is also translated as "take a beating," which may be thought of as a bitter pill. On to an ecclesiastical locution, **prendre la soutane** (lah soo-TAHN), translated as "take vows" and "enter the church," literally, "take the cassock." A cassock—in English also called a "soutane" and pronounced as in French—is a coat or jacket worn by members of the clergy. Less elevated are **prendre la vie comme elle vient** (lah vee kawm mayl vyan), literally, "take life as it comes"; **prendre le bon avec le mauvais** (luu bawn ah-VAYK luu maw-VAY), literally, "take the good with the bad"; and **prendre le maquis** (luu mah-KEE), translated as "go underground," literally, "take to the maquis," the descriptive term given to a thick scrubland on Mediterranean coastal lands within which bandits once hid to avoid capture. "Take to the maquis" became widely known in World War II, when French guerrillas, called "the maquis," carried out attacks on German troops and military installations. To turn to more common locutions, there is **prendre le mors aux dents** (luu mor roh dahn), translated variously as "apply oneself without restraint," "go all out," "be obstinately self-willed," and "fly off the handle." The literal translation is "take the bit in the teeth," the explanation behind this phrase reflecting the behavior of horses. When a horse chooses to run away, it takes the bit between its teeth, and the rider no longer can control it. Then there are **prendre le tau-**

reau par les cornes (luu toh-ROH pahr lay korn), literally, "take the bull by the horns," and well translated as "tackle a problem head-on"; **prendre le temps comme il vient** (luu tahn kawm meel vyan), translated as "take things as they come," literally, "take the weather as it comes"; **prendre le train en marche** (luu tran ahn mahrsh), translated as "climb on the bandwagon," literally, "get on the train while it's moving"; **prendre quelque chose sous son bonnet** (kaylkə shohz soo sawn bawn-NAY), translated as "take it upon oneself to do something," literally, "take something under one's hat"; **prendre quelqu'un à la gorge** (kayl-KœN ah lah gorzh), translated as "hold a gun to someone's head," literally, "grab someone by the throat"; **prendre quelqu'un à rebours** (kayl-KœN ah rəboor), translated as "rub someone the wrong way," **à rebours** meaning "the wrong way"; and, finally, **prendre quelqu'un en otage** (kayl-KœN ahn naw-TAHZH), a timely locution translated as "take someone hostage."

prends-moi tel que je suis (prahn-MWAH tayl kuu zhuu swee)
take me as I am
    Continuing, in the words of the great Broadway musical *Oklahoma*, with "or leave me be."

prenez garde! (pruu-NAY gahrd)
take care!

prêt-à-porter (pray-tah-por-TAY)
off the rack
    Clothing, that is. Better translated as "ready-to-wear." The opposite, of course, of "made-to-order."

pris à son propre piège (pree zah sawn prawprə pyayzh)
hoist by his own petard
    Literally, "caught in his own trap." The petard in the idiomatic translation above was an explosive device that was attached to enemy fortifications to blow them up. Unfortunately for the daring soul selected to set off the device, there was always great danger of expiring in the ensuing explosion.

pris de boisson (pree duu bwah-SAWN)
under the weather

Also translated as "under the influence" and "the worse for drink," **boisson** meaning the noun "drink."

profiter de l'aubaine (praw-fee-TAY duu loh-BAYN)
seize the day
Also translated as "make the most of one's chances"; more literally, "take advantage of a windfall."

projet en l'air (praw-ZHAY ahn lair)
fanciful scheme
Also translated as "pie in the sky"; literally, "project in the air."

promettre la lune (praw-MAYTRə lah lün)
promise the moon
A promise, of course, that—thus far—cannot be fulfilled.

prophète de malheur (praw-FAYT duu mah-LUHR)
Cassandra
Usually translated as "prophet of doom." Cassandra in mythology was a prophetess who could accurately foretell the future. When she refused to accept Apollo's advances, however, her prophecies from then on were not believed. Today, Apollo might have been brought up on charges of sexual harassment.

propre-à-rien (prawprə-ah-RYAN)
waster
Also translated, more literally, as "good-for-nothing" and as "ne'er-do-well."

provenance (praw-VəNAHNSS)
source
Also translated as "origin" and "pedigree." English has adopted "provenance" (PRAHV-ə-nənss), with the meaning "place or source of origin."

prudence est mère de sûreté (prü-DAHNSS ay mair duu sürə-TAY)
discretion is the better part of valor
More literally translated as "caution is the mother of safety."

quand il y a du danger, les rats quittent le navire (kahn teel lee yah dü dahn-ZHAY lay rah keet luu nah-VEER)
only quitters quit
   This proverb, which has meaning for all of us and has nothing to do with ships and rats, is translated literally as "in the face of danger, rats jump ship." It deals, of course, with human proclivities and contrasts with a modern proverb, "when the going gets rough, the tough get going."

quand le chat est loin, les souris dansent (kahn luu shah ay lwan lay soo-REE dahnss)
when the cat's away, the mice will play
   This proverb, literally, "when the cat's far away, the mice dance," shares its meaning with **quand le chat n'est pas là les souris dansent** (kahn luu shah nay pah lah lay soo-REE dahnss), literally, "when the cat's not there, the mice dance." And what do these two proverbs say to us? In the absence of someone in authority, people generally will do just what they want to do. And that suggests they will do anything but what they are supposed to be doing.

quand les poules auront des dents (kahn lay pool oh-RAWN day dahn)
in a blue moon
   Also translated as "when pigs have wings" and "when pigs learn to fly"; literally, "when hens have teeth."

quand le vin est tiré, il faut le boire (kahn luu van ay tee-RAY eel foh luu bwahr)
once the first step is taken, there's no going back
   Literally, "once the wine is drawn (from the cask), it must be drunk." Because you cannot pour it back into the cask.

quand on boit il ne faut pas faire de mélanges (kahn tawn bwah eel nuu foh pah fair duu may-LAHNZH)
don't mix your drinks

More literally, "when you drink, it's not good to mix your drinks." Or so we are told.

que ceux qui trouvent la situation intenable s'en aillent (kuu suu kee troovə lah see-tü-ah-SYAWN an-tuu-NAHBLə sahn nīyə)
if you can't stand the heat, get out of the kitchen
More literally, "let those leave who can't deal with the situation."

quelle dégoûtation! (kayl day-goo-tah-SYAWN)
what a mess!
An exclamation you should have ready for use whenever you enter your adolescent offspring's bedroom.

quelle mouche le pique? (kayl moosh luu peek)
what's bugging him?
Also translated as "what's eating him?" and "what's irritating him?"; literally, "what fly is stinging him?"

quelles sont les nouvelles? (kayl sawn lay noo-VAYL)
what's going on?
More literally, "what is the news?"

quelques privilégiés (kaylkə pree-vee-lay-ZHYAY)
privileged few
Also translated as "lucky few" and "most favored few." Everyone, that is, but you and me.

quel rasoir! (kayl rah-ZWAHR)
what a bore he is!
Literally, "what a razor!" Now figure out what this exclamation would mean to anyone encountering it for the first time whose native language is not French.

que n'ai-je le temps! (kuu nayzhə luu tahn)
oh, that I had the time!
Never said by busy people, who always have time.

qu'en dira-t-on? (kahn dee-rah-TAWN)
what will people say?
Without the question mark, this is a noun phrase translated as "a gossip."

querelle (kə-RAYL)
quarrel
Humans being what they are, this noun obviously cries out for amplification. Here are a few types of quarrels: **querelle d'Allemand** (dahlə-MAHN), translated as "groundless quarrel," literally, "German quarrel"; **querelle d'amoureux** (dah-moo-RUU), translated as "lovers' quarrel"; **querelle de famille** (duu fah-MEEYə), translated as "family dispute"; and, finally, **querelles de ménage** (duu may-NAHZH), translated as "domestic quarrels."

que sais-je? (kuu sayzhə)
what do I know?
Motto of Montaigne, a man of insatiable intellectual curiosity.

qu'est-ce que . . . (kayss kuu)
what is. . . ?
Leading inevitably to a large number of ways to complete this thought, among them **qu'est-ce que ça empêche?** (sah ahn-PAYSH), translated as "what difference does that make?" Then there are **qu'est-ce que c'est?** (say), "what is it?" and **qu'est-ce que j'y gagne?** (zhee gahnyə), translated as "what's in it for me?" and "what do I get out of it?" and **qu'est-ce que tu fais là?** (tü fay lah), translated as "what are you up to?" and "what are you doing?" Also given as **que fais-tu?** (kuu fay tü). On to **qu'est-ce que vous faîtes?** (voo fayt), translated as "what are you doing?" and **qu'est-ce que vous pouvez avoir contre moi?** (voo poo-VAY ah-VWAHR kawntrə mwah), translated as "what can you have against me?" and, finally, **qu'est-ce qu'il fabrique?** (kayss keel fah-BREEK), translated as "what is he up to?" and "what on earth is he doing?"

qui a bu boira (kee ah bü bwah-RAH)
not if AA gains a new member
Literally translated as "he who has drunk will drink again," telling us that the leopard cannot change its spots—unless bioengineering continues to blossom. (See also QUI A VOLÉ VOLERA.)

qui aime bien châtie bien (kee aym byan shah-TEE byan)
spare the rod and spoil the child
Conventional wisdom, depending on which way the child-care pendulum swings. Literally, "who loves well punishes well." Tough love?

qui a volé volera (kee ah vaw-LAY vaw-luu-RAH)
once a thief always a thief
     Literally, "he who has stolen will steal again," motto of those who be-
lieve deeply in the inevitability of recidivism. (See also QUI A BU BOIRA.)

qui casse les verres les paye (kee kahss lay vair lay payǝ)
you pay for your mistakes
     Literally, "he who breaks glasses must pay for them." The hard-nosed—
realistic?—doctrine of individual responsibility.

qui dort, dîne (kee dor deen)
he who sleeps forgets his hunger
     Literally, "he who sleeps, dines." The trick is to master the art of falling
asleep on an empty stomach.

qui est ce vieux macaque? (kee ay suu vyuu mah-KAHK)
who is that old ape?
     A far from generous way of calling attention to an old man.

qui garde son dîner il a mieux à souper (kee gahrd sawn dee-NAY eel ah
myuu ah soo-PAY)
remember to put something aside for lean times
     Literally, "he who saves his dinner will have more for supper."

qui m'aime aime mon chien (kee maym aym mawn shyan)
love me, love my dog
     Also translated as "you'll have to take me as I am," "what you see is what
you get," and, literally, "who loves me loves my dog."

qui n'a santé, il n'a rien; qui a santé, il a tout (kee nah sahn-TAY eel
nah ryan kee ah sahn-TAY eel lah too)
good health is paramount
     Literally translated as "he who doesn't have health has nothing; he who
has health has everything."

qui ne dit mot consent (kee nuu dee moh kawn-SAHN)
silence gives consent
     Literally, "he acquiesces who utters not a word."

qui ne risque rien n'a rien (kee nuu reeskə ryan nah ryan)
capitalists' creed
   Also translated as "you have to take chances" and "nothing ventured nothing gained"; literally, "who risks or dares nothing gains nothing." (See also ON N'A RIEN SANS RISQUE.)

qui paie ses dettes s'enrichit (kee pay say dayt sahn-ree-SHEE)
the rich man is the one who pays his debts
   Especially in light of the high interest rates charged for unwise use of credit cards.

qui paie les violons choisit la musique (kee pay lay vyaw-LAWN shwah-ZEE lah mü-ZEEK)
he who pays the piper may call the tune
   A French proverb, literally, "he who pays the violinists chooses the music," translated above as a seventeenth-century English proverb. Proof that money talks in every language. (See also IL FAUT PAYER LES VIOLONS.)

qui perd, péche (kee pair paysh)
nobody loves a loser
   More closely translated as "the loser is always deemed to be wrong"; literally, "he who loses, sins."

qui peut le plus peut le moins (kee puu luu plüss puu luu mwan)
he who can do most can do least
   Keep an eye out for the rich person who puts less in the collection basket than you think he ought to.

qui sème le vent récolte la tempête (kee saym luu vahn ray-KAWLT lah tahn-PAYT)
sow the wind and reap the whirlwind
   Literally, "who sows the wind shall reap the whirlwind." Hosea, in the Old Testament, tells us "they have sown the wind, and they shall reap the whirlwind," suggesting that through heedless actions, we may provoke serious consequences. So take care!

qui se ressemble s'assemble (kee suu ray-SAHNBLə sah-SAHNBLə)
birds of a feather flock together

Literally, "those who resemble each other assemble together." Which is why parents are eager to become acquainted with their children's friends.

qui se sent morveux, qu'il se mouche (kee suu sahn mor-VUU keel suu moosh)
if the shoe fits, wear it
Well translated as "if one's nose is running, let him blow it," more literally as "who has a snotty nose, let him blow it." The eighteenth-century English proverb given above is less colorful than the French proverb, but equally effective in warning us against finding fault with others when the same fault may exist in us.

qui s'excuse s'accuse (kee saykss-KÜZ sah-KÜZ)
take the Fifth!
Literally, "he who apologizes accuses himself." Better to say nothing.

qui trop embrasse mal étreint (kee troh pahn-BRAHSS mahl lay-TRAN)
grasp all, lose all
Also translated as "don't try for more than you can reasonably attain" and "who grasps at too much loses everything." Yet, as every good student of English literature knows, "a man's reach should exceed his grasp." At least that's what Robert Browning (1812–1889) wrote, but he completed the thought by asking, "or what's a heaven for?"

qui va là? (kee vah lah)
who goes there?
The question asked by alert sentries.

qui va lentement va sûrement (kee vah lahntə-MAHN vah sürə-MAHN)
more haste, less speed
Literally, "who goes slowly goes in safety."

qui vit sans folie n'est pas si sage qu'il croit (kee vee sahn faw-LEE nay pah see sahzh keel krwah)
we all make mistakes
A maxim of La Rochefoucauld; literally, "who lives without folly is not

as wise as he thinks." Most people who never make mistakes do not engage life fully.

qui vivra verra (kee vee-VRAH vay-RAH)
what will be will be
Accepting the inevitability of one's fate. Literally, "he who lives will see."

qui vole un oeuf vole un boeuf (kee vawl lœn uhf vawl lœn buhf)
who steals a penny will steal a dollar
According to this proverb, literally, "who steals an egg will steal a steer," even the smallest of crimes is unacceptable and will lead to worse crime.

raccourcir quelqu'un (rah-koor-SEER kayl-KœN)
chop someone's head off
Also translated as "cut someone down to size"; literally, "shorten someone."

racler les fonds de tiroir (rah-KLAY lay fawn də tee-RWAHR)
scrape some money together
Also translated as "empty the piggy bank"; literally, "scrape the bottom of the drawer."

raconte cela à ta soeur (rah-KAWNT suu-LAH ah tah suhr)
tell it to the Marines
Better translated as "you're speaking rubbish"; literally, "tell that to your sister."

raconter des salades (rah-kawn-TAY day sah-LAHD)
spin yarns or *tell stories*

More literally, "tell lies." **Salade**, of course, also translates as "salad," but that is not what is meant here.

raconteur (rah-kaw*n*-TUHR)
storyteller
   A noun also translated as "narrator" or "teller of anecdotes," and taken into English unchanged in meaning and pronunciation.

raison d'être (ray-ZAW*N* daytrə)
reason for being
   Also translated as "reason for existence." Often used in English without change, but pronounced RAY-zohn DEH-trə.

raisonné (ray-zaw-NAY)
methodical
   Also translated as "classified" and "systematically arranged"; literally, "reasoned." (See also CATALOGUE RAISONNÉ.)

râle de la mort (rahl duu lah mor)
death rattle
   The final sound made by some people as death approaches, adopted in English as "rale," and usually pronounced ral.

ramasser une bûche (rah-mah-SAY ün büsh)
fall on one's face
   Also translated as "take a spill" and "fall headlong." The noun **bûche** means "log," giving us a vivid literal translation of this idiom, "fall like a log." Ouch! A comparable thought is expressed by **ramasser une gamelle** (rah-mah-SAY ün gah-MAYL), but the operative noun, **gamelle**, means "mess kit." Now we have a far less colorful idiom.

rapporter sur ses camarades (rah-por-TAY sür say kah-mah-RAHD)
rat on one's friends
   Better translated as "tell tales on one's friends" or "tattle on one's friends." No matter how you translate this verb phrase, it ain't nice.

rapprochement (rah-prawshə-MAH*N*)
reconciliation
   "Rapprochement," now part of the English language and pronounced as

in French, denotes an act of reestablishment of harmonious relations between nations.

recevoir un coup de pied dans le train (rə-sə-VWAHR œn koo də pyay dahn lə tran)
get a kick in the pants
　　More literally translated as "get a kick in the ass," **train** meaning—politely—"rear end" or "backside."

réchauffé (ray-shoh-FAY)
rehashed
　　Also translated as "stale," "warmed over," or "reheated." Anything we consider to be trite may be termed **réchauffé**, in English also "réchauffé," pronounced as in French.

réchauffer un serpent dans son sein (ray-shoh-FAY œn sair-PAHN dahn sawn san)
misplaced trust
　　Usually translated as "nourish a viper in one's bosom," with the meaning of "befriend someone who proves to be treacherous."

recherché (rə-shair-SHAY)
much sought after
　　Also translated as "in great demand," "out of the ordinary," and "choice." The adjective **recherché** has been taken into English, with unchanged meanings and pronunciation. (See also C'EST QUELQUE CHOSE DE TRÈS RECHERCHÉ.)

réclame (ray-KLAHM)
publicity
　　A noun also translated as "advertisement," and taken into English with unchanged meaning and pronunciation.

réducteur de tête (ray-dük-TUHR duu tayt)
shrink
　　This term, literally, "head reducer," may be applied to a psychotherapist of any kind. The feminine form is **réductrice** (ray-dük-TREESS) **de tête**. (See also TÊTE RÉDUITE.)

refaire une virginité à quelqu'un (rə-FAIR ün veer-zhee-nee-TAY ah kayl-KœN)
restore somebody's image
This is the recognized task of the public relations expert. When we consider that the literal translation of this phrase, "restore someone's virginity," represents an impossible chore, we have a vivid demonstration of how hard it is to restore someone's reputation after it has been besmirched.

regarder (rə-gahr-DAY)
look at or *watch* or *gaze* or *see* or *view*
This infinitive leads unsurprisingly to many useful idioms, including **regarder avec convoitise** (ah-VAYK kawn-vwah-TEEZ), translated as "give someone the eye," more literally, "look lustfully at" (see below REGARDER QUELQU'UN D'UN OEIL LUBRIQUE); **regarder bouche bée** (boosh bay), translated as "gape at," literally, "look at openmouthedly" (see also RESTER BOUCHE BÉE); **regarder de haut en bas** (duu oh tahn bah), translated as "regard scornfully" or "examine from head to foot," literally, "look at from top to bottom"; **regarder de quel côté le vent souffle** (duu kayl koh-TAY luu vahn sooflə), translated as "test the waters" or "send up a trial balloon," literally, "see which way the wind is blowing" (see also BALLON D'ESSAI); **regarder l'avenir avec appréhension** (lah-VəNEER ah-VAYK ah-pray-ahn-SYAWN), translated as "feel apprehensive" or "be concerned about the future," literally, "view the future with trepidation"; **regarder quelqu'un d'un oeil lubrique** (kayl-KœN dœn nœyə lü-BREEK), translated as "give someone the eye," more literally, "gaze at someone with a lecherous eye"; and, finally, **regarder sans voir** (sahn vwahr), translated as "look at with unseeing eyes," in other words, "ignore" or "not really look at."

regonfler le moral de quelqu'un (rə-gawn-FLAY luu maw-RAHL duu kayl-KœN)
boost morale
Also translated as "bolster or jack up someone's spirits," and "cheer someone up." This meaning is also conveyed by **relever le moral de quelqu'un** (rə-lə-VAY luu maw-RAHL duu kayl-KœN). While **regonfler** may be translated as "reinflate," it also may be translated as "rebuild."

remède de bonne femme (ruu-MAYD duu bawn fahm)
folk remedy
Also translated as "old wives' remedy."

remettre quelqu'un à sa place (rə-MAYTRə kayl-KœN ah sah plahss)
put someone in his place
Also translated as "take someone down a peg or two." No matter how translated, this idiom means "take the conceit out of a pretentious person."

remonter la pente (rə-mawn-TAY lah pahnt)
make a comeback
Also translated as "fight one's way back" or "get on one's feet again"; literally, "go back up the slope."

remuer ciel et terre (rə-mü-AY syayl lay tair)
move heaven and earth
The action of a determined person, also translated as "try one's best" or "do everything one can."

remuer l'ordure (rə-mü-AY lor-DÜR)
dig up dirt
Also translated as "rake up filth," the action of an investigator or of certain publications dedicated to achieving foul ends by foul means.

rendre à César ce qui est à César (rahndrə ah say-ZAHR suu kee ay tah say-ZAHR)
obey civil authority
In Matthew, in the New Testament, the response of Jesus when asked whether it was lawful to give tribute—pay taxes—to Caesar, literally translated as "render unto Caesar the things that are Caesar's." He went on to indicate that everything else was reserved for God.

rendre tripes et boyaux (rahndrə treep pay bwah-YOH)
be sick as a dog
Literally, "vomit guts and entrails." Ugh!

renifler quelque chose de louche (rə-nee-FLAY kaylkə shohz duu loosh)
smell a rat
Also translated as "smell something fishy"; literally, "sniff something suspicious."

répondre (ray-PAWNDRə)
answer

This infinitive is part of several interesting characterizations, including **répondre avec impolitesse** (ah-VAYK an-paw-lee-TAYSS), translated as "answer rudely"; **répondre de travers** (duu trah-VAIR), translated as "give a silly answer," more literally, "give an evasive answer" (see also PARLER À TORT ET À TRAVERS); and a companion phrase, **répondre en Normand** (ahn nor-MAHN), translated as "give an evasive answer" or "give an equivocal answer," literally, "reply like a Norman," suggesting that you can't get a straightforward answer out of anyone you meet in Normandy. Surely an exaggeration, and probably based on folk history.

rester (rayss-TAY)
stay or *remain*

An infinitive that leads us into several interesting locutions: **rester à la maison** (ah lah may-ZAWN), translated as "stay at home" or "stay in"; **rester bouche bée** (boosh bay), translated as "be struck dumb," more literally, "stand with mouth wide open" (see also REGARDER BOUCHE BÉE); **rester en carafe** (ahn kah-RAHF), translated as "be left high and dry" and "be left stranded," literally, "stay in the decanter," a marvelous metaphor; **rester en retrait** (ahn ruu-TRAY), translated as "stand aside" and as "withdraw from active life," literally, "remain in retreat"; **rester garçon** (gahr-SAWN), translated as "remain single" or "remain a bachelor," the noun **garçon** having "bachelor" as one of its meanings; **rester immobile** (eem-maw-BEEL), translated as "keep still" or "stay motionless"; and, finally, **rester le bec dans l'eau** (luu bayk dahn loh), translated as "be left high and dry" or "be left in the lurch," literally, "remain with the beak in water." An apt metaphor.

restez-y! (rayss-tay-ZEE)
stay or *remain there!*

That is, "don't move!"

retourner le couteau dans la plaie (rə-toor-NAY luu koo-TOH dahn lah play)
rub salt in old wounds

Also translated as "reopen old wounds"; literally, "stick the knife back in the wound." Ouch!

revenons à nos moutons (rə-və-NAWN zah noh moo-TAWN)
back to business!

Better translated as "let's get back to the subject at hand"; literally, "let's return to our sheep."

rien (ryan)
nothing

This pronoun leads us into many interesting locutions, including **rien à faire!** (nah fair), translated as "nothing doing!"; **rien de moins** (duu mwan), translated as "nothing less"; **rien de neuf** (duu nuhf), translated as "nothing new"; **rien de nouveau sous le soleil** (duu noo-VOH soo luu saw-LAYə), also given as **rien de nouveau sous le ciel** (soo luu syayl), with **ciel** meaning "sky," both translated as "nothing new under the sun," deriving from Ecclesiastes, in the Old Testament, "there is no new thing under the sun"; **rien de plus** (duu plüss), translated as "nothing more"; **rien de plus éloquent que l'argent comptant** (duu plü zay-law-KAHN kuu lahr-ZHAHN kawn-TAHN), translated as "money talks," literally, "nothing is more eloquent than cash"; **rien n'a transpiré** (nah trahnss-pee-RAY), translated as "there were no leaks" or "nothing came to light," literally, "nothing transpired"; **rien ne marche** (nuu mahrsh), translated as "we're at a standstill," "we've reached an impasse," "nothing's working," and "nothing's going right"; **rien ne pèse tant qu'un secret** (nuu payz tahn kœn suu-KRAY), a saying of La Fontaine on the impossibility of keeping a confidence, translated literally as "nothing weighs so heavily as a secret"; **rien ne sert de courir, il faut partir à temps** (nuu sair duu koo-REER eel foh pahr-TEER rah tahn), translated as "slow and steady wins the race," literally, "nothing's gained by running; just leave on time"; **rien n'est beau que le vrai** (nay boh kuu luu vray), translated as "truth counts for everything," literally, "nothing is beautiful but the truth"; **rien n'est perdu** (nay pair-DÜ), translated as "no harm done," more literally as "nothing's lost"; **rien ne vous presse** (nuu voo prayss), translated as "no need to rush" or "there's no hurry"; and, finally, the ultimate in resignation, **rien n'y fait** (nee fay), translated as "nothing's any good" or "nothing will work."

rire (reer)
laugh

An infinitive that introduces many locutions, including the cruel **rire au dépens de quelqu'un** (roh day-PAHN duu kayl-KœN), translated as "make someone a laughingstock," literally, "laugh at someone's expense"; **rire au nez de quelqu'un** (roh nay duu kayl-KœN), translated as "laugh in someone's face," literally, "laugh in someone's nose"; **rire comme une baleine** (kawm mün bah-LAYN), translated as "split one's sides laughing" or "laugh oneself silly," literally, "laugh like a whale"; **rire dans sa barbe** (dahn sah bahrb), translated as "laugh up one's sleeve," literally, "laugh in one's beard," and three companion phrases, **rire entre cuir et chair** (rahntrə kweer ray shair), also translated as "laugh up one's sleeve," "laugh secretly," and "laugh to oneself," literally, "laugh between skin and flesh," a safe place for hiding one's laughter; **rire seul** (suhl), also translated as "laugh to oneself"; and **rire sous cape** (soo kahp), "laugh up one's sleeve," literally, "laugh under one's cape." Finally, there is **rire jaune** (zhohn), translated as "force a laugh" or "laugh on the wrong side of one's mouth," literally, "laugh yellow."

rive droite (reevə drwaht)
the right bank
   Of, for example, the river Seine, in Paris, contrasted with **rive gauche** (gohsh), the left bank of a river. Together, these two phrases divide Paris— **la Ville lumière** (lah veel lüm-YAIR), "the City of Light"—into a district known for its intellectual and student life (**la Rive gauche**), and the rest of the city (**la Rive droite**).

roman à clef (raw-MAHN ah klay)
roman à clef
   Translated literally as "novel with a key," but always given as the borrowed English phrase "roman à clef," with the French pronunciation. Both the French and the English terms may be defined as a novel in which real personages are depicted as fictional characters.

roman d'anticipation (raw-MAHN dahn-tee-see-pah-SYAWN)
science-fiction novel

Rome ne s'est pas fait en un jour (rawm ne say pah fay ahn nœn zhoor)
Rome wasn't built in a day
   In English a sixteenth-century proverb. Both the French and the English tell us that worthwhile tasks are not accomplished overnight. Patience and time are needed for anything worth doing.

ronger son frein (rawn-ZHAY sawn fran)
raring to go
   An equine metaphor usually translated as "champ at the bit"; literally, "gnaw at the bit."

rossignol d'Arcadie (raw-see-NYAWL dahr-kah-DEE)
jackass
   A humorous metaphor, literally, "nightingale of Arcadia." Arcadia—or Arcady—is an imaginary place of pastoral simplicity and happiness.

rougir jusqu'aux oreilles (roo-ZHEER zhüss-KOH zaw-RAYə)
world-class blushing
   Translated as "blush all the way to one's ears."

ruse contre ruse (rüz kawntrə rüz)
wile against wile
   An even match.

ruse de guerre (rüz duu gair)
tactics
   Better translated as "stratagem of war."

sa chambre est un vrai foutoir (sah shahnbrə ay tœn vray foo-TWAHR)
a regular boy's room
   Better translated as "his room is a pigsty"; literally, "his room is a shambles."

sacrebleu! (sahkrə-BLUU)
confound it!

sacré nom de nom! (sah-KRAY nawn duu nawn)
hell and damnation!
  Literally, "blasted name of a name!"

sa femme eut des soupçons (sah fahm ü day soop-SAWN)
she was not a fool
  More literally, "his wife had suspicions."

sa femme porte la culotte (sah fahm portə lah kü-LUHT)
his wife is the boss
  Literally, "his wife wears the pants."

sage-femme (sahzh-FAHM)
midwife
  Literally, "wise woman." (See also FEMME SAGE.)

saignant (say-NYAHN)
bleeding
  This adjective is regularly heard in French restaurants, in **entrecôte saignante** (ahn-trə-KAWT say-NYAHNT), to mean "very rare steak." **Saignante** is the feminine form of **saignant**.

sain et sauf (san ay sohf)
safe and sound
  Literally, "sound and safe."

salle (sahl)
room
  Naturally, there are many types of rooms, among them **salle à manger** (lah mahn-ZHAY), "dining room"; **salle d'attente** (dah-TAHNT), "waiting room" (see also SALON D'ATTENTE); **salle de bain** (duu ban), "bathroom"; **salle de jeu** (duu zhuu), translated as "gaming room" (of a casino) and "playroom" (for children); **salle de séjour** (duu say-ZHOOR), "living room"; **salle des pas perdus** (day pah pair-DÜ), translated as "place to cool your heels" and "outer hall of a public building," literally, "hall of the lost footsteps"—ask anyone who has ever had to wait for a bureaucrat—and, finally, **salle des urgences** (day zür-ZHAHNSS), "emergency room."

salon (sah-LAW*N*)
lounge or *salon*

Just as we have various types of **salles**, we have a number of **salons: salon d'attente** (dah-TAHNT), translated as "waiting room" (see also SALLE D'ATTENTE); **salon de coiffure** (də kwah-FÜR), translated as "beauty parlor" or "hairdressing salon"; and, sadly, **salon funéraire** (fü-nay-RAIR), "funeral home" or "funeral parlor."

saloperie (sah-law-PREE)
junk or *rubbish*

Also translated as "sluttishness" and "ribaldry" as well as "something of execrable quality." In the plural, **saloperies**, pronounced just like the singular, the meaning is "filthy remarks."

sa manoeuvre était téléphonée (sah mah-NUHVRə ay-TAY tay-lay-faw-NAY)
you could read him like an open book

Also translated as "you could easily see where he was coming from," literally "his maneuver was telephoned," expressed in baseball jargon as "his move was telegraphed."

sang-froid (sah*n*-FRWAH)
nonchalance

Also translated as "composure" and "coolness"; literally, "cold blood." English employs "sang-froid" with the same meanings and pronunciation.

sans (sah*n*)
without

Many locutions employ **sans**, among them: **sans-abri** (sah*n*-zah-BREE), translated as "homeless person," literally, "without shelter"; **sans ambages** (zah*n*-BAHZH), translated as "plainly," "in plain language," and as "without beating around the bush"; **sans cérémonie** (say-ray-maw-NEE), translated as "informally," literally, "without ceremony"; **sans changer** (shah*n*-ZHAY), translated as "without changing"; **sans-coeur** (sah*n*-KUHR), translated as "heartless," literally, "without heart"; and **sans-culottes** (sah*n*-kü-LAWT), literally, "without breeches." **Sans Culottes** was the name given during the French Revolution to the extremists of the working classes, who refused to wear knee breeches, favored by the aristocracy, and instead wore ordinary trousers. Then there are **sans Dieu rien** (dyuu ryan), translated as "without God, nothing"; **sans doute** (doot), translated as "doubtless," literally, "without doubt"; **sans éducation** (zay-dü-kah-SYAWN), translated as "uncouth" and "ill-bred," literally, "unlettered" (see also MAL ÉDUQUÉ); the noun **sans-emploi** (sahn-zahn-PLWAH), translated as "unemployed person," literally, "without employment"; **sans faute** (foht), translated as "without fail," literally, "without error"; **sans gêne** (zhayn), translated as "free and easy," "unceremonious," and "unconstrained," literally, "without embarrassment," and the noun **sans-gêne** (sahn-ZHAYN), translated as "coolness," "offhandedness," "familiarity," and "absence of constraint," as well as "unceremonious and coolly familiar person"; **sans hésitation** (zay-zee-tah-SYAWN) and **sans hésiter** (zay-zee-TAY), both translated as "unhesitatingly" or "without hesitation"; the sad phrase **sans le sou** (lə soo), translated as "penniless," literally, "without a penny" or "without a sou"; **sans mère** (mair), translated as "motherless"; **sans pareil** (pah-RAYə), translated as "unequaled," literally, "without equal"; **sans peine** (payn), translated as "readily" or "easily," literally, "without difficulty"; **sans père** (pair), translated as "fatherless"; and **sans peur et sans reproche** (puhr ay sahn ruu-PRAWSH), translated as "chivalrous," almost literally as "without fear and beyond reproach." **Le chevalier** (luu shə-vahl-YAY) **sans peur et sans reproche** was a name bestowed on the Chevalier de Bayard (1475–1524), a celebrated French knight. To continue, there are **sans racine** (rah-SEEN), translated as "rootless," literally, "without root"; **sans raison** (ray-ZAWN), translated as "groundless" and "groundlessly," literally, "without reason"; **sans rancune!** (rahn-KÜN), translated as "no hard feelings!" or, literally, "without rancor!" or "without a grudge!"; **sans remise** (ruu-MEEZ), translated as "unremittingly" and "relentlessly," literally, "without postponement"; **sans rime ni raison** (reem nee ray-ZAWN), translated as "without rhyme or reason"; **sans scrupule** (skrü-PÜL), translated as "unscrupulous" or "unprincipled," literally, "without scruple"; **sans-souci** (sahn-soo-SEE), translated as "unconcern," literally, "without care"; **sans tache** (tahsh), translated as "stainless," literally, "without blemish"; **sans tambour ni trompette** (tahn-BOOR nee trawn-PAYT), translated as "without fanfare," "without fuss," and "unobtrusively," literally, "without drum or trumpet"; **sans valeur** (vah-LUHR), translated as "worthless" and "valueless," literally, "without value"; **sans verser une goutte de sang** (vair-SAY ün gootə duu sahn), translated as "without shedding a drop of blood"; and, finally, **sans y changer une virgule** (zee shahn-ZHAY ün veer-GÜL), translated as "without changing a jot or tittle," literally, "without changing a comma in it."

saucisson à l'ail (soh-see-SAWN ah lī)
garlic sausage
   Ah!

sauf (sohf)
except or *unless*
   A preposition that serves to introduce some interesting locutions, among them **sauf avis contraire** (ah-VEE kawn-TRAIR), translated as "unless you hear otherwise" or "unless you hear something to the contrary," literally, "without contrary advice"; **sauf erreur ou omission** (ay-RUHR oo aw-mee-SYAWN), translated as "errors or omissions excepted," more literally, "except for error or omission"; **sauf imprévu** (an-pray-VÜ), translated as "barring the unforeseen" or "unless something unexpected happens"; and, finally, **sauf indication contraire** (an-dee-kah-SYAWN kawn-TRAIR), translated as "unless otherwise indicated."

saumon fumé (soh-MAWN fü-MAY)
smoked salmon
   Everybody's favorite, with or without a bagel and cream cheese.

sauter le fossé (soh-TAY lə faw-SAY)
take the plunge
   Also translated as "take the fateful step"; literally, "jump across the ditch." Of one thing you may be certain—if you do this, there's no turning back.

sauve qui peut (sohvə kee puu)
run for your life!
   A phrase literally translated as "let him save himself who can," meaning every man for himself and the devil take the hindmost.

sauver sa tête (soh-VAY sah tayt)
save one's skin
   Also translated as "save one's neck"; literally, "save one's head." So you have a choice of body parts when you can save only one.

savant (sah-VAHN)
learned or *scholarly*

This adjective is also used as a noun, with the meaning of "learned person" or "scholar." English has adopted the noun, with the same meaning and the pronunciation sa-VAHNT.

savate (sah-VAHT)
French boxing

In which the feet are used as well as the fists. **Savate** literally translates as "worn-out old slipper *or* shoe," suggesting that the boxer's feet are covered lightly.

savoir (sah-VWAHR)
know

This infinitive gives us several interesting terms and phrases, including **savoir-faire** (sah-vwahr-FAIR), translated as "tact," "know-how," and "readiness in doing the right thing," literally, "a knowing how to do"; **savoir gré** (gray), translated as "appreciate," "be grateful," and "know how to please"; **savoir prendre sur soi** (prahndrə sür swah), translated as "keep a grip on oneself," literally, "know how to contain yourself"; **savoir se faire estimer** (suu fair rayss-tee-MAY), translated as "how to win friends and influence people," more literally, "know how to gain respect"; and, finally, **savoir-vivre** (sah-vwahr-VEEVRə), translated as "being at ease in society," "good manners," and "good breeding," literally, "knowing how to live." Amen!

scène de ménage (sayn duu may-NAHZH)
domestic squabble

Also translated, more literally, as "domestic scene," a bilingual euphemism. Better to call a spat a spat!

séance privée (say-AHNSS pree-VAY)
private showing

Also translated as "private performance." The noun **séance** has been taken into English with the meaning "session"—of a particular sort, of course, especially one in which a spiritualist attempts to establish communication with a deceased person—but without change in pronunciation.

se battre contre des moulins (suu bahtrə kawntrə day moo-LAN)
tilt at windmills

A phrase from the Spanish novel *Don Quixote*, more freely translated as "fight imaginary adversaries," in which Cervantes had his protagonist give battle against windmills, which he saw as giants.

sécher son verre (say-SHAY sawn vair)
knock one back
Also translated as "drain one's glass"; more literally, "dry one's glass."

se comporter comme un enfant gâté (suu kawn-por-TAY kawm mœn nahn-FAHN gah-TAY)
behave like a brat
More literally, "behave like a spoiled child." Of course, a person so described is actually classified as an adult.

se coucher avec les poules (suu koo-SHAY ah-VAYK lay pool)
early to bed
Literally, "go to bed with the hens."

secouer les puces à quelqu'un (suu-KWAY lay püss sah kayl-KœN)
tell someone off
Also translated as "shake someone up"; literally, "shake the fleas off someone."

secret d'alcôve (suu-KRAY dahl-KOHVə)
intimate talk
Also translated, more literally, as "bedroom talk," and as "pillow talk"—between couples, that is.

se creuser les méninges (suu kruu-ZAY lay may-NANZH)
cudgel one's brain
Also translated as "rack one's brains"; literally, "dig a hole in the brains." (See also SE TRITURER LA CERVELLE.)

se crever le cul (suu kruu-VAY lə kü)
bust one's ass
More conventionally—and less literally—translated as "do one's utmost."

séducteur (say-dük-TUHR)
womanizer

Literally, "seducer." The feminine form of this noun is **séductrice** (say-dük-TREESS), translated as "seductress." In these times, one supposes, the translation of either French noun would be "seducer."

séduisant (say-dwee-ZAHN)
alluring

Also translated as "seductive" and "attractive."

se faire (suu fair)
get or *do* or *make*

This reflexive verb, which can be thought of as meaning "do *or* make oneself," forms the basis of many interesting idioms, including **se faire arroser** (rah-raw-ZAY), translated as "get drenched" or "get soaked"; **se faire bourrer la gueule** (boo-RAY lah guhl), translated as "get mugged," "suffer a terrible beating," or "get one's head bashed in," literally, "get one's mouth pummeled"; **se faire désirer** (day-zee-RAY), translated as "play hard to get," literally, "make oneself desired"; **se faire des mamours** (day mah-MOOR), translated as "bill and coo," literally, "get caresses"; **se faire du lard** (dü lahr), translated as "grow fatter and fatter" or "sit around and get fat"; **se faire écharper** (ay-shahr-PAY), translated as "get torn to pieces"; **se faire embarquer par la police** (rahn-bahr-KAY pahr lah paw-LEESS), translated as "be nabbed by the cops" or "get picked up by the law"; **se faire faire un bilan de santé** (fair œn bee-LAHN duu sahn-TAY), translated as "go in for a checkup" or "have a physical," **bilan** meaning "appraisal"; two phrases with the same meaning: **se faire flouer** (floo-AY) and **se faire gruger** (grü-ZHAY), both translated as "be conned," "be taken in," "be had," or, literally, "be swindled *or* duped"; **se faire maigrir** (may-GREER), literally, "lose weight," usually taken as "diet to lose weight"; and **se faire siffler** (see-FLAY), translated as "be hissed" and "be booed," literally, "get whistled at." In many European countries whistling is employed rather than booing. To go on, there are **se faire soldat** (sawl-DAH), translated as "enlist" and "join the army"; **se faire tout petit** (too pətee), literally, "make oneself very small," that is, "try to make oneself invisible" or "try not to be noticed"; and, finally, **se faire une montagne de rien** (ün mawn-TAHNYə duu ryan), translated as "make a federal case out of nothing," more usually, "make a mountain out of a molehill" and, literally, "make a mountain out of nothing."

se farcir la mémoire de (suu fahr-SEER lah may-MWAHR duu)
information overload

Translated as "cram one's memory with." And what do we cram our memories with? Facts, dates, batting averages, the names of French and English monarchs—all sorts of useful and useless information. When you consider that in cookery the French have given us, for example, **tomates farcies** (taw-MAHT fahr-SEE), in which tomatoes are stuffed with any manner of edible foods, you have some idea of what can be done beginning with the infinitive **farcir**, meaning "stuff" or "cram."

se fourrer les doigts dans le nez (suu foo-RAY lay dwah dahn lǝ nay)
pick one's nose

Literally, "stick the fingers into the nose." (See also FOURRER SON NEZ PARTOUT.)

se guérir d'un amour malheureux (suu gay-REER dœn nah-MOOR mah-luu-RUU)
get over an unhappy love affair

Literally, "be cured of an unhappy love affair," suggesting that a love affair gone awry should be treated as a sickness. How romantic!

se laisser vivre (suu lay-SAY veevrǝ)
take each day as it comes

Good advice, also translated as "live for the day"; literally, "let oneself live."

se livrer à des indécences (suu lee-VRAY ah day zan-day-SAHNSS)
in a plain brown wrapper, please

Translated as "indulge in indecent acts."

selon le saint l'encens (suu-LAWN luu san lahn-SAHN)
homage in proportion to importance

Literally, "according to the saint, the incense," cautioning wisely against overstatement when paying compliments or showing reverence.

se marier de la main gauche (suu mah-RYAY duu lah man gohsh)
live as husband and wife

The clear inference drawn here is that the persons so characterized have not gone through a customary marriage procedure. (For an explanation of the phrase **la main gauche**, "the left hand," see MARIAGE DE LA MAIN GAUCHE.)

se ménager une porte de sortie (suu may-nah-ZHAY ün port duu sor-TEE)
nothing like a loophole
Translated as "leave oneself a way out," which is always a sensible precaution.

se mettre au page (suu maytrə oh pahzh)
hit the sack
Also translated as "turn in" and "hit the hay," more usually, "go to bed." A word of caution: the French language can be pretty tricky, as you surely know by now. The point to be made here is the distinction between **le page** (masculine) and **la page** (feminine). The former, used in **se mettre au page**, translates as "bed," the latter as "page." (See also ALLER AU PADDOCK.)

se mettre sur son trente et un (suu maytrə sür sawn trahnt tay œn)
put on one's Sunday best
Also translated as "get all dressed up" and "be dressed to kill." The literal translation is "put on one's thirty-one," this number being taken as meaning "umpteen," that is, a fanciful and indeterminately large number. But why thirty-one? Could it be that one only dresses up in one's best once a month—and only in the seven months that have thirty-one days? Come to think of it, the French idiom is no more far-fetched than the English "dressed to the nines," for which it has been suggested that "to the nines" is a corruption of "to the eyes," written in an earlier variety of English as "to then eyne." (See also TIRÉ À QUATRE ÉPINGLES.)

s'en mettre plein les fouilles (sahn maytrə plan lay fooyə)
make a killing
Also translated as "line one's pockets"; more literally, "fill one's pockets."

s'en mettre une bonne ventrée (sahn maytrə ün bawn vahn-TRAY)
pig out
Usually translated as "stuff oneself"; more literally, "give oneself a good bellyful."

se nourrir de conserves (suu noo-REER duu kawn-SAIRVə)
live out of cans
Literally, "feed oneself canned foods."

s'entendre comme larrons en foire (sahn-TAHNDRə kawm lah-RAWN ahn fwahr)
be thick as thieves
   Literally, "get along like thieves at a fair"—where competition among thieves is not keen, since the pickings are so rich.

se rabaisser devant quelqu'un (suu rah-bay-SAY duu-VAHN kayl-KœN)
kowtow
   Also translated as "humble oneself before someone"; literally, "belittle oneself before someone." (See also S'INCLINER JUSQU'À TERRE.)

se retirer dans sa chambre (suu rə-tee-RAY dahn sah shahnbrə)
go to one's room
   Also translated as "seclude oneself" and "retire to one's room." This thought is also given as **se retirer dans sa tour d'ivoire** (dahn sah toor dee-VWAHR), literally, "withdraw to one's ivory tower."

sérieux comme un pape (say-RYUU kawm mœn pahpə)
sober as a judge
   Literally, "solemn as a pope."

se rincer la dalle (suu ran-SAY lah dahl)
have a drink
   Also translated as "wet one's whistle"; literally, "rinse the paving stone." (See also DALLE FUNÉRAIRE.)

serment d'ivrogne (sair-MAHN dee-VRAWNYə)
don't believe this man!
   Better translated as "empty vow"; literally, "drunkard's pledge."

serrer les fesses (say-RAY lay fayss)
be scared out of one's wits
   A marvelous metaphor; literally, "tighten one's buttocks."

service non compris (sair-VEESS nawn kawn-PREE)
service not included

A restaurant term meaning that the diner must dig into his pocket for a suitable tip for the waiter. The term **service compris** means service is included, so a tip is not required, although a small tip is customarily given.

se sucer la poire (suu sü-SAY lah pwahr)
neck
Also translated as "kiss passionately"; literally, "suck the pear." Wow!

se triturer la cervelle (suu tree-tü-RAY lah sair-VAYL)
cudgel one's brains
Also translated as "think as hard as one can"; literally, "grind up one's brains."

s'exiler loin du monde (sayg-zee-LAY lwan dü mawndə)
go to Tahiti
Also translated as "take to the hills" and "cut oneself off from the world."

si c'est possible, c'est fait; si c'est impossible, cela se fera (see say paw-SEEBLə say fay see say an-paw-SEEBLə suu-LAH suu fuu-RAH)
the way to get ahead in court
Freely translated as "when you say 'jump,' I answer 'how far?'" This is the reply, literally, "if it's possible, it's done; if it's impossible, it shall be done," that is attributed to French finance minister Charles de Calonne (1734–1802) to Marie Antoinette's request for money. Calonne set a record for running up state deficits—since surpassed, of course—by acceding to royal requests for funds. Incidentally, he died penniless.

SIDA (see-DAH)
AIDS
Abbreviation of **Syndrome Immuno-Déficitaire Acquis** (san-DROHM eem-myoo-noh-day-fee-see-TAIR ah-KEE), acquired immune deficiency syndrome.

si Dieu n'existait pas, il faudrait l'inventer (see dyuu nayg-zees-TAY pah eel foh-DRAY lan-vahn-TAY)
if God did not exist, it would be necessary to invent him
The words of Voltaire, at his antireligious best.

siècle d'or (syayklə dor)
golden age
Literally, "age of gold," applied especially to the reign of French King Louis XIV, **le Roi-Soleil** (luu rwah saw-LAYə).

si j'avais su! (see zhah-VAY sü)
now you tell me!
Translated literally as "if I had only known!"

si jeunesse savait, si vieillesse pouvait (see zhuu-NAYSS sah-VAY see vyay-YAYSS poo-VAY)
if youth but knew, if old age but could
An aphorism from Henri Estienne, a sixteenth-century French publisher.

s'il avait quatre sous de bon sens (seel lah-VAY kahtrə soo duu bawn sahnss)
if he had a scrap of common sense
Literally, "if he had four pennies of common sense."

simple comme bonjour (sanplə kawm bawn-ZHOOR)
easy as pie
Also translated as "easy as falling off a log," more literally as "simple as saying hello."

s'incliner jusqu'à terre (san-klee-NAY zhüss-KAH tair)
grovel
Literally, "bow to the ground." (See also SE RABAISSER DEVANT QUELQU'UN.)

si on le laisse faire il se passera lui-même la corde au cou (see awn luu layss fair eel suu pahssə-RAH lwee-MAYM lah kordə oh koo)
give someone enough rope and he'll hang himself
This has nothing to do with stringing someone up. Rather, it suggests that if we allow someone to continue doing something harmful to himself, he will suffer the consequences of his folly.

sitôt dit, sitôt fait (see-TOH dee see-TOH fay)
no sooner said than done

The performance of anyone who really has his life together; literally, "soon as said, soon as done."

si tu veux la paix, prépare la guerre (see tü vuu lah pay pray-PAHR lah gair)
be prepared!
A proverb, literally "if you want peace, prepare for war," that is translated from a Latin proverb.

sobre comme un chameau (sawbrə kawm mœn shah-MOH)
sober as a judge
Literally, "sober as a camel," apposite because the camel goes so long between drinks—of water, of course.

société anonyme (saw-syay-TAY ah-naw-NEEM)
limited company
Literally, "anonymous company," a form of business in France in which the members' names do not appear in the name of the company, and the members bear limited financial responsibility.

soigné (swah-NYAY)
well-groomed
Also translated as "carefully done," "neat," and "elegantly simple," all applied to grooming and style of dress. English has adopted this adjective without change in spelling or pronunciation.

sois un peu dans le vent! (swah œn puu dahn lə vahn)
get with it!
Translated as "be in style"; literally, "be a little in the wind."

sombrer corps et biens (sawn-BRAY kor zay byan)
disaster at sea
Translated as "go down with all hands"; literally, "founder with bodies and property." And that says it all.

son corps se moulait au sien (sawn kor suu moo-LAY oh syan)
X-rated
Literally translated as "her body molded against his."

son et lumière (sawn ay lü-MYAIR)
sound-and-light show
   Literally, "sound and light." Adopted in English as "son et lumière," and pronounced as close to the French pronunciation as one can muster.

son sang se figea dans ses veines (sawn sahn suu fee-ZHAH dahn say vayn)
his blood froze in his veins
   More literally translated as "his blood congealed in his veins." Either way, we have a vivid mental image of someone who is gripped by terror.

sortie de bain (sor-TEE də ban)
bathrobe
   Literally, "leaving the bath."

sortir de l'anonymat (sor-TEER duu lah-naw-nee-MAH)
come out of the closet
   Literally, "go out of anonymity."

soubrette (soo-BRAYT)
maid or *maidservant* or *soubrette*
   In the theater the noun "soubrette" (soo-BRET) in English, like **soubrette** in French, denotes an intriguing, coquettish, and meddlesome maid in a comedy, as well as an actress who plays such a part.

souffrir (soo-FREER)
suffer
   Obviously, we all suffer so much that French obliges us with interesting idioms, among them **souffrir comme une bourrique** (kawm mün boo-REEK), translated as "dead drunk" and "drunk as a skunk," literally, "suffer like a jackass" (see also SOÛL COMME UNE BOURRIQUE); **souffrir de la chaleur** (duu lah shah-LUHR), translated as "suffer from the heat," and its counterpart, **souffrir du froid** (dü frwah), translated as "suffer from the cold"; **souffrir en silence** (rahn see-LAHNSS), translated as "suffer uncomplainingly," literally, "suffer in silence"; **souffrir le martyre** (luu mahr-TEER), translated as "agonize," "go through hell on earth," and "undergo torture," literally, "suffer martyrdom"; and, by way of saying good-bye to suffering, there is **souffrir mille morts** (meel mor), literally, "die a thousand deaths." Man, that's dying!

soûl comme une bourrique (soo kawm mün boo-REEK)
blind drunk

Also translated as "drunk as a lord"; literally, "drunk as a jackass." (See also SOUFFRIR COMME UNE BOURRIQUE.)

soupçon (soop-SAW*N*)
a suspicion

Also translated as "a dash," "minute quantity," "mere trace," and "a taste."

soupe (soop)
soup

We can't stop there. How about **soupe à l'oignon** (pah law-NYAW*N*), "onion soup"; **soupe de l'Inde** (duu la*n*d), "mulligatawny soup," literally, "soup of the Indies"; **soupe grasse** (grahss), "meat soup"; and **soupe maigre** (maygrə), "thin vegetable soup."

sous (soo)
under

This preposition gives us several interesting locutions, including **sous le manteau** (lə mah*n*-TOH), translated as "clandestinely," "on the sly," "under cover," and, literally, "under the cloak"; **sous l'empire de la boisson** (lah*n*-PEER duu lah bwah-SAW*N*), translated as "in the grip of John Barleycorn," "the worse for drink," "entrapped by drink," and, literally, "under the empire of drink"; **sous tous les rapports** (too lay rah-POR), translated as "in all respects"; and **sous tous ses aspects** (too say zahss-PAY), translated as "in every regard," "from all sides," and, literally, "in all its aspects."

soutien-gorge (soo-tya*n*-GORZH)
bra

This important article of women's dress used to be given in English as "brassiere" (brə-ZEER), and in French was called **brassière** (brah-SYAIR), but today "bra" and **soutien-gorge** hold sway.

soyez (swah-YAY)
be

This verb is in the imperative mood, as you will see in the following locutions: **soyez ferme** (fairm), translated as "don't give in," "be firm," and "be staunch"; **soyez raisonable** (ray-zaw-NAHBLə), translated as "be sensible" and "be reasonable" (see also L'AMOUR NE SE RAISONNE PAS); **soyez sage** (sahzh), translated as "use your head," "be sensible," and "be wise"; and, finally, **soyez tranquille** (trahn-KEEL), translated as "don't worry" and "set your mind at ease."

strip-teaseuse (streep-tee-ZUHZ)
stripper
   Also translated—in a playful coinage by H. L. Mencken—as "ecdysiast."

subir le charme de quelqu'un (sü-BEER luu shahrmə duu kayl-KœN)
fall under someone's spell
   More closely translated as "be captivated by someone" and "be under the influence of someone's charm."

succès (sük-SAY)
success
   This happy noun leads us to a group of interesting locutions describing a variety of types of successes: **succès de librairie** (duu lee-bray-REE), translated as "best-seller," literally, "bookstore success"; **succès de scandale** (duu skahn-DAHL), translated as "success due to notoriety"—engendered by the sensational nature of its subject matter—literally translated as "success of scandal"; **succès d'estime** (dayss-TEEM), translated realistically as "the book *or* play *or* movie flopped—but the critics praised it," more properly translated as "success with more honor than profit," but usually given in English as "succès d'estime," pronounced as in French, rather than the literal translation "success of esteem"; and, finally, **succès fou** (foo), translated as "smash hit," literally, "mad success."

suivre son penchant (sweevrə sawn pahn-SHAHN)
follow one's bent
   Also translated as "follow one's inclination." The English noun "penchant," borrowed centuries ago from the French and still in use, was pronounced for a long time as in French, but the French pronunciation now appears to be playing second fiddle to PEN-chənt.

sujet maigre (sü-ZHAY maygrə)
barren subject
   A topic of discussion that leads nowhere.

supplément de prix (sü-play-MAH*N* duu pree)
surcharge
   A restaurant or hotel term that translates also, alas, as "additional charge."

sûrement va qui n'a rien (sürə-MAH*N* vah kee nah ryan)
he goes safely who has nothing to lose
   A streetwise proverb suggesting that the safe way to navigate city streets is to leave valuables at home and carry little money on one's person.

sur l'heure (sür luhr)
immediately
   Also translated as "at once" and "straightaway"; literally, "on the hour."

surtout, pas de vagues (sür-TOO pah də vahgə)
above all, keep it quiet
   Also translated as "above all, let's avoid a scandal," literally, "above all, no waves."

tableau vivant (tah-BLOH vee-VAH*N*)
tableau vivant
   Literally, "living picture," but usually given in English as the French phrase pronounced as in French, denoting a once-popular entertainment offering representations of a statuary group by living persons dressed in appropriate costume.

table d'hôte (tahblə doht)
fixed-price meal
   A restaurant term, literally translated as "host's table" but always given in English as "table d'hôte," pronounced as in French, to indicate a meal of preselected courses served to diners.

tâche sans tache (tahsh sahn tahsh)
an unblemished work

Literally, "a work without a fault." Notice the absence of a circumflex accent in the second **tache**. With this accent the word means "task" or "work"; without it, "blot" or "stain." Tricky language, French—at least for foreigners.

taire la vérité, c'est déjà mentir (tair lah vay-ree-TAY say day-ZHAH mahn-TEER)
not to tell the truth is as good as lying

Also translated as "withholding truth hides the truth," "incomplete disclosure hides the truth," and "we lie when we do not tell the whole truth."

taisez-vous (tay-zay-VOO)
hold your tongue!

Also translated as "be silent!" and "be quiet!" The same thought is expressed by **tais-toi** (tay-TWAH), the form used when addressing a young person or someone with whom one is on familiar terms.

talon d'Achille (tah-LAWN dah-SHEEL)
Achilles' heel

Freely translated as "weak spot," a vulnerable or especially vulnerable part of a person's character, history, or physical makeup. In Greek mythology, the mother of Achilles, hero of the *Iliad*, held the child by the heel and dipped him in the river Styx in order to make him invulnerable. And invulnerable he became—except for his heel, since his mother's hand prevented wetting of his heel. Sure enough, he was slain by an arrow wound in that very heel—giving us a durable metaphor for any chink in one's armor that plagues a person.

tant (tahn)
so much

This adverb finds use in many locutions, among them **tant bien que mal** (byan kə mahl), translated as "indifferently" and "passably," literally as "as much well as ill"; **tant mieux** (myuu), translated as "so much the better"; **tant pis** (pee), "so much the worse," also translated as "that's too bad" and, pragmatically, "never mind"; **tant qu'on a la santé** (kawn nah lah sahn-TAY), translated as "as long as you have your health," useful when a friend has recited a litany of his assorted woes; **tant s'en faut** (sahn foh), translated as "not by a long shot" and "far from it," literally, "so much is lacking"; **tant soit peu** (swah puu), translated as "ever so little"; and, finally, the proverb **tant va la cruche à l'eau qu'à la fin elle se casse** (vah lah krüsh ah loh kah lah fan ayl suu kahss), translated as "don't ask for trouble," "if you court danger, you'll get it," and "if you play with fire long enough, you're sure to be burned," literally, "if you use a water jug long enough, it finally will crack."

tartuffe (tahr-TÜF)
hypocrite

Also translated as "sanctimonious hypocrite." The title of one of Molière's popular comedies is *Le Tartuffe*, which recounts the machinations of a religious hypocrite named Tartuffe, and has given French the word **tartuffe**, also spelled **tartufe**.

tel (tayl)
such or *like* or *as*

This adjective, sometimes a pronoun, introduces several locutions, including **tel est notre plaisir** (lay nawtrə play-ZEER), translated as "such is our pleasure"; the proverb **tel est pris qui croyait prendre** (lay pree kee krwah-YAY prahndrə), translated freely as "don't be surprised when the tables are turned" and "the biter is also bitten"; **tel maître, tel valet** (maytrə tayl vah-LAY), translated as "like master, like man," the term "man" here meaning "male servant" or "valet"; **tel père, tel fils** (pair tayl feess), translated as "like father, like son"; and, finally, the sardonic **tel qui rit vendredi, dimanche pleurera** (kee ree vahn-drə-DEE dee-MAHNSH pluu-ruu-RAH), a line from Racine, translated as "laugh today, cry tomorrow," much more freely as "the Dow-Jones average won't go up forever" and, much more literally, "he who laughs on Friday will cry on Sunday."

tenez bon la rampe (tuu-NAY bawn lah rahnpə)
hold on to your hat

Literally, "hold fast to the slope." (See also LÂCHER LA RAMPE.)

tenez cela pour fait (tuu-NAY sə-LAH poor fay)
consider it done

The welcome response of a subordinate—or spouse—who knows how to take directions and execute them.

terrine de foie gras (tay-REEN duu fwah grah)
goose liver cooked in earthenware
   A most delightful dish.

tête-à-tête (tayt-tah-TAYT)
private conversation
   Translated here as a noun. As an adjective, translated as "private" or "confidential." As an adverb, translated as "privately" or "confidentially." The literal translation of the phrase, no matter how used, is "head to head."

tête réduite (tayt ray-DWEET)
shrunken head
   This is the literal translation. The phrase has nothing to do with shrinks. (See also REDUCTEUR DE TÊTE.)

tiens, un revenant! (tyan œn ruu-VəNAHN)
long time no see!
   Also translated as "look who's here!" and as "hello, stranger!"

tiré à quatre épingles (tee-RAY ah kahtrə ay-PANGLə)
dressed to the nines
   Also translated as "neat as a pin" and "well-groomed"; literally, "drawn to four pins." (See also SE METTRE SUR SON TRENTE ET UN.)

tirer (tee-RAY)
pull or *pull out* or *draw*
   This infinitive introduces several interesting idioms, including **tirer de l'argent de quelqu'un** (duu lahr-ZHAHN duu kayl-KœN), translated as "get money out of someone," literally, "pull money out of someone"; and **tirer des plans sur la comète** (day plahn sür lah kaw-MAYT), translated as "count chickens before they're hatched," literally, "draw up plans on the comet"—as though one can always count on the appearance of a comet. In short, we are being told to make sure a thing is actually yours before you act as though it is. Then there is the dismal **tirer le diable par la queue** (luu dyahblə pahr lah kuu), translated as "be on one's uppers," "live from hand to mouth," and "lead a struggling existence," literally, "pull the devil by the tail"; and **tirer les ficelles** (lay fee-SAYL), translated as "pull strings"; and, finally, **tirer les marrons du feu** (lay mah-RAWN dü fuu), translated as "do someone's dirty work for him," "be made a cat's paw," and

"get someone out of an embarrassing situation," literally, "pull the chest-nuts out of the fire." In the fable, the clever monkey wanting to get some roasted chestnuts from the fire used the paw of his friend the cat to reach them. Poor cat!

tirez le rideau, la farce est jouée (tee-RAY luu ree-DOH lah fahrss ay zhway)
it's curtains for me
Literally, "ring down the curtain, the farce is over," said to have been the last words of Rabelais.

tomber (tawn-BAY)
fall or *jump*
An infinitive that leads to several interesting locutions, including **tomber amoureux** (ah-moo-RUU), translated as "fall in love"; **tomber dans la misère** (dahn lah mee-ZAIR), translated as "take a nosedive," "fall on hard times," and "become impoverished," literally, "fall into misery"; **tomber dans les pommes** (dahn lay pawm), an intriguing way to say "pass out" or "faint," literally, "fall into the apples"; and **tomber de Charybde en Scylla** (duu shah-REEBDə ahn see-LAH), translated as "jump out of the frying pan into the fire," "try to avoid one danger and fall into another," literally, "try to avoid Scylla and fall into Charybdis." (See ENTRE CHARYBDE ET SCYLLA for further explanation.) Returning to the real world, there is **tomber de haut** (duu oh), translated as "have one's hopes dashed," literally, "fall from a height"; and, finally, **tomber de la poêle dans le feu** (duu lah pwayl dahn lə fuu)—also given as **tomber de la poêle dans la braise** (dahn lah brayz)—translated literally as "fall from the frying pan into the fire" or "fall from the firing pan (or stove) into the embers." The two idioms can be summed up as "make things worse," that is, in trying to extricate oneself from one evil you fall into a greater evil.

tombeur de femmes (tawn-BUHR duu fahm)
lady-killer
Also translated as "Casanova" or "Don Juan." The literal translation is "woman thrower." Which is a little kinder than "lady-killer."

tôt ou tard la vérité se fera jour (toh too tahr lah vay-ree-TAY suu fərah zhoor)
murder will out

Almost literally translated as "sooner or later the truth will see the light of day."

touché! (too-SHAY)
hit!

A fencing term, usually given in English as "touché!" and pronounced as in French.

toucher un bon traitement (too-SHAY œn bawn traytə-MAHN)
get a good wage

Also "get a good salary." In these times it does not matter what you call it.

toujours (too-ZHOOR)
always

The question is "always what?" Read on: **toujours gai** (gay), translated as "always gay"—"happy," that is; **toujours perdrix** (pair-DREE), translated as "too much of a good thing," literally, "always partridge"; **toujours prêt** (pray), translated as "always ready"; and, finally, **toujours propice** (praw-PEESS), translated as "always favorable."

tour de force (toor duu forss)
feat of strength

Also translated as "amazing feat." Although the translation given above is quite literal and understandable, in English we often say "tour de force," meaning "exceptional achievement," and retain the French pronunciation.

tour d'ivoire (toor dee-VWAHR)
ivory tower

The **tour** of this locution means "tower," not "feat," as in the previous entry. How this metaphor for "retreat" or "place of seclusion" or "protection against the harsh realities of life" came to use a tower made of ivory has not been explained. It is known, however, that the French phrase—credited to the great nineteenth-century French literary critic Sainte-Beuve—became part of English as "ivory tower" in the twentieth century.

tourner au vinaigre (toor-NAY oh vee-NAYGRə)
turn sour

Literally, "turn to vinegar."

tourte aux pommes (toort toh pawm)
apple pie
  Now you may be forgiven if you say "as French as **tourte aux pommes**."

tous (too)
all or *every*
  This adjective, also a pronoun, is the plural form of **tout** and, as you will see, is sometimes pronounced "tooss," but read on: **tous égaux devant la loi** (tooss ay-GOH duu-VAHN lah lwah), translated as "everyone is equal in the eyes of the law," literally, "all are equal before the law"—but it doesn't hurt to be able to hire fancy lawyers; **tous frais faits** (too fray fay), a marvelous phrase for tourists and business travelers, translated as "all expenses paid"; **tous les chemins mènent à Rome** (too lay shuu-MAN mayn tah rawm), translated as "all roads lead to Rome," that is, "all systems of thought converge in a common center": in ancient times, Roman roads led from Rome to all parts of the vast Roman Empire—and back; **tous les chiens qui aboient ne mordent pas** (too lay shyan kee ah-BWAH nuu mordə pah), translated as "don't be afraid of him," "he's all talk," "his bark is worse than his bite," and, literally, "all dogs that bark don't bite"—but don't bet on it; and **tous les goûts sont dans la nature** (too lay goo sawn dahn lah nah-TÜR), translated as "it takes all sorts to make a world." The English poet William Cowper (1731–1800) put it this way: "Variety's the very spice of life/That gives it all its flavour." But don't quit now, or you will miss two of the best: **tous les trente-six du mois** (too lay trahnt-SEESS dü mwah), translated as "once in a blue moon" and "very rarely," literally, "in all thirty-sixth days of the month"; and **tous songes sont mensonges** (too sawnzh sawn mahn-SAWNZH), translated as "all dreams are lies *or* illusions."

tout (too)
an adjective, pronoun, adverb, and noun translated in a variety of ways
  A plethora of phrases incorporate **tout** or the feminine form **toute** (toot), and the masculine **tout** in some phrases is also pronounced "toot," as you will see. Consider **tout à coup** (too tah koo), translated as "suddenly," literally, "all at a stroke"; **tout à fait** (too tah fay), translated as "entirely," "wholly," or "quite"; **tout à l'heure** (too tah luhr), translated as "presently," "in a little while," "in a moment," "just now," or "only a moment ago"; **tout au contraire** (too toh kawn-TRAIR), translated as "quite to the contrary"; **tout au plus** (too toh plüss), translated as "at the most";

tout à vous (too tah voo), a phrase used as a complimentary close to a letter, translated as "yours truly" and "sincerely yours," literally, "wholly
yours"; **tout baigne dans l'huile** (too baynyə dahn lweel), translated as
"everything's okay," or "everything's looking up," literally, "everything's
bathed in oil," as good machinery should be; **tout bien ou rien** (too byan oo
ryan), translated as "all or nothing," literally, "everything well or nothing,"
suggesting that one should always strive to do one's best; also given as **tout
ou rien**; **tout ça c'est du chinois pour moi** (too sah say dü shee-NWAH
poor mwah), translated as "it's incomprehensible" or "it's all Greek to me,"
literally, "all that is Chinese to me"—the French also say **pour moi c'est de
l'hebreu** (poor mwah say duu lay-BRUU), "all that is Hebrew to me"; the
proverb **tout ce qui brille n'est pas or** (too suu kee breeyə nay pah or),
translated as "don't be deceived by appearances," literally, "all that glitters
is not gold"; **tout comme chez nous** (too kawm shay noo), translated as
"just as with us," literally, "just as at our house"; **tout comprendre, c'est
tout pardonner** (too kawn-PRAHNDRə say too pahr-daw-NAY), literally
translated as "to understand all is to pardon all," an aphorism sometimes
and mistakenly attributed to the celebrated French writer Madame de Staël
(1766–1817); moving back to the practical, we have **tout compris** (too
kawn-PREE), a restaurant term translated as "everything included"—tips,
service charges, and the like; **tout de suite** (too də sweet), translated as
"immediately," "at once," and "straightaway"; **toute la batterie de cuisine**
(toot lah bah-TəREE duu kwee-ZEEN), translated as "the whole caboodle"
and "everything but the kitchen sink," literally as "the entire assortment of
kitchen utensils" or "the entire assortment of pots and pans"; **toute mé-
daille a son revers** (toot may-DĪYə ah sawn ruu-VAIR), translated as
"every rose has its thorns," almost literally, "every medal has two sides," in
short, "life is not uninterrupted pleasure"; **tout ensemble** (too tahn-
SAHNBLə), translated as "general effect," more literally, "the whole taken
together"; **toute peine mérite salaire** (toot payn may-REET sah-LAIR),
translated almost literally as "all effort deserves compensation," usually
translated as "the laborer is worthy of his hire," as in Luke, in the New Testament, where missionaries who work in the service of God are told not to
be averse to accepting offers of hospitality from the people they seek to
convert; **tout est bien qui finit bien** (too tay byan kee fee-NEE byan), well
translated in the fourteenth-century English proverb "all's well that ends
well," signifying that the end result of any activity is all that matters; the
unfortunate idiom **tout est frit** (too tay free), translated as "our goose is
cooked" or "it's all over but the shouting," literally, "everything is fried";

tout est perdu hors l'honneur (too tay pair-DÜ or law-NUHR), translated as "all is lost save honor," attributed to—but not actually written in these words by—French King Francis I (1494–1547), reacting to being taken prisoner at the battle of Pavia (1525), in which he fought against the English; **tout est pour le mieux dans le meilleur des mondes possibles** (too tay poor luu myuu dahn luu may-YUHR day mawndə paw-SEEBLə), translated as "all is for the best in this best of all possible worlds"—Voltaire (1694–1778), in his popular novel *Candide*, satirizing the optimistic creed of the German philosopher Leibnitz (1646–1716); **tout ira bien** (too tee-RAH byan), translated as "everything will be (*literally*, go) all right"; **tout lasse, tout casse, tout passe** (too lahss too kahss too pahss), translated as "nothing lasts forever," literally, "everything wearies or bores, everything breaks, everything passes away"; **tout le monde** (too lə mawndə), translated as "everybody," literally, "all the world"; **tout le monde est sage après coup** (too lə mawndə ay sahzh ah-PRAY koo), translated as "twenty-twenty hindsight," literally, "everybody is wise after the event"; **tout lui rit** (too lwee ree), translated as "born lucky," literally, "everything smiles upon him"; **tout mon possible** (too mawn paw-SEEBLə), translated as "my utmost," literally, "everything in my power"; **tout nouveau, tout beau** (too noo-VOH too boh), translated as "better wait until the novelty wears off," literally, "everything novel, everything beautiful"; **tout soldat français porte dans sa giberne le bâton de maréchal de France** (too sawl-DAH frahn-SAY portə dahn sah zhee-BAIRN luu bah-TAWN duu mah-ray-SHAHL duu frahnss), a saying attributed to Napoleon and translated as "every French soldier carries in his cartridge box the baton of a marshal of France"; **tout va bien** (too vah byan), translated as "all's well" and "you're all right"; **tout va de guingois** (too vah duu gan-GWAH), translated as "everything's going to pot," more literally, "everything is askew"; **tout va le mieux du monde** (too vah luu myuu dü mawndə), translated as "everything's going swimmingly"; and, finally, **tout vient à point à qui sait attendre** (too vyan tah pwan ah kee say tah-TAHNDRə), translated as "don't be impatient," literally, "everything comes to him who knows how to wait."

travailler (trah-vah-YAY)
work

This infinitive gives us a cluster of useful idioms: **travailler au noir** (oh nwahr), translated as "moonlight," literally, "work in the dark"; **travailler comme un galérien** (kawm mœn gah-lay-RYAN), translated as "work like a dog," literally, "work like a galley slave"; and **travailler dans l'ombre** (dahn lawnbrə), translated as "work behind the scenes," literally, "work in the shadow."

treize à la douzaine (trayz zah lah doo-ZAYN)
baker's dozen
   Literally, "thirteen to the dozen." In past time in France, a stern penalty was administered for giving short weight—bread was sold by weight—so bakers took no chances and gave their customers thirteen loaves rather than a dozen.

très bien (tray byan)
very well

trêve à ces niaiseries (trayvə vah say nyay-ZəREE)
no more kidding around
   Also translated as "no more of these fooleries"; more literally, "a truce to this silliness."

tripes à la mode de Caen (treep ah lah mawd duu kahn)
a dish of tripe
   A cookery term, literally, "tripe in the style of Caen," tripe being part of the stomach of a ruminant animal used for food, and Caen being a city in northwest France.

tristesse (treess-TAYSS)
gloom
   Also translated as "sadness" and "melancholy." The French novelist Françoise Sagan (1935–) gained international celebrity with her first novel, *Bonjour tristesse*, whose title, translated literally as "Hello, Melancholy," is never given in translation—justifiably.

trop de cuisiniers gâtent la sauce (troh duu kwee-zee-NYAY gahtə lah sohss)
too many cooks spoil the broth
   Literally, "too many cooks spoil the sauce."

trop de hâte gâte tout (troh duu ahtə gahtə too)
more haste, less speed
   Literally, "too much haste spoils everything."

truite meunière (trweetə muu-NYAIR)
truite meunière
    A dish of trout sautéed, literally, "in the style of the miller's wife." But on an American menu always given in French.

tu (tü)
you
    This is the familiar form of "you"—the formal pronoun is **vous** (voo)—used in many idioms and common phrases, including **tu as avalé ta langue?** (ah ah-vah-LAY tah lahngə), translated as "does the cat have your tongue?" literally, "have you swallowed your tongue?"; **tu es gentil** (ay zhahn-TEE), translated as "you're sweet," more literally, "you're kind"; the fateful sentence from Genesis, in the Old Testament, **tu es poussière et tu retourneras en poussière** (ay poo-SYAIR ay tü ruu-toor-nuu-RAH ahn poo-SYAIR), translated as "ashes to ashes and dust to dust," more fully, "dust thou art, and unto dust thou shalt return"; turning to a happier thought, **tu es mon soleil** (ay mawn saw-LAYə), translated as "you are my sunshine" or "you are my sun"; **tu le sais fort bien** (lə say for byan), translated as "you know very well"; and, finally, **tu me prends pour un naïf** (muu prahn poor rœn nah-EEF), translated as "what do you take me for?" or "you treat me like a gullible fool," more literally and elegantly as "you take me for a complete innocent."

tuer la poule aux oeufs d'or (tü-AY lah pool loh zuu dor)
ruin a good thing
    Usually translated as "kill the goose that lays the golden eggs," that is, "sacrifice future reward for immediate gain." A Greek fable relates the story of a peasant who had a goose that laid golden eggs. Thinking he could become enormously wealthy by finding the full store of all these wonderful eggs, he killed and eviscerated the goose. And how many eggs did he find? None.

tuer le veau gras (tü-AY luu voh grah)
celebrate
    Also translated, literally, as "kill the fatted calf," or as "welcome with the best of everything," as in the parable of the prodigal son in Luke, in the New Testament.

tu me rappelles mon fils (tü muu rah-PAYL mawn feess)
you look familiar
    Literally, "you remind me of my son."

tu nous pompes l'air (tü noo pawnpə lair)
we've heard enough out of you

Also translated as "you're getting us down," "we're getting fed up with you," and "we're losing patience"; literally, "you're pumping us up with air."

tutoiement (tü-twah-MAHN)
familiar address

This noun reflects the use of **tu** in place of **vous** in addressing someone, as made explicit in the idiom **tutoyer quelqu'un** (tü-twah-YAY kayl-KœN), translated as "be on familiar *or* intimate terms with someone." (See also ÊTRE À TU ET À TOI AVEC QUELQU'UN.)

un ami influent (œn nah-MEE an-flü-AHN)
an influential insider

Also translated as "a friend at court," a friend, that is, who is well connected and can pull strings for you.

un bienfait n'est jamais perdu (œn byan-FAY nay zhah-MAY pair-DÜ)
a kindness is never lost

un bikini minimum (œn bee-kee-NEE mee-nee-MUHM)
the skimpiest you can get away with

Translated as "a scanty bikini," as though there were any other kind.

un cheval qui n'a ni bouche ni éperon (œn shə-VAHL kee nah nee boosh nee aypə-RAWN)
someone with a mind of his own

Translated as "a horse that obeys neither rein (*literally*, mouth) nor spur," but applicable to any headstrong, uncontrollable person or ornery machine.

un chien regarde bien un évêque (œn shyan ruu-GAHRDə byan œn nay-VAYK)
a cat may look at a king
   A proverb, literally translated as "a dog may look at a bishop," intended when used by a subordinate as an impertinent rejoinder making it clear that he or she is as good as anyone else. Dog, cat; king, bishop? Just a difference in cultures.

un clou chasse l'autre (œn kloo shahss lohtrə)
no one is indispensable
   A sardonic French proverb telling us that anyone can be replaced, freely translated as "one man goes and another takes his place," literally translated as "one nail drives out the other." Carpenters traditionally have used a new nail as a punch to drive out old nails.

un coup (œn koo)
a blow or stroke
   Naturally, there are many types of blows or strokes, including **un coup de hasard** (duu ah-ZAHR), translated as "a stroke of luck"; **un coup de pied au derrière** (də pyay oh day-RYAIR), translated as "a kick in the pants," literally, "a kick in the behind," carrying the meaning of applying strong measures to get someone to take action; **un coup de soleil** (də saw-LAYə), translated as "sunstroke," literally, "a stroke of the sun"; **un coup de téléphone** (də tay-lay-FAWN), translated as "a phone call"; **un coup de tonnerre dans un ciel bleu** (də tawn-NAIR dahn zœn syayl bluu), translated as "a bolt from the blue," literally, "a thunderbolt in a blue sky," denoting a sudden and wholly unexpected event or catastrophe; **un coup fumant** (fü-MAHN), translated as "a masterstroke," literally, "a smoking blow" (see also COUP DE MAÎTRE); and, finally, **un coup pour rien** (poor ryan), translated as "a waste of time" or "a trial run," literally, "a blow for nothing."

un drôle de pistolet (œn drohl duu peess-taw-LAY)
a queer customer
   Also translated as "a queer fish"; literally, "a strange pistol." The same

meaning is conveyed by **un drôle de zèbre** (œn drohl duu zaybrə), literally, "a strange zebra."

une araignée au plafond (ün nah-ray-NYAY oh plah-FAW*N*)
a bee in one's bonnet
A marvelous idiom for someone obsessed by eccentric ideas, both in English and in French, in which it is literally translated as "a spider on the ceiling."

une aventure sentimentale (ün nah-vahn-TÜR sahn-tee-mahn-TAHL)
a love affair
Literally, "a sentimental adventure."

une de perdue, dix de retrouvées (ün duu pair-DÜ deess duu rə-troo-VAY)
you can't win 'em all
Also translated as "win a few, lose a few," almost literally as "lose one, find ten." No matter how translated, clearly the message conveyed is "don't worry, there are lots of good fish in the sea."

une femme assez mûre (ün fahm ah-SAY mür)
a middle-aged woman
Also translated as "a mature woman." The literal meaning of **assez mûre** is "ripe enough." No further comment.

une fois n'est pas coutume (ün fwah nay pah koo-TÜM)
just once won't hurt
Also translated as "don't make a habit of it"; literally, "once is not a habit." But isn't that how babies are conceived?

une grosse légume (ün grohss lay-GÜM)
a big shot
Also translated as "a bigwig" or "a high-muck-a-muck"; literally, "a big vegetable."

une hirondelle ne fait pas le printemps (ün nee-rawn-DAYL nuu fay pah luu pran-TAH*N*)
one uptick on the Dow may not mean a new bull market

Also translated as "one swallow does not make a summer," but literally translated as "one swallow does not make a spring," which is more faithful to the words of a fable of the Greek philosopher Aristotle (fourth century B.C.), who also spoke of spring in his account. No matter the season, "one victory doesn't mean your troubles are over," so don't jump to conclusions.

une histoire à faire dresser les cheveux sur la tête (ün neess-TWAHR rah fair dray-SAY lay shəvuu sür lah tayt)
enough to curl your hair
   Better translated as "a hair-raising story" or, more literally, "a story that will make the hairs on your head stand on end."

une jeune fille très évoluée (ün zhuhn feeyə tray zay-vaw-lü-AY)
a girl with liberated views
   Also translated as "a girl with a very independent attitude."

une maison est une machine-à-habiter (ün may-ZAWN ay tün mah-sheen-nah-bee-TAY)
a house is a machine for living in
   An aphorism of the Swiss-born French architect Le Corbusier (1887–1965).

une maladie qui ne pardonne pas (ün mah-lah-DEE kee nuu pahr-DAWN pah)
a fatal illness
   Literally, "a disease that does not forgive." The worst kind.

une minute d'hésitation peut coûter cher (ün mee-NÜT day-zee-tah-SYAWN puu koo-TAY shair)
a moment's hesitation can cost dearly
   Also translated as "he who hesitates is lost." So use every day for full living. (See also AUX AUDACIEUX LES MAINS PLEINES.)

un esprit sain dans un corps sain (œn nayss-PREE san dahn zœn kor san)
a sound mind in a healthy body
   According to English philosopher John Locke (1632–1704), "a sound mind in a sound body," a brief but full description of a happy condition in

this world. The French locution is a translation of the Latin *mens sana in corpore sano.*

une teinture de français (ün tan-TÜR duu frahn-SAY)
a smattering of French

un homme (œn nawm)
a man

What can be said of a man? Read on: **un homme averti en vaut deux** (ah-vair-TEE ahn voh duu), translated as "forewarned, forearmed," literally, "a man who is warned is equal to two"—men who have not been warned, that is; **un homme de bon conseil** (duu bawn kawn-SAYə), translated as "someone you can trust" or "a trusted adviser," literally, "a man of sound counsel"; **un homme de bonne foi** (duu bawn fwah), translated as "an honest man," literally, "a man of good faith"; **un homme de devoir** (duu də-VWAHR), translated as "a reliable man," more literally, "a man with a sense of duty"; **un homme marqué** (mahr-KAY), translated as "a marked man," one intended for punishment, if not for execution; **un homme qui parle deux langues vaut deux hommes** (kee pahrlə duu lahng voh duu zawm), literally translated as "a man who speaks two languages is worth two men"—two men who are monolingual, that is—so study foreign languages!; and, finally, **un homme qui se noie se raccroche à un fétu de paille** (kee suu nwah suu rah-KRAWSH ah œn fay-TÜ duu pīyə, translated as "desperate men cling to trifles," more literally as "a drowning man clutches at a wisp of straw."

un malheur amène son frère (œn mah-LUHR ah-MAYN sawn frair)
a misfortune brings its brother

The same thought is expressed by **un malheur ne vient jamais seul** (œn mah-LUHR nuu vyan zhah-MAY suhl), translated as "a misfortune never comes alone" and as "it never rains but it pours."

un mari complaisant (œn mah-REE kawn-play-ZAHN)
an indulgent husband

One, that is, who overlooks his wife's shenanigans.

un mari trompé (œn mah-REE trawn-PAY)
a cuckold

Also translated as "a deceived husband," a man, that is, whose wife has been unfaithful to him.

un petit service en vaut un autre (œn pətee sair-VEESS ahn voh œn nohtrə)
one good turn deserves another

un petit verre (œn pətee vair)
a shot
> Of whiskey, that is. Literally translated as "a little glass."

un poète manqué (œn paw-AYT mahn-KAY)
a would-be poet
> The infinitive **manquer** means "be lacking," from which derives the adjective **manqué**. English has adopted **manqué**, pronounced as in French and with the meaning "failed." Thus, you needn't be merely a failed or would-be poet. You can be a playwright manqué, a psychiatrist manqué, an actor manqué, or an anything else manqué. But first you must try.

un silence éloquent (œn see-LAHNSS ay-law-KAHN)
a silence that speaks volumes
> Literally, "an eloquent silence," telling us we don't always have to speak to convey an opinion or a worthwhile thought.

un sot à triple étage (œn soh ah treeplə ay-TAHZH)
a consummate fool
> Also translated as "a first-class blockhead" or "a monumental fool"; literally, "a fool to the third story"—of a building, that is.

un vin d'un bon cru (œn van dœn bawn krü)
a good vintage
> **Cru,** so often seen on bottles of French wine, means "vineyard."

valse-hésitation (vahlss-ay-zee-tah-SYAW*N*)
pussyfooting
    This French term arose back in the days when couples thought that two people waltzing around a dance floor could have great fun. A variation of the waltz was the "hesitation waltz," in which frequent use was made of a pause followed by a glide. And if you think of an important discussion in which a pause is followed by a verbal glide (or slide), you have a pretty good idea of why **valse-hésitation** came to mean "pussyfooting."

vase de nuit (vahz duu nwee)
chamber pot
    Literally, "night bowl."

vasistas (vah-zeess-TAHSS)
transom
    A term said to have originated in the nineteenth century, during the Franco-Prussian War, when Paris was occupied by German-speaking soldiers who had never before seen transoms, the windows over doors that afford ventilation without having to leave doors open. Much to the amusement of Parisians, who were accustomed to **imposte** (an-PAWST) as the term meaning "transom," the soldiers are said to have pointed to a transom and asked *Was ist das?*—"What is that?" The French ear heard this as **vasistas** and the question left its mark on the French language.

va te faire cuire un oeuf! (vah tə fair kweer rœn nuhf)
get lost!
    Literally, "go cook yourself an egg!" Another expression meaning "get lost!" or "go away!" is **va-t'en!** (vah-TAHN), the familiar form of **allez-vous-en!** (which see, under ALLER).

va vider les ordures! (vah vee-DAY lay zor-DÜR)
remember to take out the garbage!

An essential order given daily at least once by every wife, and literally translated as "Go and empty the garbage!"

velouté de tomates (vuu-loo-TAY duu taw-MAHT)
cream of tomato soup
   Velouté, here used as a noun, may be defined as "velvetiness." In the term **sauce** (sohss) **velouté**, made famous among American amateur chefs by the legendary Julia Child, **velouté**—serving as an adjective—may be defined as "given a velvety finish." The entire phrase may thus describe "a sauce soft and smooth to the palate." What could be better?

vendre (vahndrə)
sell
   This verb leads us into several interesting locutions: **vendre au noir** (oh nwahr), translated as "sell illegally" or "sell on the black market"; **vendre la mèche** (lah maysh), translated as "give the game away" or "let the cat out of the bag," literally, "sell the fuse," thus rendering a bomb useless; **vendre la peau de l'ours avant de l'avoir tué** (lah poh duu loorss ah-VAHN duu lah-VWAHR tü-AY), translated as "count one's chickens before they're hatched," literally, "sell the bearskin before one has killed the bear" (see also IL NE FAUT PAS VENDRE LA PEAU DE L'OURS AVANT DE L'AVOIR TUÉ); and, finally, **vendre son honneur** (sawn naw-NUHR), translated as "sell one's honor." For shame!

venez voir mes estampes japonaises (vuu-NAY vwahr may zayss-TAHNPə zhah-paw-NAYZ)
come up and see my etchings
   In time past, an invitation extended by a man with seduction in mind. When literally translated as "come up to see my Japanese prints," we have an indication that Frenchmen were given to the same type of heavy-handed duplicity once practiced by their American counterparts.

venons-en aux choses sérieuses (vuu-nawn-ZAHN oh shohz say-RYUHZ)
let's get down to the nitty-gritty
   Literally, "let's go on to serious matters."

ventre affamé n'a point d'oreilles (vahntrə ah-fah-MAY nah pwan daw-RAYə)
a hungry belly has no ears

Indicating that a hungry person has no stomach for advice or argument.

ventre à terre (vahntrə ah tair)
at full speed
Literally, "belly to the ground." Applicable, albeit only figuratively, even to creatures who have only two legs.

version expurgée (vair-SYAWN ayks-pür-ZHAY)
bowdlerized version
Also translated as "sanitized *or* expurgated version" of someone's remarks, a text, a movie, or the like.

vers libre (vair leebrə)
free verse

veuillez agréer l'expression de mes sentiments les meilleurs (vuu-YAY zah-gray-AY layks-pray-SYAWN duu may sahn-tee-MAHN lay may-YUHR)
sincerely yours
A complimentary close for a letter; literally, "please accept the expression of my best wishes," showing us that we must never underestimate the capacity of the French language to turn a two-word English formality into something much longer and grander. (See also DAIGNEZ AGRÉER MES RESPECTUEUX HOMMAGES.)

victoire à la Pyrrhus (veek-TWAHR ah lah pee-RÜSS)
Pyrrhic victory
Denoting a victory won at too heavy a price, like the bloody victories won against Roman forces in the third century B.C. by Pyrrhus, king of Epirus. In gaining these victories, Pyrrhus lost all his best officers and many of his men.

vider (vee-DAY)
empty
Whether translated as "empty" or as one of its synonyms, the infinitive **vider** gives us some interesting locutions, including **vider l'abcès** (lahp-SAY), translated as "root out the trouble"—any trouble—even though the locution translates literally as "drain the abscess"; **vider les ordures** (lay

zor-DÜR), translated as "empty the garbage" (see also VA VIDER LES OR-
DURES!); and **vider quelqu'un d'un bar** (kayl-KœN dœn bahr), translated
as "throw someone out of a bar." This is the work of a bouncer, in French
videur (vee-DUHR), literally, "an emptier."

vie conjugale (vee kawn-zhü-GAHL)
married life
   Euphemistically translated as "blessed state of matrimony," literally as
"conjugal life."

vieille (vyayə)
old
   The feminine form of **vieux** (vyuu). But old what? Read on. First
there is **vieille bagnole** (bah-NYUHL), translated as "old jalopy"; **vieille
barbe** (bahrb), translated as "old fogy," literally, "old beard," evocative of
the sometimes disparaging noun "graybeard"; **vieille fille** (feeyə), translated
as "spinster" or, more literally, "old maid"; and, finally, **vieille moustache**
(mooss-TAHSH), translated as "old soldier," literally, "old mustache."

vierge (vyairzh)
virgin
   This word is here defined as a noun. But it appears as an adjective in the
phrase **vierge de tout reproche** (vyairzh duu too ruu-PRAWSH), translated
as "free of all reproach," with **vierge** defined literally as "unsullied."

vieux comme le monde (vyuu kawm luu mawndə)
old as the hills
   Also translated as "very old"; literally, "old as the world." The companion phrase **vieux comme les rues** (vyuu kawm lay rü) has the same meaning, with the literal translation "old as the streets."

vieux protecteur (vyuu praw-tayk-TUHR)
sugar daddy
   Literally, "old guardian," a kinder term than "sugar daddy."

ville qui parlemente est près de se rendre (veel kee pahr-luu-MAHNTə
ay pray duu suu rahndrə)
they're close to giving in
   An excellent hint for any negotiator, literally, "a city (under siege) that

parleys is close to surrendering." So if an adversary takes a hard line but has not left the bargaining table, don't quit. Wait him out! Victory is in sight.

vin (van)
wine
   As one would expect, the French language doesn't stop there. Consider **vin coupé d'eau** (koo-PAY doh), which is given to children at a meal, translated as "wine cut with water" or "wine diluted with water"; **vin d'honneur** (dawn-NUHR), literally translated as "wine of honor," denoting wine drunk in honor of a distinguished guest; **vin du pays** (dü pay-EE), translated as "local wine" or "wine of the area," literally, "wine of the country"; **vin ordinaire** (or-dee-NAIR), translated as "inexpensive table wine," literally, "ordinary wine," and regularly given on menus outside France as "vin ordinaire," pronounced as in French; and, finally, **vin pur** (pür), translated as "uncut wine" or "wine without water added," literally, "pure wine."

vis-à-vis (vee-zah-VEE)
opposite
   Also translated as "facing"; literally, "face-to-face."

vive! (veev)
long live!
   Long live what? Read on: **vive la bagatelle!** (lah bah-gah-TAYL), translated as "long live frivolity!"; **vive la France!** (lah frahnss), translated as "long live France!"; **vive l'amour!** (lah-MOOR), translated as "long live love!"; **vive la reine!** (lah rayn), translated as "long live the queen!"; **vive la République!** (lah ray-püb-LEEK), translated as "long live the republic!"—the French Republic, of course; **vive l'empereur!** (lahn-Pə-RUHR), translated as "long live the emperor!"; **vive le roi!** (luu rwah), translated as "long live the king!"; and, finally, **vive l'impératrice!** (lan-pay-rah-TREESS), translated as "long live the empress!"

vivre (veevrə)
live
   The infinitive **vivre** introduces many ways to live, especially **vivre à la colle** (ah lah kawl), translated as "shack up" and "live together," almost literally, "live glued together"—the noun **colle** means "glue," but here is not to be taken literally; **vivre au jour le jour** (oh zhoor luu zhoor), translated as "live from day to day" and "enjoy the present," as well as "live from hand

to mouth"; **vivre aux crochets de quelqu'un** (oh kraw-SHAY duu kayl-KœN), translated as "sponge on somebody," more literally as "live off somebody's work"; **vivre ce n'est pas respirer, c'est agir** (suu nay pah rayss-pee-RAY say tah-ZHEER), the words of Jean-Jacques Rousseau, translated literally as "living is not breathing but doing," telling us that we have to do more than merely breathe to be truly alive, so let's get busy; **vivre comme chien et chat** (kawm shyan ay shah), translated as "be at one another's throats" or "fight like cats and dogs," literally, "live like dog and cat"; **vivre comme un ours** (kawm mœn noorss), translated as "live apart from the world," literally, "live like a bear" (see also VIVRE ISOLÉ); **vivre d'amour et d'eau fraîche** (dah-MOOR ay doh fraysh), translated as "live on love alone," literally, "live on love and fresh water"; **vivre dans la mollesse** (dahn lah maw-LAYSS), translated as "live the soft life," also translated as "have it made" and "live the Club Med life," literally, "live the life of indolence"; by way of contrast, there are **vivre dans la misère** (dahn lah mee-ZAIR), translated as "live in poverty," and **vivre dans la richesse** (dahn lah ree-SHAYSS), translated as "live in wealth"; **vivre dans le célibat** (dahn luu say-lee-BAH), translated as "live the single life" and "be unmarried *or* celibate"; **vivre dans l'ombre de quelqu'un** (dahn lawnbrə duu kayl-KœN), translated literally as "live in someone's shadow," that is, be eclipsed .in reputation or skill by someone; **vivre d'expédients** (daykss-pay-DYAHN), translated as "live by one's wits" and "resort to expedients"; **vivre et laisser vivre** (ay lay-SAY veevrə), translated as "live and let live," suggesting that you and I show some tolerance of the weaknesses of others; **vivre isolé** (ee-zaw-LAY), translated as "live in isolation" (see also VIVRE COMME UN OURS); and, on a happy note, **vivre vieux** (vyuu), translated as "live to a ripe old age," literally, "live old."

vogue la galère! (vawgə lah gah-LAIR)
go for it!

Also translated as "come what may!" and "here goes!"; literally, "row the galley!"

voir (vwahr)
see

Several interesting locutions are introduced by this infinitive, including **voir c'est croire** (say krwahr), translated as "I'm from Missouri," more literally as "seeing is believing"; **voir la mort de près** (lah mor duu pray), translated as "stare death in the face," more literally as "see death close up"; **voir**

la vie en rose (lah vee ahn rohz), translated as "see life through rose-colored glasses," more literally as "take a rosy view of life," and in the twentieth century made special—and poignant—by the immortal Edith Piaf (1915–1963), "the little sparrow," in her song "La Vie en rose"; **voir le dessous des cartes** (luu də-SOO day kahrt), translated as "be in on the secret," literally as "see the underside (the faces) of the cards"; **voir toujours les choses en noir** (too-ZHOOR lay shohz zahn nwahr), translated as "borrow trouble," "look always at the dark side of things," and "always take a dark view of things," literally translated as "always see everything in black"; and, finally, **voir trente-six chandelles** (trahnt-SEE shahn-DAYL), translated as "see stars," literally, "see thirty-six candles." Why thirty-six? No answer here. Why stars?

voler de bouche en bouche (vaw-LAY duu boosh shahn boosh)
spread like wildfire
　　Literally, "fly from mouth to mouth," as with news and gossip.

volte-face (vawltə-FAHSS)
reversal or *change of policy*
　　Literally, "a facing about." Used in English, with the same meaning and the pronunciation vohlt-FASS.

vouloir c'est pouvoir (voo-LWAHR say poo-VWAHR)
where there's a will there's a way
　　An upbeat proverb, literally "to want is to be able." So they say.

vous avez raison (voo zah-VAY ray-ZAWN)
you're right
　　Which naturally leads to **vous avez tort** (tor), translated as "you're wrong."

vous déraillez (voo day-rah-YAY)
you're off your rocker
　　Also translated as "you're raving" and "you're talking through your hat." More literally, "you've jumped the tracks."

vous êtes vraiment le roi des imbéciles (voo zayt vray-MAHN luu rwah day zan-bay-SEEL)
you're a prize idiot
　　More literally translated as "you are truly the king of the idiots."

vous et vos pareils (voo zay voh pah-RAYǝ)
people like you
   Also translated as "you and your kind"; literally, "you and your equals."

vous me mettez le couteau sous la gorge (voo muu may-TAY luu koo-TOH soo lah gorzh)
you're holding a gun to my head
   More literally, "you're holding a knife to my throat." A complaint alleging unfair tactics, uttered against someone who holds the upper hand in a negotiation—not something one says to an assailant, who surely doesn't have to be told what he's doing with his gun or his knife.

vous vous faites rare (voo voo fayt rahr)
you're not around much these days
   Also translated, more literally, as "you're making yourself scarce" and as "we rarely see you anymore" and "we haven't seen much of you lately."

vous y perdrez vos pas (voo zee pair-DRAY voh pah)
you'll be wasting your time
   Also translated as "you'll be going to a lot of trouble with nothing to show for it" and, more literally, "you'll be wasting your steps there."

voyeur (vwah-YUHR)
peeping Tom
   The noun "voyeur" has been adopted in English and is best pronounced as in French.

zinc (zank)
a bar or *a counter*

zut alors! (züt tah-LOR)
darn it!

Also translated as "shut up!" A fitting way to close this recital of French idioms and proverbs.

$\mathcal{I}$ndex